Born Fighting

BORN FIGHTING

*How the Scots-Irish
Shaped America*

JAMES WEBB

Broadway Books

NEW YORK

BROADWAY

PRINTED IN THE UNITED STATES OF AMERICA

BROADWAY BOOKS and its logo, a letter B bisected on the diagonal,
are trademarks of Random House, Inc.

Visit our website at www.broadwaybooks.com

First edition published 2004.

Book design by Fritz Metsch

Library of Congress Cataloging-in-Publication Data
Webb, James H.
Born fighting : how the Scots-Irish shaped America / James Webb.—1st ed.
p. cm.
Includes bibliographical references and index.

1. Scots-Irish—United States—History. 2. United States—Ethnic relations I. Title.
E184.S4W43 2004
973'.049162—dc22   2004045741

ISBN 0-7679-1688-3

3   5   7   9   10   8   6   4   2

To those who went before us.

And to those we will someday leave behind.

Acknowledgments

THIS BOOK IS the product of decades of research and thought. Over those years many people encouraged me to write it. Many others gave me valuable emotional support during the difficult months it took to do so. But I would especially like to thank Oleg Jankovic and Nick Gardiner for their time and insights as the manuscript progressed, and my editor, Charlie Conrad, who believed in the value of the book from its inception, and resolutely steered me to its final conclusions without diluting its emotional and intellectual content. No writer can ask for more.

Contents

PART ONE

Rulers and Rednecks

Of the different racial strains that mingled their blood with the earlier English—Irish, Huguenot-French, German, Scotch-Irish—the last was by far the most important. . . . They were desperately poor; the available lands near the coast were already preempted; so armed with axes, their seed potatoes, and the newly invented rifle, they plunged into the backwoods to become our great pioneering race. Scattered thinly through a long frontier, they constituted the outposts and buffer settlements of civilization. A vigorous breed, hardy, assertive, individualistic, thrifty, trained in the democracy of the Scottish kirk, they were the material out of which later Jacksonian democracy was to be fashioned, the creators of that western type which in politics and industry became ultimately the American type.

—VERNON LOUIS PARRINGTON,
Main Currents in American Thought

1

Big Moccasin Gap

GATE CITY IS more than four hundred miles from Arlington, down the long spine of mountains that marks Virginia's western border. It takes seven hours to drive there, interstate highway almost all the way. I go west on I-66 until it hits the mountains, then hang a left on I-81, keeping those low, blue ridges off to my right as I tear my way south, heading through history. I-81 is a busy road, lots of New York and Pennsylvania license plates weaving in and out of heavy traffic. The exit ramps whiz past my vision, heading off the interstate to towns like Staunton, Lexington, Roanoke, Radford, and Wytheville. I recognize the counties, Rockbridge, Botetourt, Franklin, and others, places where my ancestors once built log cabins and scraped corn patches out of the mud before heading farther south or west.

The mountains are beautiful, smoky from the haze that the sun makes when it burns into the pine. My mind plays tricks. I tell myself that I've been right over there, once upon a time, or at least my blood has, taking water straight from a stream and staring out into the wild unknown, dreaming of the majestic deliverance that must be just over the next horizon, hiding in a valley that no white man has ever seen before. Or maybe the next horizon, or the next one, or the next one after that. Which is why my people kept on going, some of them getting hung up, staying behind in the cul-de-sacs of Appalachian hollows while the more adventurous worked their way, ratlike, through the maze until it broke out into Kentucky and then Missouri, Texas, and Colorado, and one day even hit the palm-lined beaches of California.

Because that is the story of my people, not for a generation or for ten generations but for forever. There was a time more than two thousand years ago when the Celtic tribes dominated middle Europe. They made beautiful jewelry and carvings. They were poetic and warlike. They followed strong leaders, even to their deaths. They brought their women and children to the battlefield and put them behind their ranks so they would be sure not to retreat. And they did not retreat. But they refused to recognize leadership beyond their local tribes and thus would not become a nation. And they had a permeating discontent that caused the more determined of them to keep pushing, every generation, a little bit farther into the wild unknown.

Until God played his greatest trick on them. Up the English island they moved, a generation at a time, ever northward, each generation seeing the more restless and aggressive push farther, breeding a new generation of even more restless and aggressive travelers. To the far north they moved, into what is now called Scotland, and when it ended or became too bleak they found sea bridges into Ireland. And so after hundreds or thousands of years of insistent wandering, the most migratory and curious among them found that they were caught in a cruel genetic joke, all their energies bottled up in wild, desolate places that only faced each other or the sea. So back and forth they went, across the sea bridges from Ireland to Scotland and then back again, waves of them that they now called "clans" taking out their fury on each other, then uniting once in a while when the Romans or the English sought to conquer them. The wildest, most contentious people on all the earth, trapped in a sea-bound bottleneck, their emotions spattering out into poetry and music and brawls, calling each other Irish and

Scottish now, or Catholic and Protestant, anything that might make another reason for a good, hard fight.

Until they became the British Empire's greatest voyagers, indeed its greatest export, settling in odd places all around the world. And for that splinter of them that became my people, the Scots-Irish, this meant the Appalachian Mountains, their first stop on their way to creating a way of life that many would come to call, if not American, certainly the defining fabric of the South and the Midwest as well as the core character of the nation's working class.

You yourself may see cars and Burger Kings when driving along I-81. But I am watching my own ghosts: tough, resilient women on the buckboards of narrow wagons, hard men with long rifles walking alongside, and wool-clad kids tending thin herds of cattle as they make their way down the mud trail called the Wilderness Road.

That rough road, as Johnny Cash once sang. That old Breezy Creek Road. That low-down, troublesome road through Moccasin Gap.

Nearing Gate City, I dip for a few miles into the hills and ridges of Tennessee, then drop off the interstate and come down a mountain until I am back in Virginia. Soon I pass a sign that remembers Big Moccasin Gap. This was Indian hunting ground for thousands of years. Arrowheads are almost as common as acorns if you scrape the thin soil around Gate City. It was also Daniel Boone's home. His son Jim was killed by an Indian war party in Castlewood, barely twenty miles away. And from this point in 1775, Daniel Boone blazed the first trails through the mountains into Kentucky. Big Moccasin Gap. Johnny Cash wrote the song about it many years ago, probably to honor his wife, June Carter Cash, whose famed musical family was from Hiltons, six miles up the road.

I have family here, too.

From Gate City, I follow narrow, winding roads along rushing streambeds and past small frame houses built at the bottom of the ridges. The mountains loom above me. Trucks are parked along the roads. Little wooden footbridges cross the streams, leading to the front doors of the houses. American flags are frequent, on the trucks and in the yards and on the porches. America got bombed and mountain people don't forget, even if it happened in New York and Washington, because when it comes to fighting wars, mountain people have always been among the first to go.

A few miles outside of town I turn left onto a far narrower road. It has no marker other than a small hand-painted sign with an arrow and the name of a Baptist church, but I know it by heart. It wasn't so long ago that the road was still dirt. This is the entrance to Alley Hollow. My great-great-grandfather lived in this hollow. My great-grandfather left from here to move up to Kentucky. A lot of people back in Alley Hollow share my blood. And all of them share a large part of my history.

My great-great-grandparents are buried back here along with maybe a dozen others in a rough patch of woods on top of a nearby mountain. There are no headstones, only large rocks that mark individual graves. When David G. Webb died, he owned no property and the value of his possessions totaled ten dollars, neither of which was unusual in these hills. Years ago I contacted the Veterans Administration and obtained a Confederate headstone for him and my great-great-grandmother, but there is no road leading to the top of the mountain and it is a laborious trek by foot, so the heavy marker has yet to find its proper resting place. Thinking of the anonymity of their graves, I remember a time when I visited a Protestant cemetery in Northern Ireland, in a little town along the coast just north of Larne. Most of the oldest headstones were unreadable, their etchings washed away by centuries of cold rain coming in from the sea. When I asked why they had not been replaced, I was told, simply, that the families that had buried those people had moved on.

The mountain is on someone else's property, back in the hollow. My cousins have called to ask permission for us to visit it. We drive in a truck down dirt roads. Old frame houses mark our journey, their porches buckling and the springhouses along the rushing streams falling into ruin. Folks here are still moving on. They always have. That is the story of our people. The road roughens even more, ribbed like an old washboard from the rains. We pull up in front of a haunted, empty farmhouse and walk across its back pasture. Two yapping barn dogs appear from nowhere and stay with us as we head slowly up the mountain.

On top of the mountain the wind, heavy with oxygen, hits my face. I look over at the deep green waves of mountains that surround me, thinking on the one hand that it reminds me of being in the open sea, and on the other that I can now see all the way to Tennessee. And I know this is what my ancestors must have thought as well. Another mountain, and then another. Why should I stop here? And I think not only of my great-great-grandparents lying underneath my very feet, but of all the others who made me, whose lives passed through these mountains and others just like them to the north and south. Perhaps they were brave. Perhaps they were merely desperate. But they were daredevils, not only to have shown up, but also to have had the courage to leave.

On top of this mountain you can understand the Pioneer's Creed: The Cowards Never Started. The Weak Died Along the Way. Only the Strong Survived.

The names jump at me, up from the front-porch chronicles of my grandmother, out from the pages of the past. Webb, Hodges, Smith, Doyle, McKnight, Marsh, Cox, Long, Leach, Condley, Murphy, Walker, DeHaven, McBride, Miller, Jewell, Cochran, Johnson, Leckie, Chitwood, Stuart, Lane. And the others whose names just now escape me, all of them coming here from one unknown, stopping for a while, and then heading out again into another.

The earth is a ravisher in these mountains, its vines and tangles swallowing up the memories of those who went before, and in their place the wild things are moving back into the hollows. Deer are so thick that my cousin finds it hard to keep them from the alfalfa he grows for his small herd of cattle, and even from his garden. Someone nearby reported seeing elk up in the far woods. And at night if you listen close, you can hear an occasional coyote.

Standing on the mountain, I worry that when this generation dies, the memory of those who went before me will be lost just as completely, buried under the avalanche of stories that have on occasion ridiculed my people and trivialized their journey. They came with nothing, and for a complicated set of reasons, many of them still have nothing. The slurs stick to me, standing on these graves. Rednecks. Trailer-park trash. Racists. Cannon fodder. My ancestors. My people. Me.

This people gave our country great things, including its most definitive culture. Its bloodlines have flowed in the veins of at least a dozen presidents, and in many of our greatest soldiers. It created and still perpetuates the most distinctly American form of music. It is imbued with a unique and unforgiving code of personal honor, less ritualized but every bit as powerful as the samurai code. Its legacy is broad, in many ways defining the attitudes and values of the military, of working-class America, and even of the peculiarly populist form of American democracy itself. And yet its story has been lost under the weight of more recent immigrations, revisionist historians, and common ignorance.

Walking down the mountain and driving back toward the world that these people made possible for me, I make a simple vow. Or maybe I simply hear them, calling to me from the place where I will someday join them.

The contributions of this culture are too great to be forgotten as America rushes forward into yet another redefinition of itself. And in a society obsessed with multicultural jealousies, those who cannot articulate their ethnic origins are doomed to a form of social and political isolation. My culture needs to rediscover itself, and in so doing to regain its power to shape the direction of America.

2

The Radical Individualists

THE SCOTS-IRISH (sometimes also called the Scotch-Irish) are all around you, even though you probably don't know it. They are a force that shapes our culture, more in the abstract power of emotion than through the argumentative force of law. In their insistent individualism they are not likely to put an ethnic label on themselves when they debate societal issues. Some of them don't even know their ethnic label, and some who do know don't particularly care. They don't go for group-identity politics any more than they like to join a union. Two hundred years ago the mountains built a fierce and uncomplaining self-reliance into an already hardened people. To them, joining a group and putting themselves at the mercy of someone else's collectivist judgment makes about as much sense as letting the government take their guns. And nobody is going to get their guns.

But this is who they are, and where they came from.

Their bloodline was stained by centuries of continuous warfare along the border between England and Scotland, and then in the bitter settlements of England's Ulster Plantation in Northern Ireland. Their religion was a harsh and demanding Calvinism that sowed the seeds of America's Bible Belt, its on-your-feet independence instead of on-your-knees rituality offending English Anglicans

and Irish Catholics alike. On occasion they sold themselves as indentured servants in order to escape Ulster's harshness, although
unsurprisingly, they quickly became known in America as disagree-
able and in-your-face when in that role.

Mostly they came in families and even large groups of families,
and thus retained their cultural identity long after leaving Ireland.
They came to America on small boats that took months to cross the
Atlantic, as many as 30 percent of their passengers dying on a typical voyage. They settled not in the plantations along the Southern
coast or in the bustling towns of New England, but in the raw
and unforgiving mountain wilderness, some spilling out from
settlements in New Hampshire, but the overwhelming majority
populating an area along the Appalachians that stretched from
Pennsylvania to Georgia and Alabama. It was not unusual to find
that their first task beyond building a cabin was to defend themselves against the bloodcurdling attacks of Indian war parties.

They fought the Indians and then they fought the British, comprising 40 percent of the Revolutionary War army. They were the
great pioneers—Daniel Boone, Lewis and Clark, and Davy Crockett
among them—blazing the westward trails into Kentucky, Ohio,
Tennessee, and beyond, where other Scots-Irishmen like Kit Carson
picked up the slack. They reshaped American politics, taking hegemony away from the aristocratic English-Americans and creating
the populist movement. In this role they gave us at least a dozen
presidents, beginning with the incomparable Andrew Jackson and
including Chester Arthur, Ulysses S. Grant, Theodore Roosevelt
(through his mother), Woodrow Wilson, Ronald Reagan (again
through his mother), and, most recently, Bill Clinton. It is even said
that the patrician George W. Bush has a Kentucky-born, Scots-Irish
ancestor.

They formed the bulk of the Confederate Army and a good part
of the Union Army as well, and even in later wars provided many of
the greatest generals and soldiers our nation has ever seen. Stonewall Jackson comes to mind, as do Sam Houston, Nathan Bedford

Forrest, Ulysses S. Grant, George S. Patton, and a slew of army chiefs of staff and Marine Corps commandants. Not to mention Sgt. Alvin York, the most remembered hero of World War I, Audie Murphy, the most decorated soldier of World War II, and David Hackworth, America's most decorated veteran from Korea and Vietnam. Indeed, they have fed dedicated soldiers to this nation far beyond their numbers in every war—for instance, the heavily Scots-Irish people of West Virginia ranked first, second, or third in military casualty rates in every U.S. war of the twentieth century. As one comparison, West Virginia's casualty rate was twice that of New York's and Connecticut's in Vietnam, and more than two and a half times the rate experienced by those two states in Korea.[1]

The intense competitiveness that makes them good soldiers also has produced a legion of memorable athletes, business leaders, and even such completely American pastimes as NASCAR racing, which evolved from the exploits of the daring moonshine runners of the Appalachian Mountains during the days of Prohibition.

They created and still dominate country music, which along with jazz and soul is a truly American musical form. Indeed, it would be fruitless to single out country music legends from this culture, because to name a dozen would be to leave another hundred out. Country music is at the heart of the Scots-Irish culture. It percolated for more than a century in the remote and distant mountains until WSM radio took it national in the 1930s through the Grand Ole Opry. In the hollows through those isolated earlier years the dulcimer found its plaintive notes, the traditionally exquisite violin turned into such a hot fiddle that some warned it came from the devil, and the *banjar*, a native African instrument made with a gourd, evolved into the hillbilly banjo.

And they gave us so many brilliant writers—Mark Twain the lion among them, Horace Greeley, Edgar Allan Poe and Margaret Mitchell not far behind, and Larry McMurtry a good honorable mention—that their style of folklore became one of the truest American art forms. Not to mention a horde of thespians, including

Tallulah Bankhead, Ava Gardner, Andie MacDowell, the legendary Jimmy Stewart, John Wayne, Robert Redford, and George C. Scott, who hailed from Wise County, Virginia, just a few miles down the road from Big Moccasin Gap. A thousand years ago, English monasteries searched out Scots, Welsh, or Irish monks to be their scribes, calling their native artistic talent "the Celtic curve." And in the American South it has always been said that one cannot shoot an arrow up into the air without having it land on a soldier, a musician, or a writer.

Paradoxically, the Scots-Irish are also a culture of isolation, hard luck, and infinite stubbornness that has always shunned formal education and mistrusted—even hated—any form of aristocracy. In this sense they have given us the truest American of all, the man the elites secretly love to hate (except in Hollywood, where he is openly reviled to the point of caricature), the unreconstructed redneck. Blamed for slavery even though only a minute percentage actually owned slaves, they suffered for generations after the Civil War due to the twin calamities of Reconstruction and the ever-increasing seclusion of the Appalachian and Allegheny Mountains.

Enduring poverty at a rate that far exceeded the rest of the country, over the last century they scattered far and wide, following (most famously) the Hillbilly Highway up to the North-Central factory belt and the *Grapes of Wrath* roads into California, often taking their poverty with them. Conditioned by a thousand years of conflict, those who stayed behind resisted the Northern-dominated structure of the civil rights movement as an invasion from the outside just as vociferously as they had viewed the Civil War in such terms. The reformers who worked to help end segregation failed to understand the vital historical distinctions among white cultures in the South, forcing a fight with a naturally populist people who might otherwise have worked with them, at least on some points, if they had taken a different approach.

The Scots-Irish did not merely come to America, they became America, particularly in the South and the Ohio Valley, where their culture overwhelmed the English and German ethnic groups and defined the mores of those regions. And the irony is that modern America has forgotten who they were (and are) so completely that it is rare to find anyone who can even recognize their ethnic makeup or identify their amazing journey and their singular contributions. It is no exaggeration to say that despite its obsession with race and ethnicity, today's America has a hole in its understanding of its own origins. Not a small hole, as for instance the need to rediscover and recount some long-ago incident in an isolated backwater, but a huge, gaping vacuum that affects virtually every major debate where ethnicity plays a role.

This lack of cultural awareness applies to many people of Scots-Irish heritage as well.

The story of the Scots-Irish has been lost in the common understanding for a variety of reasons. First, due to their individuality and the timing of their migration—roughly the first seventy years of the 1700s—the Scots-Irish never really desired to define themselves by their ethnic identity. In their rush to become Americans, the "hyphens" didn't matter, except in the telling of family histories in the front-porch chronicles that persisted into my own generation. Indeed, although they were the dominant culture of these regions, they were not ethnically exclusive and often intermarried with those who accepted the mores of their communities. A good example of how this phenomenon has affected self-identification is that fully 38 percent of the city of Middlesborough, Kentucky (in the heart of Scots-Irish America), listed their ethnicity on the 2000 census simply as "native American," compared to 7 percent nationwide. America's "ethnocentric retreat" of the last few decades caught this culture unaware and by surprise.

Second, many of the most literate observers of American culture tend to lump the Scots-Irish in with the largely English-derivative New England Protestant groups and the original English settlers of the vast Virginia colony as "WASPs" (White Anglo-Saxon Protestants) under the rubric of "British" ancestry. But these were, and are, distinctly separate and different peoples. In terms of historical background, education, religious formality, and experiences here in America, the people who made up the New England settlements had nothing in common with the Scots-Irish or even with the English who settled in Virginia. Alexis de Tocqueville was instructive on this point in his 1835 classic *Democracy in America.* "The settlers who established themselves in New England," he pointed out, "all belonged to the more independent classes of their native country.... These men possessed, in proportion to their number, a greater mass of intelligence than is to be found in any European nation of our own time. All without exception had received a good education, and many of them were known in Europe for their talents and acquirements."[2]

The New England migrations were well planned, carefully structured, and organized from their beginning to create townships and the advantages of urban infrastructure. The townships were platted out with a careful sense of equality, and families were given their own pieces of land. Academic institutions were created early on, including Harvard, Yale, Princeton, and many of our other great learning institutions. The WASP societies of New England were indeed formidable, dominating America's intellectual and economic institutions for centuries.

The original English settlements in Virginia were quite the opposite, immediately creating an agrarian economy and a three-tiered class system that often caused members of the lower classes to regress rather than advance as the generations moved forward. Of those English settlements de Tocqueville wrote, "The men sent to Virginia were seekers of gold, adventurers without resources and without character.... They were in nowise above the level of the inferior classes in England."[3] Even the later migrations of "Cavalier aristocracy" that eventually made up the famed first families of Virginia had little to do with the WASP cultures of New England— and were not interconnected with the Scots-Irish themselves at all. The Scots-Irish migrations were separate from this three-tiered structure along the Virginia Tidewater, in geographic, religious, and cultural terms.

And thus the Scots-Irish had nothing in common with either the English aristocracy in Virginia or the New England WASP settlements. Nor, for that matter, did the typical English who made their way into the mountains to join them. Some of the English in the mountain communities had come from Ulster with the Scots-Irish. Some came from the border areas between England and Scotland and were, in contrast to the New England English, heavily Celtic in their origins. And others, such as those depicted by de Tocqueville, drifted into the mountains from the ugly, class-based system that characterized lowland Virginia.

These three distinctly separate cultural groups approached almost every important issue differently as the nation took shape, and were affected in dramatically different ways by social and economic policies. Analysts who attempt to analyze American history and political views by combining all those with "British Protestant origins" under one rubric will invariably end up with a false understanding as well as a mass of useless and conflicting data.

Third, there is a tendency in many academic and literary quarters to lump the Scots-Irish in with the Irish themselves. More than 40 million Americans claim Irish descent, exclusive of those Scots-Irish who have self-identified themselves on census reports under other categories such as Scottish or "native American." Interestingly, more than half of these are of Scots-Irish ancestry. This fact is rarely recognized even by Protestants of Scots-Irish descent, many of whom may be found happily wearing the green and marching in St. Patrick's Day parades. A considerable number of Scots-Irish immigrant families did carry Irish as well as Scottish blood, just as many of them also carried English blood. My own ancestors included Murphys, Doyles, and Connollys, among others. But at some point they all became Protestant, and the cultural migration as well as the experiences of the Scots-Irish were widely different from their Celtic kin, the Irish Catholics.

Early America experienced three great "Celtic waves" of migration from Ireland. The first, numbering between 250,000 and 400,000, included many Northern English and Scots, but consisted principally of Scots-Irish Presbyterians emptying out of Ulster.[4] Although the migration began in the late 1690s, its heaviest years were between 1717 and the American Revolution. The second, spurred on by Ireland's potato famine in the late 1840s, was most heavily, but not exclusively, Catholic. In its peak years during the 1860s, about 100,000 Irish immigrants were flooding into America every year.[5] The third, centering on the two decades that bracketed the beginning of the twentieth century, was in many ways a continuation of the second wave but at about half the immigration rate, with 84 percent of all Irish emigrants from 1876 to 1921 coming to the United States.[6]

Once removed from Ireland, the common Celtic origins of these two groups brought many similarities, especially in their military traditions, their affinity for politics, and their literary prowess. But the timing, geography, and cohesion of these respective migrations resulted in starkly different experiences in America. The first, Protestant wave centered on the Appalachian and Allegheny Mountains. The other, principally Irish Catholic migrations flowed mostly into Boston, New York, Philadelphia, and Baltimore, with a secondary outflow to Chicago. They were not only urban in their first instance, but also competitive with other large ethnic migrations such as those from Italy, Greece, and Eastern Europe. They were also up against a truly dominant WASP establishment that quickly became identified as an adversary to be overcome as well as a benchmark against which to measure their success. However, in contrast to the Scots-Irish, these migrations benefited from having landed smack in the middle of America's rich and thriving Northeast corridor. Although they met early resistance from the entrenched elites, the availability of quality schooling and the ability to organize themselves politically allowed many Irish Catholics to assume positions of power and influence very quickly, including in the worlds of publishing, mass media, and academia.

Another division between these two cultures pops up from time to time from the perspective of some Irish Catholic Americans. The unresolved issues between Protestant and Catholic factions in Northern Ireland are closer in their experience than they are to the Scots-Irish, and this remembered bitterness at times affects their views of Americans of Irish Protestant descent. To a few Irish Catholics, the Scots-Irish remains a people apart who should still be battled or at best kept at a distance. If you are Protestant, the logic goes, you have no claim to being truly Irish. This viewpoint amounts to an unfair judgment even as it relates to Irish history itself, as many of Ireland's greatest figures have been Protestant and, in the parlance, "Anglo-Irish." Nationalist leaders Theobald Wolfe Tone and Charles Stewart Parnell come to mind, as do legendary writers Jonathan Swift, William Butler Yeats, and George Bernard Shaw. Musician Van Morrison is also an Irish Protestant of Scottish descent. And the highest-ranking native-born Irishman in the Civil War, the legendary Confederate general Patrick Cleburne, was a Protestant who had once served in the British army.

There is another reason that the Scots-Irish story has been lost to common identification. In the age of political correctness and ultraethnic sensitivities, it has become delicate, to say the least, to celebrate many of this culture's hard-won accomplishments when teaching American history in today's public schools.

The Scots-Irish settled the Ulster Plantation in Northern Ireland at the urging of the English, a position that is anathema to some Irish Catholics, who look at this migration as having sown the seeds of the current Troubles in Ireland. No matter that Presbyterians and Catholics suffered many of the same legal and political difficulties at the hands of the Anglican hierarchy.

They came to America and took the land that no one else wanted, a difficult movement to sell in today's politically correct environment, since in many eyes they took it from the Indians.

Their legacy is stained because they became the dominant culture in the South, whose economic system was based on slavery. No

matter that the English aristocrats of Tidewater were slavery's originators and principal beneficiaries, or that the typical Scots-Irish
yeoman had no slaves and actually suffered economic detriment
from the practice.

They suffered 70 percent killed or wounded in the Civil War
and were still standing proud in the ranks at Appomattox when
General Lee surrendered—but in today's politically correct environment this means that they were the "racist" soldiers of the Nazi-
like Confederacy.

They are a culture founded on guns, which considers the Second Amendment sacrosanct, while literary and academic America
considers such views not only archaic but also threatening. And yet
it is not hyperbole to say that Al Gore lost the 2000 election by going against them on this issue, causing Tennessee and West Virginia
to vote for George W. Bush.

And they are the very heartbeat of fundamentalist Christianity,
which itself is largely derived from the harsh demands of Scottish
Calvinism. As such, they have produced their share of fire-and-
brimstone spiritual leaders, whose conservative views on social issues continually offend liberal opinion-makers.

Because "sophisticated" America tends to avert its eyes from the
bellicose and often warlike nature of their journey, it also is inclined to ignore or misunderstand this culture, even though the
Scots-Irish continue to hold enormous social and political sway.
Other than the occasional student that they are usually able to tame
through the educational process of their high-end universities, or
the Southern politician that they can indoctrinate and mold into
their version of a respectable presidential candidate, America's
elites have had very little contact with this culture. As with African-
Americans fifty years ago, they rest comfortably with the false notion that the "redneck world" does not comprise a social or political
force outside of the narrow and often invented social issues that are
necessary to get its vote. The elites do not have to deal with people
from this culture on a daily basis in their classrooms or their neigh-

borhoods or at work. They do not see them in their clubs or go to the same parties. They do not need their goodwill in order to advance professionally. But they ignore them at their peril. Because in this culture's heart beats the soul of working-class America.

These are loyal Americans, sometimes to the point of mawkishness. They show up for our wars. Indeed, we cannot go to war without them. They haul our goods. They grow our food. They sweat in our factories. And if they turn against you, you are going to be in a fight.

Historian Walter Russell Mead, who won the 2002 Lionel Gelber Prize for outstanding writing on international affairs, illuminated the validity of these last points in an essay examining what he termed "the Jacksonian Tradition" in American foreign policy.[7] Defining a movement that came out of the Scots-Irish settlements and later migrations and was personified by President Andrew Jackson, Mead contrasted the Jacksonians with other foreign policy cultures such as the Wilsonians, Hamiltonians, and Jeffersonians. The Jacksonians, he indicated, are "instinctively democratic and populist." They believe "that the government should do everything in its power to promote the well-being—political, moral, economic—of the folk community. Any means are permissible . . . so long as they do not violate the moral feelings or infringe on the freedoms that Jacksonians believe are essential in their daily lives."[8]

Mead asserts that this political movement takes its views from the Scots-Irish definitions of personal honor, equality, and individualism,[9] and then makes two vitally significant observations. The first is that despite this reality, the Jacksonians are virtually invisible to America's elites. "Jacksonianism is less an intellectual or political movement than an expression of the social, cultural and religious values of a large portion of the American public. And it is doubly obscure because it happens to be rooted in one of the portions of the public least represented in the media and the professoriat."[10]

The second is that the tenets of Jacksonianism have expanded beyond the Scots-Irish to become the dominant political code of

America's working class, including the more recent immigrant communities in the North. "American Catholics, once among the world's most orthodox, remained Catholic in religious allegiance but were increasingly individualistic in terms of psychology and behavior. . . . Urban immigrants may have softened some of the rough edges of Jacksonian America, but the descendants of the great wave of European immigration sound more like Andrew Jackson from decade to decade."[11]

It is one of the odd paradoxes of modern America that this movement has had such an impact while at the same time those who brought it to this country have been so frequently reviled, and their history has been allowed to melt into obscurity. To understand the movement and its future implications, one must understand the people who created it and still sustain it. And to understand the people who created it, one must comprehend their journey, which has been not simply one of hardship or disappointment, but rather of frequent and bitter conflict. These conflicts, from which they have never in two thousand years of history retreated, have followed a historically consistent cycle of, among other things, a values-based combativeness, an insistent egalitarianism, and a refusal to be dominated from above, no matter the cost.

That mind-set promises to play an even greater role in American politics as the philosophical debates shift into unpredictable new territory. We have now entered an era where the old labels of liberal and conservative no longer resonate, and where the most comfortably predictable alliances of both Democrats and Republicans may soon begin to fall away. On these shifting political sands, the hyperindividualistic Scots-Irish and their Jacksonian allies will very likely have more influence than at any time since the age of Andrew Jackson himself.

To understand the forces that drive this culture, one must begin in Scotland, a very long time ago.

PART TWO

The Making of a People — and a Nation

Oh, Flower of Scotland
When will we see your like again?
That fought and died for your wee bit Hill and Glen?
And stood against them, Proud Edward's armies
And sent them homeward, tae think again

—*"Flower of Scotland,"*
a Scottish traditional song

1

Hadrian's Wall

ON MARCH 6, 1997, I buried my father in Arlington National Cemetery. It was bitter cold on Arlington Ridge. The sky was cloudless, so blue that it reminded me of robins' eggs. The wind blew in hard from the northwest, just as it always does in this part of Virginia when bringing in a cold front. It whipped our faces as my family and a few dozen friends stood at his grave site, listening to the Air Force chaplain utter his final prayers.

I had done my duty, as it is demanded of the eldest son in my culture. I had met his casket at the front door of the Fort Myer chapel when the Air Force burial detail ushered it inside from the hearse. I had welcomed the guests and delivered the eulogy. I had chosen the four-verse poem "Crossing the Bar" by Alfred, Lord Tennyson so that each of his children could read a verse and in some small way say good-bye. It was the same poem that my father's mother had asked to be read at her own funeral, many years before. He had made me memorize it when I was eight years old, but there would be few other times in my life that he would have to force me into poetry. Poetry was one of our little games, a shared passion, along with hunting and fishing and long, intense discussions about how to lead, and how to fight, and who had led the best and who had fought the hardest.

Sunset and evening bell, and after that the dark
And may there be no sadness of farewell when I embark

But at the grave site, as the biting wind blew my tears into salt streaks along my face, my eyes were on my brother. He stood farther up the hill, near an old tree, shivering in a kilt. And as the chaplain finished the eternal, never-ending prayer that committed my father's remains forever into the honored soil of Arlington, my brother's bagpipes filled the air, his music washing over us. Standing alone on that knob of earth, like a sentry guarding the gates of our distant past, my brother played "Amazing Grace," and then "Scotland the Brave."

The music reached inside me, to a place that I can neither identify nor explain, and I thought of the long, impossible journey that had brought my blood to this very spot. I was, I reasoned, so very different from the first of my people who had come to the mountains those hundreds of years ago. And yet I also was so very much the same. We were pioneers, that was what my father and mother had so strongly urged upon us when we were small. Scots-Irish, with a smattering of Irish and English and even Cherokee thrown in. Out of Ulster, into the mountains, off to other places. *Your people carried this country on their backs, and don't you ever forget it.*

Did America change us? Or did we change America? And who were we—was there really a consistency that could be defined?

The answer, I decided, was some, some, and definitely yes. And I knew that the best way to examine that consistency was to go back to where it was formed.

Some might think it absurd to reach back two thousand years in order to fully comprehend the temperament of a cultural piece of today's America. And yet, many people are comfortable looking into the biblical Scriptures for evidence of how they should conduct their lives, and others argue firmly that the basis for Western ideals in government, philosophy, and even drama can be found in ancient Greece. Indeed, the Japanese people can trace the direct ancestry of their emperor and thus the movement of their culture through a line that begins before the time of Christ.

For many centuries the ancestors of today's Scots-Irish Americans carried on an oral rather than a written tradition. They were a warlike culture that indulged in little trade and left few tangible records, other than the observations from the more learned peoples who observed them. But strong cultures come together in the face of challenge and cannot help but leave their mark. To fully comprehend the forces that created the Scots-Irish mind-set of today, one must actually begin nearly two thousand years ago, and then trace a series of events that culminated in the Battle of Bannockburn in 1314. It is best to start from atop the ruins of an ancient structure built by Roman soldiers at the command of an emperor named Hadrian.

The enduring character of the Scots-Irish people was formed first and foremost in Scotland. Geography shaped it, cultural traits related closely to survival were its grist, and a peculiar form of struggle hardened and refined it. At Hadrian's Wall, one can consider the interplay of all of these. For along this wall, give or take a few miles, is where the Scottish nation took its physical shape. And it was the resistance of one people as well as the ebbing of another that drew its southern boundary.

The wall stretched for seventy-three miles from sea to sea across the island's narrow neck a few miles south of where modern-day England and Scotland share their border, from Carlisle in the west to the other side of Newcastle in the east. It took Rome's soldiers six years to build it. Made principally of stone, it was in most places fifteen feet high and ten feet across. The wall was marked along the way by a series of signal towers—about eighty "mile castles" where small Roman garrisons manned outposts, and seventeen larger forts with gateways into and out of the northern "wilderness" that we now call Scotland. A thirty-foot-deep ditch ran in front of it, and another ditch was dug behind it.

The wall's ruins are not much to look at—mostly crumbling

stones now set in overgrown fields, where it seems far more sheep pass their days than humans. But if one considers the energies that propelled the building of it and the cultural forces that thereafter stacked up behind each side of it, Hadrian's Wall assumes a magic all its own. Indeed, it becomes a nesting place for remembering a tale of dissipating empires, and of new peoples emerging from the seeds of past defiance.

Fifty-five years before the birth of Christ, Roman legions crossed what someday would be called the English Channel and invaded Britain. Behind them lay the societal wreckage and reassembly from their conquest of much of Central Europe and Gaul. The tribes that the Romans had defeated on this journey were largely Celtic. The Celts were a warlike but emotional people known for their flowing oratory as well as their mastery of metallurgy, both in personal adornments and in weaponry.[1] They had lost to the Romans because they were consistently hampered by one tragic flaw: they were adamantly tribal, gathering not as nations but instead following the lead of a long succession of warrior princes, and thus defied modern notions of political unity. Nora Chadwick illuminated this point in her classic work, *The Celts*. "In any conflict between Celts and Romans, the superior powers of organization, sense of discipline and general orderliness of the Roman culture were bound to overcome the volatile and undisciplined Celts whose sense of loyalty, powerful though it may have been, was normally centered on an individual rather than on an institution or an ideal."[2]

But although defeated, the stronger warriors among the Celtic tribes did not submit to Roman conquest. Some chose to die on the battlefield with sword in hand. The others moved on, expanding outward in several directions from the Roman areas, in some cases swooping south to attack Rome itself.[3] In fact, there is considerable evidence to indicate that the Teutonic tribes that later emerged in Germany were yet another division of the Celtic people.[4]

The invading Romans faced a similar assortment of Celtic tribes in Britain, which were doomed to meet similar results. In a series of campaigns that ran intermittently for more than a hundred years, the Romans conquered most of what is now termed England, and then Wales after that. Again, the stronger, the luckier, and ultimately the freer among the Celts avoided the yoke of conquest, refusing to go through that mandatory ritual of defeat, the bowing of heads as the vanquished were required to walk under a low bar in order to "bend the knee to Rome." Many of them headed for the untamed areas of Cornwall, Wales, and especially Scotland, and from these redoubts continued to resist the Roman occupation. In the words of Winston Churchill, "In the wild North and West freedom found refuge among the mountains, but elsewhere the conquest and pacification were at length complete and Britannia became one of the forty-five provinces of the Roman Empire."[5]

And resist they did. In A.D. 71, after brutally suppressing a rebellion in East Anglia, the Romans headed north in an attempt to conquer the southern areas of what is now Scotland. In Scotland the Romans met up not only with the tribes that had migrated away from their earlier invasions, but also with a fierce native people they later named the Picts, due to their tradition of painting important tattoo-like symbols on their bodies. Many campaigns followed, including, as Chadwick writes, an eastward march where the Romans "were met by a vast array of Caledonians, presumably the immediate ancestors of the historic Picts, with whom they fought a great pitched battle at an unidentified place called Mons Graupius."[6] Factual accounts of such campaigns are difficult to verify, since the Celts of Scotland did not commit records to writing until the fifth century,[7] but some estimates, probably taken from Roman reports, indicate that thirty thousand Caledonians were killed in this battle.[8]

But it was not only the wild Celts of the north who took fearsome casualties. As Churchill writes, the positions the Romans "had won in Scotland had to be gradually abandoned. The legions fell back on the line of the Stangate, a road running eastward from

Carlisle. The years which followed revealed the weakness of the British frontier. The accession of Hadrian was marked by a serious disaster. The Ninth Legion disappears from history combating an obscure uprising of the tribes in Northern Britain. The defenses were disorganized and the province was in danger."[9]

In A.D. 122 the Romans decided to partition their conquered lands from the wilderness they had been unable to tame. Roman emperor Hadrian visited Britain, and in a trip to the north he decided to build a boundary stretching from sea to sea in order to defend Rome's holdings from further attacks. And thus was built the wall that bears his name. A second wall called the Antonine Wall was built farther to the north twenty years later, but the Romans found themselves surrounded on both sides by the ferociously resisting barbarians, and this structure was quickly abandoned. One can get a hint of the nature of the Celtic people the Romans were up against at the Antonine Wall in the works of Cassius Dio (c. A.D. 150–235). Dio, one of Rome's most influential "mid-period" historians, described the tribes that were to the front and rear of the Roman position.

There are two principal races of the Britons, the Caledonians and the Maeatae, and the names of the others have been merged in these two. The Maeatae live next to the cross-wall which cuts the island in half, and the Caledonians are beyond them. Both tribes inhabit wild and waterless mountains and desolate and swampy plains, and possess neither walls, cities, nor tilled fields, but live on their flocks, wild game, and certain fruits; for they do not touch the fish which are there found in immense and inexhaustible quantities.

They dwell in tents, naked and unshod, possess their women in common, and in common rear all the offspring. Their form of rule is democratic for the most part, and they are very fond of plundering; consequently they choose their boldest men as rulers. They go into battle in chariots, and have small, swift horses; there are also foot-soldiers, very swift in running and very firm in standing their ground. For arms they have a shield and a short spear, with a bronze apple attached to the end of the spear-shaft, so that when it is shaken it may clash and terrify the enemy; and they also have the dagger.

They can endure hunger and cold and any kind of hardship; for they plunge into the swamps and exist there for many days with only their heads above water, and in the forests they support themselves upon bark and roots, and for all emergencies they prepare a certain kind of food, the eating of a small portion of which, the size of a bean, prevents them from feeling either hunger or thirst.

Such is the general character of the island of Britain, and such are the inhabitants of at least the hostile part of it.[10]

Once the Antonine Wall was abandoned, Hadrian's Wall became the permanent dividing line between the forces of Rome and those who refused to be assimilated. But Rome's retreat to this wall did not stop these burgeoning and volatile tribes from making war on the Romans. Nor did it put an end to punitive raids by the Romans into northern territory. Its intention, and its main effect, was to enable Rome to consolidate its political control in the south by clearly defining its boundaries.

And still the tribes of the north persisted. Cassius Dio went on to describe the costly and exhausting nature of the military operations undertaken by the Romans when they sought to subdue these Celtic warriors and their families, as well as the draconian measures the Romans were inclined to take when things went wrong. On the one hand, his accounts demonstrate the strategic and tactical acumen of the loosely knit tribes the Romans faced. On the other, they give fresh meaning to the importance of the concept that we now term "the laws of war."

Severus, accordingly, desiring to subjugate the whole of it, invaded Caledonia. But as he advanced through the country he experienced countless hardships in cutting down the forests, leveling the heights, filling up the swamps, and bridging the rivers. . . . The enemy purposely put sheep and cattle in front of the soldiers for them to seize, in order that they might be lured on still further until they were worn out; for in fact the water caused great suffering to the Romans, and when they became scattered, they would be attacked. Then, unable to walk, they would be slain by their own men, in order to avoid capture, so that a full fifty thousand died.

When the inhabitants of the island again revolted, he summoned the soldiers and ordered them to invade the rebels' country, killing everybody they met; and he quoted these words:

"Let no one escape sheer destruction,

No one in our hands, not even the babe in the womb of the mother,

If it be male; let it nevertheless not escape sheer destruction."[11]

These raids by the emperor Severus in A.D. 208 were uncommonly vicious. They did not break the spirit of the northern tribes, but they did succeed on another level. Failing to defeat the enemy that inhabited this harsh wilderness, Severus decided for once and for all to permanently seal them off. As Churchill wrote, Severus "flung his energies into the task of reorganization [along the wall, and] stability was achieved. So great had been the destruction, so massive were his repairs, that in later times he was thought to have built the Wall, which in fact he only reconstructed. He died at York in 211; but for a hundred years there was peace along the Roman Wall."[12]

The Romans could conduct all the punitive raids they wanted and kill all the Caledonian men, mothers, and babies that they desired, but in the context of history it did not matter. Their empire in Britain had reached its high-water mark, and there were a whole lot of people on the northern side of the wall whom they had not conquered and would never be able to conquer. And thus the peoples of the north, ragged and barbaric though they were, could forever make one important boast: they had never bent a knee to Rome.

Hundreds of years passed. Differing bloodlines mixed on both sides of the wall. Different forms of government were attempted. On the southern, English side of the wall, the Romans eventually disappeared, replaced as rulers and occupants by a continuing mix of Angles and Saxons, Jutes and Danes, and, eventually, after the 1066 Battle of Hastings, by the scions of the Norman Conquest.

And on the northern, Scottish side of the wall, a different sort of mixing and adaptation was taking place, leading to the creation of a different sort of people.

2

Tribalism Versus Feudalism:
The Celtic Tie of Kinship

AS THE CENTURIES progressed south of Hadrian's Wall, the Romans and then the Saxons and especially the Normans who followed them developed a cultural and governmental system that would be recognizable in some form in England today. Their methods and structures are also visible when one looks at the early New England settlements, whose townships in America comprised a distant mirror. By contrast, the basic formation of society on the northern side of Hadrian's Wall can still be identified in Scotland and to some extent in Ireland, and are clearly recognizable in the Scots-Irish cultures that dominated the making of the American South.

England became Anglo-Saxon and then Norman while Scotland remained Celtic. England became highly structured, top-down, and feudal while Scotland remained atomized, bottom-up, and in many respects tribal. The English (particularly under the Normans) built a military caste system coldly imposed from above as a sort of tax. The Celts retained a no-less-warlike tribal system, but the personal loyalties that fueled it, emanating as they did from below, made it more democratic and compelling, based on an individual's honor in belonging to the tribe. And the implications of these distinctions, subtle as they may seem, are in fact enormous.

Below Hadrian's Wall, in the words of Churchill, "there was law; there was order; there was peace; there was warmth; there was food and a long-established custom of life. The population was free from barbarism without being slunk into sloth or luxury. Roman habits percolated; the use of Roman utensils and even of Roman speech steadily grew. The British thought themselves as good Romans as any. . . . To be a citizen of Rome was to be a citizen of the world, raised upon a pedestal of unquestioned superiority over barbarians or slaves."[13]

This benefit was structural as well as material and emotional. "The gift which Roman civilization had to bestow was civic and political. Towns were planned in chessboard squares for communities dwelling under orderly government. The buildings rose in accordance with the patterns standardized throughout the Roman world."[14] This standard held its pattern and was not dissimilar to the structure of the New England towns in the early settlements of the seventeenth century.

The most telling modification of the Roman system came after the Norman Conquest of England, when William the Conqueror crossed the English Channel from France and defeated the Saxons in the Battle of Hastings in 1066. For four years thereafter, William, the bastard son of the duke of Normandy, conducted a vicious slash-and-burn campaign throughout England, subduing the countryside, ousting the Saxon nobility, and installing French-born masters in every manor and castle. Dramatic changes were literally thrust down England's throat. As Churchill put it, "Everywhere castles arose. These were not at first the massive stone structures of a later century; they were simply fortified military posts. . . . From these strongpoints horsemen sallied forth to rule and exploit the neighborhood; above them all, at the summit, sat William, active and ruthless, delighting in his work, requiring punctual service from his adherents and paying good spoil to all who did their duty."[15]

For a while, the ever-adaptable English paid homage to their

new French masters, learning French and taking on French customs. Within a few generations, however, the French royalty had
been absorbed through intermarriage and became simply another
layer of ethnicity that blended in with past conquests to define
what it meant to be English. The lasting impact of the Norman invasion proved to be structural, not ethnic, for it ushered in the feudal system with its heavy-handed diminution of the common man.
It is grand in these modern days to think of fanciful tales of knights
in shining armor with their fair maidens and their squires and their
jousting fests as well as the effusive toasts to brotherhood before famous battles that are well remembered in William Shakespeare's
better plays. But this was a system that thrived on camaraderie
among a band of elites and was fed by the unthinking subjugation
of those below them. The lowly serf who toiled hard for his daily
crust of black bread was given no toasts, and very little thanks, in
feudal England.

In fact, the tie between lord and serf in England's feudal society
was clearly incidental to the stronger tie between the lord and his
owned properties. Churchill termed Norman feudalism "a sudden
acceleration of the drift toward the manorial system . . . even in
Wessex the idea still persisted that the tie of lord and man was primarily personal, so that a free man could go from one lord to another and transfer his land with him. The essence of Norman
feudalism, on the other hand, was that the land remained with the
lord, whatever the man might do. Thus the landed pyramid rose up
tier by tier to the King, until every acre in the country could be registered as held of somebody by some form of service."[16] This bond
of service was unbreakable to be sure, but only in the same sense as
a property tax that must be paid.

North of Hadrian's Wall the centuries passed more harshly, and
yet in a way were far more just. Different migrations, severe terrain, and a primitive but insistent form of populism bred a different
kind of people. The Romans and their Saxon/Norman progeny
were quite used to systems based on inflexible notions of class. The

Celts, by contrast, refused to be so rigidly regulated despite their penchant for following strong leaders. In addition, while Scotland's rough topography made it difficult to conquer, it made it equally difficult to rule. This affected both the ethnic makeup of the area whose borders had been defined by Hadrian's Wall, and the manner in which its peoples finally succeeded in "coming together" as a true nation.

Not unlike Appalachia, Scotland is a land of difficult water barriers, sharp mountains and deep hollows, soggy moors and rough pastures, and of thin, uncultivable soil that lies like a blanket over wide reaches of granite. Armies such as the Roman legions described by Cassius Dio tended literally to become bogged down as they advanced into Scotland's interior. And (again not unlike Appalachia), a central government that wished to impose its will on the tough, weapons-wielding folks who dwelled back in the hollows would be guaranteed a hostile reception unless it had the full cooperation of local leaders.

Unlike in England, the settlements of ancient Scotland grew haphazardly and emphasized a rugged form of survival that had links neither to commerce nor to the developing world. Again we find a cultural evolution and a fundamental lifestyle very much like those that would emerge later in the Appalachian Mountains. Professor T. C. Smout, who once held a personal chair at the University of Edinburgh, described these early patterns in his seminal *A History of the Scottish People, 1560–1830.*

> Virtually everyone lived by some form of agriculture. Pastoral farming, herding rough-haired cattle, goats and sheep . . . represents a survival into modern times . . . In the steep, rain-sodden, peat-covered mountains of the west, however, hunting and fishing were probably then, as they were much later, as important as agriculture. The peoples of Scotland do not in these early times seem to have lived in large nucleated villages, except in parts of Lothian. . . . More typically their houses were grouped in small

settlements that were, later at least, often called baile or farm-touns. The buildings were of turf or stone, skin or brushwood, and often partly subterranean in their struggle with Scottish weather. . . . [There was] little that we would have identified as urban life—there was no coinage until the twelfth century, few sophisticated crafts and evidently no organized trade with the outside world.[17]

Hadrian's Wall had succeeded all too well, for in addition to their independence, the tribes of Scotland had also retained their primitivity. Furthermore, Scotland's rough topography meant that invading armies of any size coming from the south were limited in their approaches to the eastern and western extremities. In the west this would later result in centuries of so-called "border wars" involving the ancestors of America's Scots-Irish as well as a contin-ual mixing of the blood and lifestyles between the lowland Scots and the English in the area where the English and Scottish borders were so ill-defined. But away from this narrow land border, Scotland is surrounded on three sides by the sea. And in the early centuries, the greatest and most important migrations came to her soil from Ireland.

Although some historians mention Viking invasions from Nor-way and possible early forays from Spain, Scotland was principally inhabited by four different early peoples, and it would take nearly a thousand years for these peoples to finally cohere into a true Scottish nation.[18] The strongest of them, and the oldest inhabitants of the land, were the Picts, a Celtic people who believed in matrilin-eal descent and whose origins will probably never be fully known. These were the wild, combative tribes who stood so strongly against the Romans, entering their journals as large-limbed, tattooed, red-haired madmen, which probably was not much of an exaggeration.

The most learned and diplomatic of the four peoples were the Scots, or *Scotti*, a powerful Irish tribe that had gained ascendance in Northern Ireland. By the fifth century the *Scotti* were joining a larger Irish migration across the narrow sea into western Scotland. Nora Chadwick mentions this "invasion from Ireland which, beginning in a small way, grew in importance till it imposed the Irish language on the whole of the Highlands in what is known today as Gaelic, and gradually extended its political sway over the Picts."[19] In the southwest of Scotland were the Britons, a Celtic tribe that once had dominated England itself and now straddled the border roughly created by Hadrian's Wall. And in the southeast, in an area below modern-day Edinburgh called the Lothians, were the Angles, a largely Germanic tribe that had swept northward from the border areas during the seventh century.

It was the *Scotti* who were principally responsible for the union of the different kingdoms, beginning in the ninth century when they defeated the Picts and united their peoples into a single kingdom called Alba.[20] Over the next two centuries the Scots continued their consolidation through warfare and intermarriage, and by 1034 "the Picts, the Scots, the Lothian Angles and the Strathclyde [southwestern Scotland] Britons owed common allegiance to an Alban king."[21]

But the story of the rise of Scotland cannot be told through a simple enumeration of kings and royal houses, although in the ancient Celtic tradition its people continued to rally behind and fight on behalf of strong leaders. Just as the mountains and the hollows broke up the flow of peoples, so also did they contain and bind personal loyalties to more local chieftains. And these loyalties could never be demanded by some faraway prince or regent based on land ownership or on mere royal blood that by some circumstance had captured a distant throne. Loyalty, as well as the military service it entailed, was given by an individual as a matter of personal honor and kinship to the leader of one's local tribe, which over the centuries took up the now-familiar name of "clan." And it was up to these leaders to decide whether to join a larger cause.

As Professor Smout points out, "Celtic society was clearly tribal, based on a real or fancied kinship between every free man and the head of his tribe. The tribes occupied fairly distinct areas of the country, had reached the stage of individual ownership of land among the tribesmen, were organised [sic] in social strata . . . and possessed differing tribal laws that were memorised [sic] by hereditary wise men who handed them down unaltered to their sons. . . . Feudalism is the antithesis of tribalism."[22]

This "Celtic tie of kinship" has survived in some form through the ages, even in America. An offshoot of this ancient concept defines the unusually strong feelings about military service held by so many Americans of Scottish and Irish descent, and helps explain why such a high percentage of American combat units in today's volunteer military are from Scots-Irish and Irish Catholic backgrounds. From the earliest known history of the Celts, military service was viewed not simply as an obligation, but as a high honor. Fighting for—and alongside—the tribal leader (or, later, the Great Captain, or, as now, one's branch of military service) brought one into the family. And at this level—the willingness to face danger collectively—every family member was equal regardless of rank or wealth. Fighting especially well turned one into a favored son, and in time could even allow him to evolve into a new tribal leader.

Another aspect of this notion of extended kinship was that it tended to embrace members of other ethnic groups rather than demean them. An individualistic society based on loyal service reaches to the person rather than to his or her ethnicity, although it certainly is capable of opposing an enemy on racial or national grounds if it is threatened. It was the later Norman society that attempted to break apart the Celtic notion of kinship and replace it with impersonal, territorial loyalties that pyramided their way up to the English king, a system that encouraged the more nationalist form of racism.[23] Religious and other barriers could complicate this notion, but in the Celtic societies, if one stepped forward to serve, he was "of the kin" so long as he accepted the values and mores of the extended family.

And so when the Scottish people began to form a nation, they

were already an eclectic lot, bound not so much by previous origins
as by their loyalties to the tribes (or clans) that absorbed them.
Again, Professor T. C. Smout comments, " 'That wicked army,' said
the English chronicler of the host advancing to the Battle of
Standard in 1138, 'was composed of Normans, Germans, English,
of Northumbrians and Cumbrians, of men of Teviotdale and
Lothian, of Picts who are commonly called Galwegians, and of
Scots.'. . . Scotland, in fact, was much less an identifiable state than
a confederacy of peoples with distinct characteristics and traditions,
each prone to rebellion and to internecine war, held together only
by allegiance to the person of the king."[24]

One could see this phenomenon just as clearly in the Appalachian settlements of the eighteenth century, where the Scots-Irish
quickly assimilated the English, Irish, German, Welsh, French, and
other settlers among them, bending them to their "characteristics
and traditions" while also accepting them as equals in their communities.

Further evidence of this notion was brought home to me rather
succinctly during a trip to Ireland in the early 1990s while I was
visiting a very thoughtful gentleman who, thirty years before in
his youth, had been a member of the Irish Republican Army.
Ruminating on the often violent struggle between Irish Catholics
and Protestants that has now gone on for more than three centuries, I suggested that new blood might leaven the brawl and even
shake away old hatreds. Half facetiously, I commented that perhaps [then prime minister] Maggie Thatcher could alleviate the
problem in Hong Kong and help resolve the Troubles in Northern
Ireland by allowing a hundred thousand Hong Kong Chinese to
emigrate to Ulster.

He laughed, then grew deadly serious. "You're wrong, you see,
because you underestimate the power of the Celtic culture.
We'd absorb them," he said. "Within ten years we'd have the
IRA [Catholic-supporting] Chinese and the Orange [Protestant-
supporting] Chinese."

The union of the Scottish peoples beginning in the eleventh century did enthrone a monarchy and as a result enabled national leaders to look outward. As this was occurring, the powerful, ever-aggressive Anglo-Norman barons reached northward into Scotland, establishing themselves in a series of fortified castles and controlling their holdings through the use of heavily armed horsemen that the local Scots found impossible to turn away.[25] The result of these two realities was that the Scottish kings found themselves on the one hand vulnerable to this power and on the other seduced by its sophistication. The Norman pattern of military pressure and royal intermarriage saw a succession of Scottish kings accommodating English royalty and also engaging in periodic flirtations with the French. And by 1212 an English commentator was writing that the Scottish royal house "was Norman in blood and heart, French in race and manner of life, in speech and in culture."[26]

This "Normanization" of the highest levels of Scottish royalty had implications both inside and outside Scotland. In England's eyes, their rulers were changing the character of Scotland, just as the Normans had done in the south. However, in the layers below the national throne, nothing could have been further from the truth. True, the powerful Celtic earls who, in Smout's words, had "been the backbone of the indigenous aristocracy in Alba,"[27] had now been brought into a semblance of feudal relations with the king. But in Scottish eyes, at least at the level below the monarch, they had done so only by applying the traditional notions of Celtic kinship to their obligations. The lower Scottish nobility had committed neither themselves nor those who served under them in the manner envisaged by the Scottish monarch and the English invaders. The Norman system based on land ownership would have bound them to the monarch for as long as they held their properties. But they had rejected the Norman concept of feudalism and relied explicitly on their own tradition of blood fealty to the Alban monarch—a loyalty that could be withdrawn if they and their kin decided it was not being wisely placed.

This is not to say that the English overlords failed to establish feudalism in Scotland, but rather that its concepts never fully penetrated the culture in a way that changed the character of either the tribal leaders or the common people. As Smout put it, "Even knights and castles, the effective teeth of feudalism, could do no more than grip the fringe of this fierce country for the king."[28]

The end result was predictable. The Scots had grown together from the bottom up over many centuies, through a myriad of interlocking loyalties that began with the independent spirit of an individual offering his service to the leader of his local clan. Especially at the level below the monarch, they were ready to declare themselves an independent nation. Meanwhile, the English had evolved from their Roman, Saxon, and Norman models and emerged into a powerful, ever-expanding nation based on a highly organized system of controlling its people through the implications of land ownership. Applying the lessons of their own history, their rulers had decided that it was time to bring Scotland permanently inside their sphere.

Thus began the Wars of Independence, which would ebb and flow for nearly a century, from 1286 to 1371. However, the key period of this conflict began with English king Edward I's massacre of almost the entire city of Berwick in 1296 and ended with the Scottish victory over England at Bannockburn in 1314. Between these two dates the Scottish people showed their unyielding character not only to the world but also to their own frequently hesitant royalty. That royalty finally responded by declaring the Land of the North to be a true nation.

3

Braveheart

THE SCOTTISH MONARCHS had intermarried and intermingled with the English and the Normans, the French and the Norwegians, until the throne became something of a foreign playground. The Scottish people had kept their distance from this enchantment, assimilating the occasional outsider who came into their midst but not wishing to mimic the ways of the world beyond the next mountain or quick stream. The Scottish monarchs had become fascinated by the goings-on in such places as London and Paris, an ancient version of jet-setting as they cavorted with the foreign glitterati of their day, often living overseas for years at a time. The Scottish people had kept to their lochs and moors and glens, entranced by the meter and the cadence of their ancient oral culture, which now was finding a written voice in rhetoric and poetry and song. The hybrid Scottish monarchy was seduced by what it viewed to be its new place in the larger world, daring to dream that it had become part of the international elite. The Scottish people did not care much for the larger world, and they especially did not care much for elites.

Having themselves been altered in their blood and traditions by intermarriage with Norman and English royalty, the high families of Scotland now embraced further schemes. In 1286 a quirk of history had made Margaret—at the age of three—the only direct heir to the throne of her grandfather, King Alexander III of Scotland, and thus she was in line to be the queen. Margaret was known in Scotland as the Maid of Norway since her late mother had married King Eric II of that country. Born in Norway, she had never even set foot in Scotland.

"Proud" King Edward I, England's ruthless and unusually powerful monarch, saw opportunity where others saw tragedy. In his eyes, Alexander's death could quickly deliver him the prize of Scotland itself.

The thirteenth century had begun a period of great change in Europe that over the next few centuries would cause the transition from the feudal system to the concept of the modern sovereign state. In sovereign terms, the great irritation of a feudal estate was that it could cross national boundaries. As the modern state evolved, this created difficulties not only in terms of military obligations, but also in such issues as taxation and local government. As Princeton's Joseph Strayer wrote in his classic text *Western Europe in the Middle Ages*, "Overlapping political authority was just as natural under feudal conditions as it is unnatural in the modern state; the transition from the first to the second was bound to cause conflict. The concept of distinct boundaries, within which one ruler has supreme authority, was new at the end of the thirteenth century. In attempting to draw such boundaries, overlapping rights had to be ignored and tenuous claims of suzerainty exaggerated."[29]

King Edward I was a master of this process of exaggerating claims to contested land areas, using it to good effect in the "final conquest" of North Wales, and then setting his sights, or rather his obsessions, on Scotland. Noting the fragility of the Scottish throne, Edward seized the moment, gaining agreement among Scotland's and Norway's high royalty that the infant girl should marry Edward II, his eldest son, who would one day succeed him. The arrangement was formally agreed to among Margaret's four guardians and the king in the Treaty of Birgham-on-Tweed. Ominously, the treaty also guaranteed that young Edward would gain an irrevocable personal right to "the Scottish inheritance" if he produced an heir, with Margaret or any other wife, so long as he and the infant queen had once been married.[30] Thus, Edward I had arranged to deliver to England by royal fiat that which it had been unable to accomplish through a thousand years of military effort—a Scotland that would be firmly ruled by English royalty.

The Scottish people and their tribal leaders watched and listened, having already rejected the entire basis of this odd Norman concept whereby the ownership of land somehow equated to the subjugation of peoples. And they were not convinced.

The child-queen mooted the point in 1290 when she died in a stormy sea as she was being rushed from Norway to the royal court. But after her death, civil war threatened Scotland as the Scottish kingdom had no clear line of succession to its throne. Thirteen people stepped forward and claimed the right to rule, and the Scots had no legal apparatus that would resolve their claims. Instead, Scotland's high families invited the notorious Edward I to reconcile the question, and predictably he acted not as a mediator but as a firm-handed regent. His appetite having been whetted by his earlier attempt to wed his son to little dead Margaret, Edward chose John Balliol, the weakest among the possible successors. At the same time, Edward made clear that he considered himself to be the true overlord of Scotland.

John Balliol might be king, but Edward was going to rule.

Balliol was crowned at historic Scone on St. Andrew's Day, 1292. He was now king of Scotland, but many of the castles and their soldiers were already in Norman-English hands. Edward I himself lost no effort in humiliating Balliol, and within a year he had claimed the three largest towns in Scotland as his own due to Balliol's alleged contempt of the throne. Two years later Balliol appealed to the French for help, and in October 1295 he signed a weakly worded treaty with the French. Edward seized upon this desperation as a breach of fealty and decided to march on Scotland.

March Proud King Edward did. Burn he did. Kill he did, earning along the way the nickname "the Hammer of Scotland." In a campaign more vicious than anything Scotland had seen since the pillage by Roman emperor Severus a thousand years before, Edward set upon the flourishing port of Berwick, then the richest city in Scotland, and literally destroyed everything in it, including its people. On March 30, 1296, Edward entered Berwick with some 5,000 cavalry and 30,000 infantry, and in one day killed an estimated 17,000 people. As Churchill rather dryly put it, "Berwick sank in a few hours from one of the active centres [*sic*] of European commerce to the minor seaport which exists today."[31]

Why did Edward do this, and indeed, how could a supposedly Christian monarch have lived with such blood on his hands? Centuries later, in 1937, the Japanese would coin a phrase for such ruthless conduct as they took similar (though not so completely brutal) measures in Nanking, China. In Asia the concept was called "killing the chicken to scare the monkeys." Laying waste to Berwick was a deliberate act of state terrorism, the medieval equivalent of a strategically placed atomic bomb. It was meant to create such fear in the rest of Scotland that the people would hurry to show their deference to the powerful English king.

Wrong country. Wrong people.

Edward should have read his history more carefully, for he then would have understood that Roman emperor Severus also had underestimated the intransigence of the people of the North in the face of foreign brutality. The English king did predict accurately the actions of many of the high Scottish nobles, but he vastly underestimated the people themselves. The high royalty ran from Edward, but the people did not. In fact, the rape of Berwick had inflamed them.

Edward discounted the people, content with the notion that his intimidation of the Anglo-Norman high nobility had been success-ful. After Berwick, the hapless Balliol was trapped into a fight, hav-ing no choice but to renounce his homage to England, which he did a month later. The trap thereby sprung, a month after that the English routed the Scottish at Dunbar, where ten thousand Scots died and their high nobility literally fled the battlefield. Soon after that, all the great castles belonged to the English. In July, Balliol surrendered himself and his "kingdom" to Edward, and he was taken to England, where he lived a comfortable life for a few years and then retired, equally comfortably, to France. Just after Balliol's surrender, Edward himself rampaged through Scotland, marching freely throughout the kingdom to demonstrate his invincibility. On his way back to England the avaricious king looted jewelry, relics, and the famed Stone of Scone from Scone, symbolically "uniting" the two countries with the capture of Scotland's most important ceremonial accoutrements.

Scotland had been subdued, or so it might have seemed. But Proud Edward's fatal mistake was thinking that Scotland was merely ruled from above rather than driven from below. Instead of frightening the Scots, Edward's promiscuous violence had roused in them an uncompromising nationalism. The English king had set into motion a spirit of vengeance and independence among the "monkeys." Indeed, he had awakened, in Churchill's words, "a race as stern and resolute as any bred among men."[32]

Even as the high nobles were crumbling before Edward's ad-vance, the Scottish people were coming together, and soon they were actively resisting. They had built their nation from below, family by family, glen by glen, oath by oath, not through some im-personal, didactic Norman pyramid based on obligations tied to real estate but instead through the Celtic way of blood loyalty, locked elbows, and the honor of raising swords in unison. They would march and they would fight and many of them would die, all for a new and rare concept that even then they dared to label freedom.

When the moment for fighting and dying came, it fell on two very different leaders to deliver the Scottish people to their future. One leader was a commoner whose fighting spirit, moral courage, and charisma were so unusual that the world has seen his sort only rarely in the entire annals of history. William Wallace gave the individual Scot his patriotic "brave heart" as well as the certainty of this new national identity, and even today his legacy has the power to inspire great acts and shame those who shirk from challenge. The other leader was of the hybrid–royal blood caste, a ruthlessly ambitious and deeply conflicted man who gained his countrymen's loyalty and respect only after he had shown a unique form of perseverance that transcended his royal titles. Robert the Bruce gave Scotland its first true moment of independence from England, providing structure and validity to the dream of Wallace. And from that point forward the Scottish people made clear that they might endure, but would never accept, subjugation from the outside in any form.

It is not surprising that King Edward so vastly underestimated William Wallace. So also did the high Scottish nobility. For William Wallace was a historic phenomenon, perhaps the first commoner in modern Western history to lead a national movement. And like the remarkable Andrew Jackson, who would rise up nearly five centuries later from the chaos of the American frontier, Wallace accomplished this unique feat by winning the allegiance of his countrymen through his insistence on their equality, and by his own performance on the battlefield.

Tales of Wallace still resonate, passed down through the centuries until fact, legend, and myth have commingled into an inseparable collage. The millions around the world who have watched the Oscar-winning film *Braveheart* will be familiar with a stylized but emotionally accurate depiction of his life. Born in the wild part of southwest Scotland that would later provide the bulk of the Scots-Irish migration to Ireland and then America, Wallace was the land-less second son of a minor laird who was brutally killed by an English knight. He came of age during the years leading up to the massacre at Berwick and learned early to hate—and to fight—the local English authorities that had been installed by Edward I.

A charismatic leader and smart guerrilla warrior, Wallace avenged his father's death by assembling fifty men and ambushing the knight, remembered only as Fenwick, killing him and another one hundred English soldiers. Similar successes fed both his repu-tation and his army. Operating out of the roadless and impenetra-ble Etterick Forest, he quickly demonstrated military gifts of a high order, not only on the battlefield but also in organization. Charac-teristically, he built his army from the bottom. As Churchill de-scribed it, "Every four men had a fifth as a leader; every nine men a tenth; every nineteen men a twentieth, and so on to every thou-sand; and it was agreed that the penalty for disobedience to the leader of any unit was death. Thus from the ground does freedom raise itself unconquerable."[33]

The famed "fire team" system of the United States Marine Corps took similar shape in later centuries, built tightly from below through interlocking leaders. A four-man fire team is its founda-tion, three teams building into a squad, three squads into a platoon, three platoons into a company, and four companies into a battalion, making each leader's span of control efficient and yet complete. The effectiveness of this modern concept remains as testimony ei-ther to Wallace's legacy or his logic.

The incendiary event that launched Wallace's national reputa-tion grew out of another act of revenge. When Hazelrig, the En-glish sheriff of Lanark, learned that Wallace had courted and apparently married a beautiful woman named Marion Baraidfute, who lived in his jurisdiction, he ordered her brother killed. Wallace responded by raiding the town at night with a handful of guerrillas and killing several dozen English soldiers before melting back into the woods. The sheriff, angry that he had not caught Wallace, retaliated by killing the innocent Marion. And then, as they say, the lid blew off. The grieving Wallace raised a larger force and again entered Lanark at night, overpowering the castle guards and killing the sheriff in his bed. He and his men then rampaged through the town, killing some 240 English soldiers, merchants, and commoners, sparing only women, children, and priests.

For this, Edward branded Wallace a traitor and an outlaw, but among common Scots he quickly became a national hero. Only months before, Edward had massacred virtually the entire population of Scotland's most important city and destroyed its infrastructure. His army had then burned and sacked the countryside. He had taken the sacred implements of Scone. The high nobility had fled, fearing Edward's sword more than their loss of honor. Who but Wallace would lead the fight for Scotland?

Thousands flocked to Wallace. The entire country, down to the smallest of landowners, was in revolt. Their unabated guerrilla tactics stunned the English as Wallace's army swept the countryside. Wallace's soldiers took Scone, and for a brief time a handful of nobles, including Robert the Bruce, rallied to Wallace's side. But then Edward, distracted in France, sent an English army north to quell the rebellion. And upon that army's arrival, every member of the high nobility again abandoned Wallace except for the redoubtable Sir Andrew de Moray, who had brought a band of Gaelic warriors down from the north.

Edward, thinking of Wallace as a mere outlaw, did not believe that the Scottish rebel could actually lead an army. Ever the medievalist, the English king simply could not fathom that thousands of soldiers would fight under a man who was not of high nobility. And he gained comfort in this view from the actions of Scotland's own high royalty, which collectively had decided that Wallace and his men were a rabble and in some cases dangerous to their own aspirations.

Thus Edward and Scotland's high nobility seemed quietly to

agree on one notion, no matter their lack of accord on others: William Wallace was a threat to their own personal interests.

In September 1297, only a year and a half after the Berwick massacre, Wallace led his fledgling army against the larger and far better equipped English force, whose mission was to break apart his brigands and capture him, thus ending the rebellion. The English were 60,000 strong, with another 8,000 held in reserve. Their ranks included heavily armored cavalry, seasoned longbow archers, and well-provided infantry. Against them Wallace was fielding 40,000 lightly armed infantry and fewer than 200 horses. The high Scottish nobility had deserted him. His soldiers were men from the roughest ends of Scottish life. They wore animal skins or coarse homespun cloth for uniforms. A few had fashioned metal skullcaps, but none had armor. Most had made their own weapons as well, the deadliest being the standard twelve-foot-long spear, or pike, that Scottish soldiers used when fighting from a circular formation called the *schilltron*. Others simply carried axes, some even knives.

The English army was advancing westward from Berwick. If forced to fight them in open terrain, Wallace's army would have been quickly decimated, both by the English cavalry and by the highly skilled Welsh longbow archers, many of whom had recent combat experience in France. In a brilliant tactical move, Wallace chose to accept the English advance near the town of Stirling, where the rivers Forth and Clyde would narrow the English advance into hilly, broken terrain. He placed his forces on the steep slopes of the Ochil Hills near the Abbey Craig, looking down on the River Forth, where the English were advancing toward him from the far side.

Watching the English cavalry approach the river, Wallace gave an order that would be repeated five hundred years later by Andrew Jackson as he waited for the British to advance on his position just before the Battle of New Orleans: we are outnumbered, don't fight too soon. Wallace carried a horn, and the word went out among his men to attack only when they heard its sound.

The English, apparently thinking Wallace's army was little more than a gang of ruffians, could not have been more accommodating. Instead of fording the river on a wider front upstream, the English cavalry crossed to the other side over a narrow bridge. The crossing was slow. On the Scottish side of the river the ground was boggy, further frustrating the English horsemen. In time the English army was divided on both sides of the river, with its cavalry floundering at the marshy base of the steep hill. And then Wallace's horn pierced the September air, followed by the unearthly screams of thousands of fiercely charging Scottish spearmen.

The Scots made quick work of the English, decimating their cavalry by killing the stalled horses and finishing off the knights, and within a few hours sent its shocked army into full retreat. Wallace and Andrew de Moray followed with a retaliatory offensive that covered much of Scotland and also included a fierce raid into England, although Moray, wounded at Stirling, died shortly after the battle. Wallace was now preeminent. Just as important, the nation had been fully awakened to its possibilities, and even for a short time the ever-vacillating high nobles genuflected toward the rebel leader. In March 1298, Wallace was knighted and given the title "Guardian of Scotland." Characteristically, he chose to hold the title as a fiduciary for the absent King John Balliol rather than seeking the monarchy himself.

But the indecisive high nobles remained quietly against Wallace, measuring their lands, titles, and personal ambitions against the prospects of his long-term success. If Wallace were to win, he surely would turn against the Anglo-Norman version of the royal system. If he were to lose, Proud Edward would make mincemeat of those who had supported him. And so they waited him out. In July 1298, Edward I again personally invaded Scotland, adamant in his determination to avenge Stirling and destroy Wallace's nationalist movement. Shortly thereafter, two Scottish lords secretly revealed Wallace's positions to Edward, and the English army caught Wallace by surprise in the gently sloping, open terrain near

Falkirk. As a further blow, a large portion of the Scottish army led by the high nobles marched off the battlefield when the vastly superior English army approached, including the forces under John Comyn, the lord of Badenoch, who remained one of the claimants to the Scottish throne. And Wallace, as well as his army, was doomed.

The unspoken alliances of the powerful had overwhelmed him. The hybrid nobility had betrayed him. Wallace's army was slaughtered and shattered. Edward was resurgent. For five more years Wallace avoided Edward's grasp, first hiding in the remote crags and glens where no English army dared to travel, then traveling to France in an attempt to gain foreign assistance for the cause of Scottish independence. Unsuccessful in that effort, he returned to Scotland in 1303 and resumed his smaller scale guerrilla activities. In short measure he was betrayed again and captured by the English, then transported to London for a show trial and a viciously barbaric execution.

On August 23, 1305, Wallace was tried at Westminster Hall. The charges were treason, as a traitor to the king. Edward I, known for having created the system of barristers still in use today, did not provide Wallace any such legal rights at the trial. Nor was Wallace allowed to reply directly to the charges against him. The records do indicate, however, that Wallace could not be silenced when he was accused of treason against the king. His response to this charge was eloquent and has echoed through the centuries to succeeding generations of Scots. "I can not be a traitor, for I owe him no allegiance. He is not my sovereign; he never received my homage; and whilst life is in this persecuted body, he never shall receive it. To the other points of which I am accused, I freely confess them all. As Governor of my country I have been an enemy to its enemies; I have slain the English; I have mortally opposed the English King; I have stormed and taken the towns and castles which he unjustly claimed as his own. If I or my soldiers have plundered or done injury to the houses or ministers of religion, I repent me of my sin; but it is not of Edward of England I shall ask pardon."

Nor did Edward give it. Wallace was quickly convicted, then marched outside and tied to a team of horses and dragged through the streets of London to a gallows erected outside the city walls. A large crowd cheered as the Scottish hero was hanged until semi-conscious, then disemboweled while still alive. After that he was "drawn and quartered," four horses pulling his body apart by moving in four different directions, and, just to be sure, he was beheaded as well. Edward ordered Wallace's head impaled on a pole along London Bridge. He then sent the four pieces of the rebel's body to Newcastle, Perth, Stirling, and the luckless Berwick.

Edward's goal in such brutality was in many ways similar to his goal in the massacre and destruction he had overseen in Berwick nine years before: the deterrence of a people through unspeakable terror. However, just as in Berwick, Edward vastly misread the Scottish people. Rather than striking fear into them, Edward's treatment of William Wallace elevated the charismatic rebel so that even in death he quickly became the national symbol of Scotland itself.

Wallace was the first great populist leader of any Western nation. Here was a warrior to remember, up from the backward wilderness of the wild southwest, who had dared to take on the most powerful army in Europe. Here, in contrast to the calculating royal class, was a leader who fought not for fame or reward, but in pursuit of his nation's honor. Here was a man who had persisted despite the betrayal of the self-seeking higher nobility that always had seemed more concerned about their titles and their lands than their nation. And here was a national martyr who, with his last words in the face of a certain and horrible death, spoke only about the justness of his people's cause.

William Wallace in his life and in his dying had shown a resoluteness of spirit and grace under pressure that won the respect even of many of his enemies. And once the people grieved him, his courage certainly must have shamed many of the higher nobility who had run from Edward on so many occasions when a united Scotland might have carried the day.

Among those whom Wallace must have both shamed and inspired was, beyond doubt, Robert the Bruce, who within months of Wallace's death had picked up the great rebel's cudgel and vowed to finish the job.

4

Bannockburn

ROBERT THE BRUCE earned his place in history by wielding the terrible, swift sword that finally obtained, from England and from the pope, Scotland's recognition as a separate nation. And yet when it came to personal honor and loyalty, Bruce was made from a far different mold than Wallace. Indeed, from all historical accounts it must be said that he was a shrewd, ethically conflicted, and violently dangerous man. To be fair, Bruce was of the royalty, and he lived in an ethically conflicted and violently dangerous time. But in the year 1305 there was little reason for the average Scot or even his fellow high nobles to trust him.

The Bruce family, which also had been known as de Brus, was said to be Celtic in its origins. But it had been granted extensive landholdings in southwest Scotland and also across the border in northwestern England after the Norman invasion, and probably was a beneficiary of the Anglo-Norman advance into Scotland. Thus from the outset Bruce, who held the Scottish title of earl of Carrick, was more closely tied to the English Crown than with the Scottish yeomanry of that rough-hewn region. The conflict of these mixed origins was reflected in his immediate family. When the infant Maid of Norway died in 1290, Bruce's grandfather, who was known as Robert the Competitor, was one of the claimants to the

Scottish throne. But once the wars of independence began in earnest, Bruce's father fled for a while to Norway to live with one of his daughters and later retired to his holdings in England rather than return to Scotland.

Many have speculated that Bruce as well as his grandfather worked actively against the hapless "King" John Balliol and later against William Wallace. What is clear from historical accounts is that Wallace's populist agenda would have been seen by Bruce as a threat to his more regal ambitions, and it is fair to say that Bruce did little to support the famed rebel. Indeed, whenever Wallace stumbled, Bruce seemed available to carry on the race, and it was Bruce who became the immediate beneficiary of Wallace's efforts once Proud Edward had posted Braveheart's head on London Bridge.

The years between Wallace's ascendancy and his execution in London found Bruce and other members of the high nobility in a swirl of competition and betrayals as they attempted to position themselves both inside Scotland and with King Edward. In 1298, after Wallace had been abandoned on the battlefield at Falkirk and was forced to flee into the wilderness, Bruce and his archrival John "Red" Comyn, who was known as the principal representative of English interests, were chosen to replace Wallace as Guardians of Scotland. The next year Comyn, who had betrayed Wallace by marching his troops off the battlefield at Falkirk when the English army appeared, asked Bruce to meet him privately in the seclusion of the Selkirk Forest. When Bruce arrived, Comyn nearly killed him in an ambush. In 1300, Bruce resigned from the Guardianship, and in 1302 he actually went over to King Edward's side, ostensibly because the Bruce family had never recognized John Balliol as king. Then in 1304, a year before Wallace's execution, Bruce's father died. This event, plus the passion that Wallace's fate aroused throughout Scotland, led Bruce to seek the Scottish crown and unite the nation.

His ambitions were hardly met with great rejoicing in Scotland, but Bruce did have a plan. Six months after the death of Wallace, Bruce asked Comyn, now his most dangerous competitor for the country's leadership, to meet him in the Minorite church at the border town of Dumfries. Inside the sanctuary of the church, Bruce coldly killed Comyn, opening himself up to charges not only of murder and treason, but also of sacrilege, and he was in fact excommunicated shortly thereafter.

Killing his major rival was obviously a huge personal and political gamble, but in the context of the times it also had its logic. First, it was a preemptive strike against a man who had already tried to kill him once, and might try again. Second, he had done it personally, which in its own odd way could be considered, if not honorable, at least not cowardly. And finally, the deaths of Wallace, the hero whom Scotland had loved, and Comyn, the rival who could have beaten him to the throne, left Bruce with no major competitors.

Hardly a month later, on March 25, 1306, Bruce declared himself king of Scotland and arranged his own coronation in the royal seat at Scone. In many eyes this was the ultimate form of Scottish chutzpah—having killed Comyn, the best way for Bruce to avoid charges of murder and treason was to place himself quickly and firmly above anyone who might bring them. The coronation itself was sparsely attended, including only members of his family, a few bishops, and Isabella, the countess of Buchan, whose brother was then a prisoner of the English. Comyn's powerful family swore a blood oath against Bruce. Many ordinary Scots also opposed him, unable to forget that only a few years before, while William Wallace was on the run, Bruce had joined forces with Edward himself.

In London, the news of Bruce's crowning sent Proud Edward into a mad fury. Ridiculing Bruce as "King Hob" (old English slang for a clownish lout), Edward swore a famous "oath upon the swans" that he would not rest until Scotland was finally conquered. And within weeks the now-aging Hammer of Scotland was leading yet another army into the land of the north, slashing and burning a path toward his latest impetuous usurper. Within three months the English had smashed Bruce's small army in a battle at Methven Park near Perth, summarily hanging their captured prisoners and driving Bruce north into the Highlands.

As Bruce avoided him, Edward's retribution was ferocious. Isabella, who had attended Bruce's coronation, was put into a cage in Berwick and kept there for four years, never fully set free for the rest of her life. Bruce's brother Nigel was seized and executed without a trial, and two other brothers were also soon killed by Edward. His wife and daughter, attempting to escape to Norway, were captured and kept prisoner. Over the next year Scotland itself fell into civil war as several powerful families took up arms against him.

But Bruce did indeed have a saving grace: resoluteness. He kept fighting, and in fighting he kept adapting, matching the strengths of his smaller forces against the weaknesses of those who sought to destroy him. And then he started winning. Bruce knew that his only hope was to gain the respect of the typical Scot. Ironically—but also predictably—the common penchant for disliking Bruce was eased by the passions that Proud Edward had set loose, both with the execution and desecration of William Wallace and his latest foray into Scotland. Quite simply, the whole of Scotland was finally ready to repulse the English, and this time they were in search of a leader. And in historic Celtic fashion, Bruce finally won over the doubters by his unrelenting efforts on the battlefield.

In the summer of 1307 fate intervened in his behalf. Edward I, aged and in ill health, died while moving toward yet another battle in Scotland. As Churchill put it, "Edward was now too ill to march or ride. Like the emperor Severus a thousand years before he was carried in a litter against this stern people, and like him he died upon the road. His last thoughts were on Scotland and on the Holy Land. He conjured his son to carry his bones in the van of the army which should finally bring Scotland to obedience."[34]

The Hammer of Scotland passed his throne on to Edward II,

whose skills were far less than those of his father and in the end were no match for Bruce's.

The battles piled up, some against the English and others against powerful Scottish families who had their own ambitions. But other Scots, now including the leaders of many of the powerful Celtic families just beneath the high nobility, gradually came over to Bruce's side. He began to win more than he lost and he kept on fighting. On the battlefield, Bruce was a smart tactician and a skillful innovator. As Professor Mackie writes, Bruce developed a highly effective battlefield doctrine against the English, relying on smart defenses of his own choosing and a maneuverable offense that allowed him to concentrate his forces. In sum, he "denied ground to hostile cavalry by digging trenches to prolong his short battle line; he avoided pitched battle; he destroyed the castles which he captured, and moved swiftly while his enemy, relying on heavy horses, were sometimes unable to stir until the fields could supply fodder."[35]

One can question Bruce's ethics and recoil from the extremes he took to eliminate personal enemies, but such judgments must be balanced against his goals as a national leader and his brilliance as a fighter. Wallace had the heart. Bruce had the stomach, and the brains.

By early 1314, Bruce's forces had taken all the major castles in Scotland except Stirling, and it was there, not far from where William Wallace had first defeated the English fourteen years before, that Bruce lured the English into the most decisive battle in Scotland's history. Laying siege to the castle, Bruce obtained an agreement from its commander, Philip de Mowbray, that if the English were unable to lift the siege by midsummer's day, the castle would be surrendered. In London, Edward II ordered a general levy of the whole power of England and marched northward with an army of 30,000 men, including some 3,000 knights and men at arms and his famous Welsh longbow archers.

On the face of it, Bruce would appear to have erred. The English outnumbered his army by more than three to one. Having carefully avoided static defenses for years, he was now placing his soldiers into fixed positions. By interposing themselves between the English and Stirling Castle, they would have no room to maneuver, and they also could be devastated by cavalry charges and the type of longbow arrow showers that had taken apart the pikemen of Wallace's army at Falkirk.

But Bruce brought two intangible advantages to this fight. First and foremost were his highly disciplined soldiers. Under his feudal authority, Edward had levied an army that was, in Churchill's words, "hard to gather, harder still to feed," so massive that "it took three days to close up from rear to front." But the clans had come together for Bruce, forming his army from the bottom up. His fighting force, as always with the Scots, was unbreakable in spirit, its common soldiers locked at the elbows and determined to fight—"the hard, unyielding spear men who feared nought [sic] and, once set in position, had to be killed."[36]

Bruce's second advantage was his own tactical brilliance. Anticipating both the English advance and the makeup of its army, he chose his terrain carefully and as a result was able to control the tempo of the battle. Edward's force was better suited for the open fields of Flanders, where the cavalry might penetrate much like the armored forces did during World War II seven centuries later, and the longbow archers might wreak the same kind of havoc in the wide terrain as did machine guns and artillery. Instead, Bruce carefully prepared his defenses with a keen eye to sloping hills, boggy marsh, and the protection of nearby woods, so that he might channel the English into a narrow attack and at the same time take away their ability to maneuver.

Taking a page from Wallace's earlier battle plan at Stirling, Bruce set his forces on the far side of the Bannock Burn, or stream, which the English would cross while approaching the castle. But he went further; his tactical acumen sharpened by years of constant fighting, Bruce added a few twists of his own. By placing his main forces on the high ground above the stream with both flanks merged into thick woods, he precluded an envelopment by English cavalry so that their only approach to his main forces would be through a frontal assault as they crossed the Burn. Then he made the low ground between his forces and the Bannock Burn a minefield of surprises; his soldiers dug and then camouflaged trenches and deep holes that would break a cavalry charge and utterly confuse the English side of the battlefield. And finally, anticipating that young Edward would move the Welsh archers on a flank, Bruce kept a small force of horsemen under his direct command, ready for an immediate counterattack.

As the English forces formed for battle, one of their knights provided Bruce what turned out to be a divine opportunity to motivate his army. Henry de Bohun rode forward in an apparent surprise move toward Stirling Castle and ended up challenging Bruce to individual combat. The knight charged him. In full view of his cheering army, Bruce turned his horse away from Bohun's lance and then smashed the knight's head apart with one blow of his battle-ax.

On the morning of June 24, 1314, the English began their assault, their cavalry leading the charge across the Bannock Burn and into the killing ground Bruce had prepared. The camouflaged ditches and holes disoriented them, but still they moved forward, up the hill toward the unmoving spearmen who made up the Scottish *schilltrons*. One cannot tell this tale better than Churchill himself.

> As neither side would withdraw the struggle was prolonged and covered the whole front. The strong corps of archers could not intervene. When they shot their arrows into the air . . . they hit more of their own men than of the Scottish infantry. At length a detachment of archers was brought round the Scottish left flank. But for this Bruce had made effective provision. His small cavalry force charged them with utmost promptitude, and drove

them back into the great mass waiting to engage, and now already showing signs of disorder. Continuous reinforcements streamed forward toward the English fighting line. Confusion steadily increased. At length the appearance on the hills to the English right of the camp-followers of Bruce's army, waving flags and raising loud cries, was sufficient to induce a general retreat, which the King himself, with his numerous personal guards, was not slow to head. The retreat steadily became a rout. The Scottish schilltrons hurled themselves forward down the slope, inflicting immense carnage upon the English even before they could re-cross the Bannock Burn. No more grievous slaughter of English chivalry ever took place in a single day. [The Scottish] feat in virtually destroying an army of cavalry and archers mainly by the agency of spearmen must . . . be deemed a prodigy of war.[37]

Other battles were fought over the next several years, but after Bannockburn there was no doubt that Scotland would win its independence. King Edward II had been humiliated, retreating first to Stirling Castle and then narrowly escaping across the border to England before being captured. Many English nobles were indeed captured, some of them later used for ransom or to redeem Scottish captives, among them Bruce's wife and daughter. The English attempted to use the authority of the pope to subdue the Scots, but without avail.[38] And the resoluteness of the Scots after Bannockburn was reflected in the famed declaration of the Abbot of Arbroath, Bruce's own chancellor, who wrote to the pope in April 1320:

For so long as one hundred of us shall remain alive we shall never in any wise consent to submit to the rule of the English. For it is not for glory we fight, for riches, or for honours [sic], but for freedom alone, which no good man loses but with his life.

This declaration was not merely an expression of the will of a monarchy, for it had become clear that neither Bruce nor any other Scottish leader could fight or rule without the consent—and the unique notion of kinship—of those who had brought him victory. Arbroath's words reflected the coda of an entire people, born largely through resistance to the yoke of Rome and hardened through centuries of warfare. Nor was it simply the attempted rule of the English that would spur Scottish defiance. A people had been formed, from the bottom up. Later centuries would scatter them across the globe. And wherever they traveled, they would bring with them an insistent independence, a willingness to fight on behalf of strong men who properly led them, and a stern populism that refused to bend a knee, or bow a head, to anyone but their God.

PART THREE

The Ulster Scots

No Surrender.

—*The blood oath of Londonderry, 1689*

1

The Ulster Plantation

IN THE MID-1980s, while I was serving as assistant secretary of defense, a high-ranking British army general with whom I was meeting learned that most of my ancestors had come to America from Northern Ireland. The general was a highly respected officer throughout Europe and in America, both for his operational skills and his intellectual prowess. The author of several well-received books, he also had extensive "ground time," as the infantry likes to put it, in some of the more turbulent areas of Asia and Africa. But upon hearing of my Ulster origins, within minutes the general was telling me of his most difficult assignment—commanding British troops in Northern Ireland during the period in the late 1970s known as the Troubles, when violence flared continuously between Catholic and Protestant factions.

"They are the hardest, toughest people on earth," he said with the kind of quiet conviction of one who has had many chances for comparison. "Both sides, Catholic and Protestant alike. That is why Ulster is such a nightmare. Both sides would rather die than take a step back."

I could not restrain a knowing smile, for the culture had hardly changed after it crossed the Atlantic Ocean three hundred years ago and set up its communities in the Appalachian Mountains.

There's an old saying in the mountain South. Insult a Yankee and he'll sue you. Insult a mountain boy and he'll kill you.

The blood feuds of today's Ulster—and their legacy in the journey of America's Scots-Irish—have their roots in a decision made in 1610 by King James I of England, who also reigned as James VI of Scotland, to form a Protestant plantation on Irish soil. Three years earlier, James, an enthusiastic colonizer, had created a similarly structured colony in Virginia, known appropriately as Jamestown.

James had several different motivations for establishing the Ulster Plantation. Some dealt with the problems inside Ireland. Some reflected England's concern about the strategic moves of competing foreign powers such as Spain and France. Some ineluctably boiled down to the politics of religion. And some had to do with the geography and demographics of Scotland itself.

As with Scotland, the English had attempted to subdue Ireland for centuries, with similarly negative results. The major difference in these two countries' experiences with the English were on the one hand that for centuries the sea protected Ireland from large-scale invasions, and on the other that the Irish, by clinging even harder than the Scots to the reign of powerful tribal chieftains, were slower to configure themselves in political terms as a nation. But that did not mean that the English would prevail over Irish culture as a whole. As in Scotland, during the centuries well before 1600 the English dotted the Irish countryside with Anglo-Norman royalty, which in the case of Ireland was followed by a small gentry class of professionals and tradesmen. But time and distance caused these early "Anglo-Irish" families to be assimilated until they eventually became more Irish than English in both outlook and loyalties.[1]

This relatively comfortable balance among the various ethnic groups was to change as Ireland moved to the front burner of English politics during the reign of Elizabeth I (1558–1603). England had gone through the Protestant Reformation beginning in the reign of Elizabeth's father, the notorious Henry VIII, while the Catholic Church and particularly the Jesuits had chosen Ireland as a strategic focal point of a "Counter-Reformation." The Jesuits had begun this fervent movement in 1561 with all the determination of a guerrilla force. They "preached to the people in their own tongue, performed pastoral duties with devotion, taught the catechism to children, identified themselves with the patriotic struggles of the Irish against the English, and so won the hearts and loyalties of the people."[2]

In addition to its religious goals, this effort had clear political overtones, since the Church had for centuries played heavily in international politics, and the Protestant Reformation had confronted and diminished the power of Rome. As longtime Princeton professor Joseph Strayer pointed out, in each country of Europe during this period, "the Church became closely connected with the government. The Protestant Reformation was merely the extreme stage of this process. The kings of France and Spain remained within the Catholic Church largely because they were able to gain special privileges from the pope. . . . The rulers of England and north Germany set up state churches which gave them a large degree of control over the religious life of their countries."[3] Thus in English eyes the missionary work of the Jesuits in Ireland represented something of a political flanking movement engendered by Rome, made more dangerous by the alliances some Irish chieftains were seeking with powerful Catholic nations such as Spain and France.

Queen Elizabeth sought to address this threat by encouraging larger numbers of Protestant English to settle in Ireland. In this quest she enacted policies that stripped many native Irish of their property in order to provide land grants to English lords and gentry. This practice, which represented a change from the notion of merely settling in Ireland to that of actually colonizing it, was first attempted in Leinster and Munster during the 1560s and twice in Ulster during the 1570s. Predictably, it infuriated the local and dispossessed Irish, who persistently attacked the English immigrants, driving most of them back to whence they came.

England's hostile relations with Spain toward the end of the century put an even more intense focus on Ireland and resulted in renewed efforts to encourage non-Irish Protestants to migrate there. In 1588, Philip II of Spain sent a large naval fleet into the North Atlantic with the mission of crushing both the Dutch and English navies, justifying his acts largely in the name of Catholicism while desiring eventually to dominate Europe's foreign affairs. Able, highly experienced English seamen, with the help of smaller, more maneuverable ships as well as some bad Atlantic weather, thoroughly decimated the famed Spanish Armada. But Philip's ambitions remained intact, and after the armada's defeat he looked toward placing Spanish naval bases in Ireland, which would have had a powerful strategic impact on both England and the Netherlands.

In 1595, Hugh O'Neill, the powerful earl of Tyrone, set off a rebellion in Ulster whose end result might have accomplished Philip's ends. O'Neill's personal goal was to unite the Gaelic lords of Ulster under his sway. He was himself a rather curious figure, in many ways as personally contradicted as Scotland's Robert the Bruce. He was Irish but had been reared in England as a Protestant. Although he rebelled against the English, he had served in the English army, in Ireland. Denounced as a traitor by the English when he claimed an Irish title, "The O'Neill," by Gaelic ritual, he was nonetheless accepted in the court of James I in 1603 after his final defeat. Ever mercurial, he then in 1607 chose to lead the famed "flight of the earls" into exile from Ireland and died in Rome nine years later.[4]

But by 1598, three years into his rebellion, The O'Neill had ignited the imagination of Ireland, largely by giving the English their worst-ever defeat at the hands of the Irish, in the Battle of Yellow Ford. Native Irish resistance was spreading south and west from Ulster all across the island, with religion as its rallying cry. The

O'Neill was developing an alliance with Spain. And Queen Elizabeth decided that she must crush The O'Neill and conquer Ulster, if not Ireland itself.

In 1601, King Philip, who had supplied The O'Neill with arms and munitions, finally sent a Spanish military expedition to Ireland. In a display of lamentable seamanship on a par with that of the ill-fated armada thirteen years before, the Spanish managed to land their army on the remote peninsula of Kinsale in County Cork, as far away as one can get from Ulster without leaving Ireland. The O'Neill's army traveled the length of Ireland to link up with the Spanish, but the English beat them to Kinsale and intercepted their advance. On Christmas Eve, 1601, the English cavalry attacked at dawn, devastating the weary and disoriented Irish army as it was preparing to break its encampment. After also smashing the Spanish, the English then turned north in a savage campaign that laid waste to Ulster itself.

Led by the ruthless Charles Blount, the eighth Lord Mountjoy, who had been appointed lord deputy of Ireland by Elizabeth in 1600, the English army turned Ulster into a sparsely populated no-man's-land. Killing any Irishman found to be carrying arms, destroying homes, confiscating food and livestock, the English deliberately brought about a famine that caused the native Irish to move elsewhere and eventually broke the back of the rebellion. Mountjoy's campaign, which took a terrible toll on civilians, was based on a plan to "make Ireland a 'razed table' on which the Elizabethan State could transcribe a neat pattern."[5] It had as its implicit justification among many English the notion that the Irish were a lesser race. That callousness sowed the seeds of a bitterness and desire for revenge that carry on even into today.

One by one, the lords of Ulster capitulated until The O'Neill was isolated and fighting a desperate rearguard action. Finally, Queen Elizabeth authorized Mountjoy to offer him a pardon. The O'Neill accepted this pardon in 1603, just as Elizabeth herself was dying and James I was ascending the English throne. And in the ensuing seven years the groundwork was laid, partly by design and partly by happenstance, that brought about the formal creation of the Ulster Plantation.

First, in 1603, two Scottish lairds from Ayrshire, Hugh Montgomery and James Hamilton, arranged the private purchase of large tracts of Ulster from Con O'Neill, an Ulster chieftain then imprisoned by the English. The complicated formula that allowed these purchases included their assistance in obtaining Con O'Neill's pardon, his release from prison, and, oddly, a knighthood for O'Neill balanced by a pledge from the two lairds to King James that the land would be "planted with British Protestants."[6] Almost immediately, Montgomery and Hamilton began arranging the migration of large numbers of lowland Scots into their Ulster lands.

Second, also in 1603, Sir Arthur Chichester, the new English lord deputy for Ireland, received a sizable land grant from the king as a reward for his services during The O'Neill's rebellion. His lands were "on the East Coast of Antrim, near the modern city of Belfast. Determined to 'plant' his estates, he brought farmers from his own county of Devon and attracted others from Lancashire and Chesire. His colonization so prospered that much of southern Antrim became English in character."[7]

Finally, in August 1607, the cream of Ulster's Irish aristocracy, including Hugh O'Neill himself, left Ireland for permanent exile. Other Irish were to follow these hundred or so key leaders until by 1614 "there were 300 Irish students and 3,000 Irish soldiers in Spanish territories alone."[8] This famous "flight of the earls" provided "the symbolic image of the last great Gaelic chieftain joining the world of the Irish exiles."[9] Importantly, it also allowed the English to confiscate their lands. In the next year, "all the holdings of their clans in six of the nine northern counties were declared escheated to the King."[10] The seizure of almost all the lands of Ulster brought with it even more bitterness from the native Irish, as it ignored the less formal but still binding Irish tradition of subownership, thus dispossessing many Irish of property they held under their own honored codes.[11]

This is not to imply that there was an immediate nationalistic resistance from the Irish to migration on their soil, particularly when it came from Scotland. For centuries small bands of Scots and Irish had flowed back and forth across the narrow straits that separated their two countries. As was previously mentioned, the *Scotti* who provided the diplomatic backbone of Scottish unification and for whom the country is named were originally an Irish tribe. And as R. F. Foster points out, by 1600 "there was a sense, indeed, in which some of the [Ulster] province was 'planted' already; Scots had been spilling back and forth across the narrow straits since time immemorial, and Antrim and Down were densely Scottish in population. In many ways the Antrim coast was closer to the Scottish mainland than to its own hinterland."[12]

But this time the issues were different and overwhelming, both in their emotions and in the number of people involved. They included Irish memories of the rapacity with which the English had starved, burned, and otherwise forced them from their lands, coupled with the collapse of the Irish chieftains. The volatile tinderbox of religious differences would be ignited again and again for many generations, fed by undeniable political implications that would soon cut not two but three ways, since many English and Scottish in the Ulster settlements would battle fiercely over vastly differing views of Protestantism. And the confrontations would become far more serious due to the sheer volume of migrations that followed the creation of the Ulster Plantation. In 1600 less than 2 percent of Ireland was of English or Scottish descent. Within a century that number would rise to 27 percent, almost all of it in Ulster.[13]

Characteristic of traditional Anglo-Norman precision, the 500,000 acres of the original Ulster Plantation were laid out with exactitude. Half would be divided between "Undertakers"—lords and gentry from England and Scotland who would agree to "plant"

Protestant farmers and also provide fortifications behind which their planters might defend the allotted areas, and "Servitors"— proven soldiers who could be used in further military operations in Ulster. One-tenth (50,000 acres) would be allotted to the twelve municipal corporations that comprised the government of London and would be responsible for developing trade. These same companies had underwritten the Jamestown Plantation in 1607. Two-tenths went to the Episcopal Church, now to be called the Church of Ireland. One-tenth went to the establishment of forts and towns. And finally, only one-tenth would go to native Irish "of good merit," who would be free to take on Irish Catholic tenants.[14]

And so the die was cast. Over the next four hundred years, two passionate viewpoints, each technically supportable based on their respective cultures, would clash again and again. Under English law the departed earls had participated in a rebellion, consorted with the Spanish, and then fled the country, leaving their properties behind to be properly confiscated. And from the English perspective, bringing other British subjects into Ulster would prevent future rebellions as well as strategically protect their flank from foreign powers. But in Irish eyes, their traditional rights of subownership had been ignored and the land had been dishonorably taken. The end of the rebellion had brought overwhelming violence against innocents, confiscation of property, and colonization from the outside rather than a resolution from within.

The Catholic Irish would be left with an unending bitterness and a perpetual desire for revenge. But for the Protestants, the situation would become far more complex. For rather than attracting large numbers of English settlers, by far the largest percentage of "British Protestants" to come to Ulster would be the hard-bitten, unbending, tightly knit lowland Scots who would migrate from the war-ravaged areas along Scotland's southwest border. These were desperately poor people, as accustomed to armed conflict as the London English were to commerce and trade. Except for those equally rugged northern English who had faced them for centuries across that brutal border, neither the English nor the Irish in Ulster had seen their likes before. The Scots had their own history of struggle against English attempts at conquest. And as the last four hundred years in Ireland and elsewhere have shown, they have never been a yielding people.

True to a pattern that has played itself out in many forms during their historic journey, those who emerged from the hills and glens of the southwestern Scottish lowlands brought with them no real stake in the previous feuding between the English ruling class and the rebellious, wronged Irish. But they would not hesitate to fight when attacked, and they were not above extending the battle once it was engaged. The "Ulster Scots" would shape the character and conduct of the Protestant elements of the Ulster Plantation. And then many of them would move on to the mountains of America.

2

Border Warriors —
and Bible Beaters

THE BORDER DWELLERS of southwestern Scotland were still William Wallace's people. They were also, after a fashion, the descendants of Robert the Bruce, whose family had held vast land grants in southwestern Scotland and northwestern England. The centuries after the historic victory at Bannockburn had not been kind to them, or to their land. Their numbers had ebbed and flowed, periodically visited by smallpox and the plague, which thirty years after Bannockburn had wiped out one-third of the population. But by 1600 the number of inhabitants in the region had grown so large that the thin soil could not support their agrarian ways, and famine had become a common malady. The once thick forests that had hidden Braveheart and his men so well from their English pursuers were now denuded. As an English visitor of the time pointed out, southwestern Scotland had turned into "a bleak and bare solitude, destitute of trees, abounding in heather and morass and barren hills; soil where cultivation was found only in dirty patches of crops, on ground surrounded by heather and bog."[15]

The Scottish victory at Bannockburn had resolved two vital issues: gaining an acceptance from the English that Scotland was indeed a nation, and getting a guarantee from Rome that the Scottish king deserved to be recognized by the Church and thus by other rulers as a national sovereign. But it was not in the character of the English to slide away into obscurity just because they had lost a battle. Scotland may have established a somewhat separate existence, but the exact boundaries of the nation itself had not been agreed upon. And in addition, a continuous stream of ineffective or reckless Scottish monarchs ensured the country's instability.

The issue over where, exactly, England ended and Scotland began had resulted in hundreds of years of continuous warfare, turning farms and hamlets in the contested areas into repeatedly ravaged battlegrounds that call to mind the free-fire zones of the Vietnam War. Although Hadrian's Wall had provided an emotional and historical line of demarcation, the English wanted more, and over time they succeeded, rolling back the Scottish border in the west and especially in the east. The bitter fights during these middle centuries caused many areas that were ethnically and historically Scottish to end up on the English side of the border. Indeed, most of the English province of Northumbria as well as a portion of Cumbria lie north of Hadrian's Wall, and during this period were populated by people of similar heritage to the Scots.

The death of Robert the Bruce was quickly followed in 1333 by an English incursion into Scotland that amounted to the "systematic destruction of the Scottish lowlands as far north as Edinburgh."[16] This campaign included a vast massacre of Scots outside the hapless city of Berwick, which later fell permanently to the English. After that, in the words of Professor Smout, "There followed a hundred years of fluctuating and intermittent warfare in which the Scots strove to evict the English from the southern counties all the way from Haddington to Dumfries, not ending until 1460 when James II fell regaining the castle of Roxburgh. . . . Half a century of peace between monarchs ensued, though it was no longer observed by their subjects along the Border. In 1513 official warfare erupted again with the tragic campaign of Flodden and the death of James IV. After Flodden came another truce, then the Scottish defeat at Solway Moss in 1542, the 'Rough Wooing,' and the further defeat at Pinkie in 1547."[17]

King Henry VIII's "rough wooing" campaign in the 1540s harkened back to the days of Roman emperor Severus and Edward I's first slaughterhouse campaign against Berwick. Henry had ordered his battlefield commander, the earl of Hertford, to put "man, woman and child to fire and sword without exception where any resistance shall be made against you." The earl would later proudly report that he had "plundered and burnt Edinburgh, Leith and Holyrood, with Newbattle Abbey, Haddington, Burntisland and Dunbar, taking 10,000 cattle and 12,000 sheep . . . sacking seven abbeys, sixteen castles, five 'market towns,' and no less than 243 villages."[18]

As these campaigns ensued, bringing with them continuous local turmoil, the national leadership of Scotland also remained chaotic. "Seven monarchs ruled between 1406 and 1625, and of the seven, five had been infants or mere children upon their accession."[19] In addition, "James I (1406–37) was assassinated by his own henchmen; James II 'of the fiery Face' (1437–60) was blown to pieces while attacking the English at Roxburgh; James III (1460–88) was murdered by a family of rampaging border warlords; and James IV (1488–1513) died fighting the English at Flodden Field."[20]

Such turbulence at the center of the national government not only empowered the local clan leaders, it also demanded that they be strong, both for their own survival and also for the well-being of their extended families. And again a familiar pattern reinforced itself in what would become the Scots-Irish character: the mistrust of central authority, the reliance on strong tribal rather than national leaders, and the willingness to take the law into one's own hands rather than waiting for a solution to come down from above.

In addition to frequent warfare with the English, the people of lowland Scotland, particularly along the border areas with their ever-shifting boundaries, became dominated by unending blood feuds, rampant acts of group violence, and the settlement of contentious issues by force or tradition rather than formal law. The celebrated feud between the Hatfields and the McCoys in America's Appalachian Mountains had numerous predecessors in sixteenth-century Scotland, many of them far lengthier and more violent.[21] Professor Smout notes that one Ayrshire vendetta between the Cunninghams and the Montgomerys and parts of the Kennedys lasted for more than a century. He then points out that "Border families from both sides were quite happy to gang up to help in each other's feuds, an English surname joining a Scottish surname against another Scottish or English family as occasion required. As Borderers they all had more in common with one another than with the tiresome governments in Edinburgh and London."[22]

David Hackett Fischer writes of these ethnically similar peoples on both sides of the borders in his magnificent book *Albion's Seed*, quoting historian George Fraser. "English and Scots Borderers had everything in common except nationality. They belonged to the same small, self-contained, unique world, lived by the same rules and shared the same inheritance."[23]

The centuries after Bannockburn ushered in a predictable, even naturally populist result. If the conditions of daily life had remained harsh, the effect on the lowland Scots themselves was peculiarly the opposite. Living continuously on the edge of warfare created a society founded on military rather than economic principles. The shared risk inherent in frequent conflict developed an egalitarian, if not democratic, set of personal relationships. And the hardships of this existence, plus the frequent attacks by organized English armies designed to break their spirit, bred a peculiar form of nationalism among the lowland Scots. Such dangers fused "the Lowlanders into a single people . . . [They] all lost their old ethnic loyalties and became part of a coherent Scottish nation, assertive, warlike, resilient, patriotic and freedom loving. 'Scotland was born fighting' was an old saying and a true one."[24]

Such a concept was not conducive to commercial success, however, and in fact seemed to ignore economic conditions altogether. "Scottish rural society was so largely organized to face war and feud and was so closely bound in blood and duty to its lords that it had no conception of itself as divided along other lines by economic interest. . . . Land tenure had to be organized to maximize fighting power rather than productivity; the best warriors rather than the best farmers got the best holdings."[25]

The impact of the centuries was to accentuate rather than ameliorate the strongly individualist tendencies that had become so apparent in the wars of independence leading up to Bannockburn. The typical lowland Scot was bound to a complicated set of loyalties to his clan and willing to serve his laird, but he answered in his honor to no one. "It is a notable fact that in Scotland, probably alone among all the countries of Europe, there was never anything approaching a general uprising against the lords. On the contrary, the sense of personal and reciprocal loyalty between barons and underlings, lairds and tenants, usually made the farmers devoted retainers."[26]

As Professor Smout points out, the notion of Celtic kinship and its emphasis on soldierly virtues thrived during the centuries following Bannockburn. "The poor man did not in fact claim the rank of an earl or a baron. What he claimed was something he valued more, to belong to a family of incomparable nobility and martial valour [sic], and by virtue of that to be as good as any earl, baron or commoner of different family in the land. . . . The whole atmosphere of kinship was a complex one, compounded both of egalitarian and patriarchal features, full of respect for birth while being free from humility. It appeared uncouth beyond Scotland mainly because it was a legacy of Celtic influence unfamiliar to the outside world."[27]

Thus the lowland Scots as well as many of the northern English who faced them in the border areas grew to be similar in many respects and far different than other British peoples. They were insistently and even gladly warlike; they were destitute but did not measure themselves by wealth; their properties were frequently attacked and they did not risk their slim assets in fancifying an abode. They became mobile, moving easily from one temporary, hastily built lodging to another—Fischer mentions their rough homes of wood or stone or beaten earth called "cabbins," which predated both the primitive settlements on the American frontier and today's resultant culture of trailer parks and prefabricated houses.[28] And in a tradition that carried with it their historic rejection of feudalism, they concerned themselves more with personal ties than with the ownership of a specific piece of land.

ANOTHER POWERFUL FACET played into the cultural development of those who would become known as the Scots-Irish, and it is impossible to overstate its importance, for it still resonates in American culture and politics four hundred years later. The impact of the Protestant Reformation was far greater—one is tempted to say "more nearly total"—in Scotland than in any other country, and this impact went well beyond religion itself. Unlike its positive and even messianic contribution in Ireland, by the early 1500s the Catholic Church in Scotland had become characterized by incessant corruption on every level and was detested by many Scots of all classes. And the hard-driven Calvinism that replaced it melded neatly with Scotland's traditional populism. In time, these twin forces of Calvinism and populism came together to create both the fundamentals of American-style democracy and the embryo of what would in the twentieth century be called America's Bible Belt.

The rejection of a corrupt form of Catholicism while embracing the harshest form of Calvinism at first threatened to turn Scotland into a theocracy. But in the end its far-reaching changes would carry with them the veritable signature of the Scots-Irish people. The struggle with Scotland's Catholic bureaucracy would reinforce a long-held tendency to view higher authority with suspicion and also affect attitudes toward Irish Catholics once the Ulster migrations began. Calvinism's insistence upon accepting responsibility for one's personal actions would help create an even stronger sense of individualism. And the very structure of this new form of Christianity also reflected the beginnings of a fresh type of democracy, built from the bottom up just like the Scottish nation itself rather than evolving slowly from the top down, as with the English and other systems. It is no accident that the Scots-Irish people became quickly known after their arrivals in both Ireland and America as rebellious, difficult to control from the top, and inclined toward a volatile political radicalism.

How did this happen? We begin with twin phenomena: the bastard bishops, and the bishops' bastards.

Through the Middle Ages, as nations began to form their modern borders and government became more sophisticated, the Catholic Church had begun to recede from its overwhelming dominance of European affairs. In Scotland the Church had largely transitioned from a religious into a commercial power, and at the same time had allowed its positions of religious authority to become little more than sinecures to be held at the pleasure of an ever-fickle royalty.

Commercially, "the church had too great a share of the national wealth. On the eve of the Reformation its revenue amounted at least to £300,000 a year whereas the Crown's patrimony brought in only about £17,500."[29] As Leyburn points out, "By 1560 it had amassed . . . property estimated to consist of more than a third of all the land in the country and half of its wealth."[30]

Spiritually, the Church was bankrupt. As one example of how badly its sanctions were abused, in 1532, King James V, while only twenty, "had wrung permission from the Pope . . . to appoint three baby sons, all illegitimate, to be titular abbots of Kelso and Melrose, priors of St. Andrews and Pittenweem, and abbot of Holyrood respectively; a fourth was later made prior of Coldingham and a fifth abbot of the Charterhouse. The king thus got his bastards beautifully provided with an income at the churches' expense, but the monasteries were lumbered with the face of a baby master."[31] As another, in the same decade Scotland's top priest, Cardinal Beaton, was known to have at least eight illegitimate children. Beaton had accumulated so much wealth through his priesthood that he had given one of his daughters "a marriage portion as large as that given by the greatest Earl in Scotland to his daughter."[32]

Such conduct was not limited to the high priesthood. Nor was it isolated. Smout points out that "ecclesiastical sources abound with evidence of priests coming to the altar half drunk, of priests hardly able to read the services either in Latin or in English, and of a 'profane lewdness of life' in general at all levels. . . . [L]egitimations of priestly offspring were so numerous that, in mid century, when perhaps two Scotsmen in six hundred were priests, no less than two legitimised [*sic*] children in seven were the bastards of priests. In these circumstances society at large treated the church and its services with open irreverence."[33]

Based on similar complaints of Church corruption as well as the perception that Church doctrine had erected structural barriers between God and Man, the Protestant Reformation had begun in Germany and spread quickly throughout Europe. By the mid-1500s, half of Europe had left the Catholic Church. "Parts of Germany and the whole of Scandinavia followed the revolutionary theology of Martin Luther, first enunciated at Wittenberg in 1517, while other parts of Germany, of the Low Countries, of France and of Switzerland followed the still more radical teaching of John Calvin of Geneva."[34]

Calvin was indeed more radical; he can safely be called the founder of the modern Christian evangelical movement. Born into a well-off French family with close ties to the Catholic Church, Calvin had briefly studied to be a priest before switching over to law, and then converted to the Reformed faith in 1533 at the age of twenty-four. By 1536 he had broken with the Roman Catholic

Church altogether, and from that point on until his death in 1564 he resided principally in Geneva, where he wrote, preached, and lectured on Reform theology.[35] And perhaps his most determined and successful follower was the Scotsman John Knox.

Knox, himself a former priest, embodied the utter fearlessness of William Wallace. A born rebel who had defended an early Protestant leader by wielding a two-handed sword during his services and who had once served nineteen months as a galley slave for participating in a religious rebellion, he turned his energies against the hierarchy of the Church rather than the English Crown. Mary, Queen of Scots, the Catholic ruler who fled Scotland as the Reformation took hold, is reputed to have said, "I fear the prayers of John Knox more than all the assembled armies of Europe."[36] And well she should have. Her reign had been characterized by her marriage to the Dauphin of France, who later became King Francis II, as well as by an importation of many Frenchmen to high offices. These gestures had caused ordinary Scots to fear annexation by France as their price for that country's assistance during the time of Henry VIII's "rough wooing."[37]

Mary's life ended when an English court later put her to death in 1587, ostensibly for plotting to assassinate her cousin, Queen Elizabeth I. Although her Catholicism did inspire several plots against the Protestant Elizabeth's life, in reality this was a cold-blooded murder-by-fiat by England's high lords. Her death was designed to quell the seemingly unending series of conspiracies in England and in Europe that were designed to put a Catholic back on the throne of England, and thus end the momentum of the Reformation throughout Europe. The conspirators knew that the childless Elizabeth would die without heirs. If Mary had survived her, under the laws of succession she would have become queen. But the earlier death of Elizabeth's cousin would allow the throne to pass, as it did, to Mary's son, the Protestant Scot who became James I.[38] In this sense the Scottish Reformation took on international overtones in addition to its rebellion against church corruption, and it began a period of closer cooperation between England and Scotland.

The impact of all these twists and turns on the Scottish people was that the Catholics were out, the followers of John Knox had won in Scotland, and at the same time Scotland had become closer to England and estranged from France. And from that point forward, Knox and his supporters moved quickly to change the shape of religion in Scotland. Their major structural move was to destroy papal authority and replace it with the power of local religious bodies called the Kirk. Under this concept, the only head of the church was Christ, who was represented not by a pope but by local ministers elected by the church members themselves. The congregations would also elect key church leaders such as deacons and elders rather than having them foisted upon them from above. There were to be only two sacraments, baptism and Holy Communion. Every individual was to be held responsible for his own actions, and the church elders would be fierce in enforcing notions of "godly discipline." And as a harbinger of things to come when America's Bible Belt hit full swing, sexual misconduct of all kinds would rank high among those offenses inviting such "godly discipline."[39]

Most interestingly, although they had joined together against the Catholic powers, the English and Scottish had absorbed the Protestant Reformation in characteristically different ways. As Mackie points out, "In England the Crown arrogated to itself all the power of which the Pope was deprived," thus preserving England's top-down religious, social, and governmental structure. In other words, the Anglican Church, also called the Episcopacy, was little more than a makeover of the Catholic Church itself, with the king replacing the pope. But Scotland "developed the Calvinistic doctrine that civil government, though regarded as a necessity, was to be recognized only when it was conducted according to the word of God."[40] This meant not only that the Kirk would have the power to organize religious activity at the local level, but also that Scots had reserved the right to judge their central government according to the standards they themselves would set from below.

This decision—that the laity at the lower levels of society would directly participate in judging their higher-ups—was a daring and astonishing concept for its times, even though it had emerged naturally from more than a thousand years of historical experience. The high Scottish nobility and religious authority had never fully penetrated beyond the clan leaders and thus had never directly controlled the people. And now the people, in concert with their local leaders acting through the Kirk, had firmly declared a measure of independence from those above them.

The lowland Scots would carry this fresh philosophy of government with them when they ventured across the narrow straits and took their place as settlers in the Ulster Plantation. As Mackie put it, "The Kirk they produced trained up a people strong in faith, patient of discipline, ready to venture, and even to die, for their beliefs."[41] These tenets as well as the embryonic strains of true democracy that propelled them would meet a stern, century-long first test in Ulster.

3

The Problem Children of Ulster

———————————

AND SO WE can imagine these families heading out from their heather-covered, denuded hills for the coastlines, where they would catch the boats that took them a few miles across the stormy North Channel of the Irish Sea and into the new world that awaited them in Ireland's Ulster Plantation. The men would be dressed simply in the wool sweaters and plaid trousers of their day, the women in "linen skirts with a plaid draped over their heads and pinned across their bosom and falling to their knees."[42] Some would be shoeless. They would be carrying few possessions; weapons, certainly, and perhaps a few days' supply of the ever-vital oatmeal to be mixed with milk into porridge or with water into gruel. They would be traveling not simply in families but more likely among a group of families, on their way to settle in little pockets of farmland that their lairds had marked for them.

As with all voyagers who leave behind the security of a known world in order to thrust themselves into the flurry and confusion of an unproven existence, these were the dreamers and daredevils of their lot, the ones whose veins pumped with adrenaline and who were willing to take large risks. What was it that they risked as they abandoned the admittedly infertile soil and incessantly war-torn valleys of what would soon become their pasts? Certainty, however difficult. The continuity that came from their clan relations and their communities. The end of their family's full association with Scotland. And their lives.

Can we put a face on them? Can we imagine their banter and their spirit? We are told that the harsh disciplines of Calvinism had turned the Scots into a dour and even humorless people, and that the wars and isolations of the centuries had given them little chance to appreciate literature or the arts. But we know that they were a people who had a strong love of oratory and music, who invented many types of dancing, and who relished all forms of competition. And we also know that any community or family gathering ended up with bonfires, gaiety, and all of those other things, especially singing and games of physical challenge such as racing and wrestling. Further, the evidence is clear that despite Calvinism's heavy hand against sexual transgressions, the lowland Scots were an openly sensual people who not only delighted in teasingly aggressive sexual banter but also married early, quite often with a child already on the way. Indeed, much of Calvinism's harsh discipline could be attributed to the attempt by church leaders to tame this highly spirited people.

These were not monks and nuns trudging along the roadways toward the western Scottish seaports or stepping off the long boats at the Irish port of Larne. Nor were they Talmudic scholars. Most of them had little or no schooling, knew no refined trade, and had read no book except perhaps the Bible. Few would have had any idea why someone would even want to sit down in front of an easel with a dozen pots of colored oils and paint a picture of a Madonna or a bunch of flowers.

But they were strong, keen of practical intellect, and reliable. They were hard-faced, thick-palmed farmers who doubled when necessary as ferociously dedicated soldiers. They were women who married early, bore numerous children, worked alongside their men in the fields, and frequently ran things by themselves when their men were gone. They were children who grew up quickly and learned from an early age to expect hardship and physical confrontation as a way of life. They willingly served their leaders, not as serfs but as emotional and spiritual coequals. They accepted the judgments of their ministers, but prayed while standing on their feet and not bent over on their knees. And if any man, no matter how highly born, should strike or offend them, it was their credo to strike back twice as hard.

Thinking of them, I cannot help but remember a favorite uncle, a man of fearsome but unpolished intellect who in his youth was known both for an uncanny mechanical aptitude and for his ability to fight. In the ring, he fought professionally. Outside of it, despite being only five feet, seven inches tall, he became a local legend for, among other things, having fought and beaten three grown men at the same time. Another fight, over a woman, ended with a knife thrust deep into his chest, missing his heart by less than an inch. Having never gone beyond grade school, he spent his entire life working with his hands, first in the meatpacking houses of St. Joseph, Missouri, then as an electrician, then in the shipyards of Long Beach, and finally making an independent living as a TV repairman and fixing air conditioners. He was also deeply emotional. When my father shipped out for World War II, my uncle Tommy Lee Webb took a train ride nonstop from Long Beach to the Midwest, thirty-six hours each way over a single weekend, just to have a cup of coffee with him. He shook his younger brother's hand, gave him a survival knife that had been handmade by another brother, and on Monday morning was back at work in the shipyard.

When I was in my teens, I asked Uncle Tommy what he considered to be his proudest accomplishment. He thought about it for a moment, and then he grinned.

"I never kissed the ass of any man."

Uncle Tommy was, as my grandmother would have put it, poured white-hot, right out of the mold.

These were the kind of people you would want covering your back in a barroom brawl or protecting your flank in the next foxhole while waiting for an enemy to make a night attack. They were the kind of people who would fight like madmen, then after it was over, look down at a dead friend or relative and cry like babies. They were the kind of people who would die in place rather than retreat if they had given you their word that they would be there for you. And they were not the kind of people you would ever, ever, want to set in action against you.

They were the lowland Scots, leaving the ancient battleground of the borders, heading across the North Channel of the Irish Sea to endless fights in a beautiful, blood-soaked countryside called Ulster. If they thought they might find respite in Ireland, they were quickly dispossessed of that fantasy, for in the native Irish they found a similarly emotional and combative people. That itself was hardly an accident of nature. For who are the Irish, but their closest blood cousins?

———————

AS THE FARMLANDS, towns, and textile mills of the Ulster Plantation began to fill up with these new Scottish arrivals in the early and mid 1600s, the entire British Isles fell into the gravest internal crisis of its modern history. This period of chaos and disruption would continue in several different renditions for nearly a century. At stake were the shifting notions of power among the competing centers of religion, monarchy, and representative government as Great Britain evolved from monotheistic feudalism toward a modern liberal state.

The initial series of explosions was in many ways brought about by the Scots themselves. The Calvinist notion that fundamental freedom and the rights of the common individual transcended religion to the point of defining politics had a huge impact on the British government, shaking the foundations of the Parliament, the monarchy, and even the English military. Ireland became a frequent and sometimes symbolic battleground, with its continuous clashing of a wronged Catholic people against both the English government and a fresh influx of Protestant immigrants. As this chaos played itself out, it would be the Ulster Scots rather than the English or the Irish who would take stock of later English policies and decide in the greatest numbers to leave Ireland for America. Thus would start the first great Celtic migration out of Ireland, which began in the early 1700s and did not cease until the beginning of the American Revolution in 1776.

———

IT IS A small irony that, after all the centuries in which England sought to bring Scotland into the fold and thereby "unite the crowns," it was a Scot who actually did the uniting, in the process becoming the first king of Great Britain. James I, the only son of Mary, Queen of Scots, was raised as a Calvinist but had no particular love for the rigors of this demanding version of Protestantism. More important, he detested and feared the democratic implications of the faith, sensing early on that its fundamental independence carried with it grave dangers to the throne. As Churchill put it, "James had had enough of the Kirk. He realized that Calvinism and monarchy would quarrel in the long run and that if men could decide for themselves about religion they could also decide for themselves on politics."[43]

At the core of this century of internal conflicts was the transition of the monarchy away from the unilateralist whimsy of what had been called "the royal prerogative" toward a more representative form of government embodied in the powers of Parliament. In short, the Parliament increasingly stood up to the Crown, and as events progressed the common people learned new ways of standing up to the aristocracy. And swirling around these new concepts, never far from the center of the debates, was the part that religion played in determining individual freedoms, in conducting governmental affairs, and inevitably in the enunciation of Great Britain's foreign policy.

In 1625, James I gave way to his son Charles I. After a series of

altercations with the Parliament, Charles simply dissolved it, sending it home and beginning a period that historians have called
the Personal Rule. But in attempting to rule without Parliament,
Charles cut himself away from his ability to raise funds through taxation and in the process lost much of his standing army. With an
alienated Parliament and not much of an army, Charles then made
the—literally—fatal error of unnecessarily taking on the Scots.

In 1637 the archbishop of Canterbury convinced Charles to attempt a unification of the Protestant faiths under the Anglican
Church through a common prayer book. This ignited a ferocious
rebellion among the Scots, who in 1638 formed a countermove-
ment through the mass signing of a covenant that bound the entire
nation to support the Calvinist Church of Scotland. Many Scots
signed the covenant using their own blood as ink. Scottish leaders
then formed a General Assembly to confront the king, comprised
heavily of the populist lay elders and ministers elected by the Kirk.

Charles I, irritated and perhaps naive about the extent of his
moral authority, ordered the General Assembly to disband. Refusing to do so, the Scots instead took to arms, recalling from Germany thousands of hardened soldiers and officers who had fought
many campaigns under the Protestant leader Gustavus Adolphus,
known widely as the father of modern warfare. Within a few
months Scotland had assembled the strongest military force in
Great Britain. Filled with the emotional resolve of a people daring
to confront the powers above them, the Scottish army marched on
England and shortly was occupying the ancient Scottish territory of
Northumberland and parts of Durham below it. And King Charles
had little to stand in their way.

In a truly ironic twist, the Scots seized the initiative, now demanding that Charles replace the Anglican Church with their own
Presbyterian system. Charles, without either a full army or funds,
decided that his only hope was to recall Parliament after an eleven-
year hiatus. Instead of helping him, the returning Parliament re-

volted, demanding greater powers. The nation became paralyzed. In 1642, Great Britain fell into civil war.

As the civil war spread, the forces aligned against Charles split between the Scots and another "dissenting" Protestant sect termed the Congregationalists, which became the dominant force in Oliver Cromwell's Roundheads, in opposition to Charles's cavalier Royalists. The Congregationalists strongly opposed both the Anglicans and the Presbyterians. Also important, they made up a large percentage of the Roundhead army, which was led by Cromwell himself and became known as the Ironside Army. This army eventually marched on London, overthrew Charles I, and, after arranging his beheading in 1649, installed Oliver Cromwell as dictator with the title of Lord Protector.

Churchill observed that Cromwell's ascendancy was "the triumph of some twenty thousand resolute, ruthless, disciplined, military fanatics over all that England has ever willed or ever wished. . . . Cromwell was dictator. The Royalists were crushed; Parliament was a tool; the Constitution was a figment; the Scots were rebuffed, the Welsh back in their mountains; the Fleet was reorganized, London overawed."[44]

The butchering, Bible-quoting Oliver Cromwell would remain dictator for eleven bloody years until the "Lord Protector's" sudden and unexpected death in 1658. Then, although Cromwell had attempted through his will to establish his son as the follow-on "Protector" of England, the British Parliament finally reasserted itself again and managed to recall Charles's son from exile in 1660. Charles II, "the merry monarch," brought a much-needed respite to a nation shell-shocked by Puritanism. He ruled with a playful, often distracted hand filled with mistresses and self-indulgence until his death in 1685. His most glaringly unfortunate legacy was in personally seeking religious tolerance but officially acceding in a series of harsh discriminatory laws against non-Anglicans, Protestants and Catholics alike.

Failing to leave any heirs, Charles II was followed in 1685 by his brother James, who ruled as James II. James dreamed of reinstating Catholicism as the national religion and immediately began appointing Catholics to numerous key positions in government and the military. In 1688 a group of English Protestant leaders drove James II into exile, bringing in William of Orange from his position as Stadtholder of Holland to rule Great Britain, justifying their action because he was the grandson of Charles I and thus formally in the "direct line of succession." William III would rule until 1702. James II did not disappear, however. Having aligned himself in exile with the French, he attempted to reclaim the throne through a determined campaign in Ireland. He lost, famously. But he did, for a time, establish his own regency in Dublin.

The implications of all this turbulence fell hard on Irish soil, bringing conflict from the outside as well as from within. A seemingly unending series of rebellions and retaliations swept the land, affected by attempts from London to invoke a plethora of constantly changing political policies that favored certain religious groups while punishing others. Contrary to the romanticism of many modern accounts, these battles were not precisely drawn as ethnic Irish versus non-Irish. Nor were they two-sided fights between Protestant and Catholic. Rather, they usually pitted the old-line Irish, which included the long-established Anglo-Irish, against the newer Anglicans of English descent, with the predominantly Scottish Calvinists thrown in as the wild card, sometimes matched by a small percentage of English Protestants who were neither Anglican nor Presbyterian. If it sounds complicated, well, it was a complicated time.

In late 1641, as England was on the edge of civil war after the Scots had signed their covenant and King Charles I had recalled a rebellious Parliament, a violent Catholic uprising broke out in Ulster. English and Scottish settlers throughout the plantation were unexpectedly attacked by rogue individuals as well as organized private armies. Many were driven from their homes and had their properties confiscated. The rebellion spread, quickly taking on a life of its own. Thousands were killed. Estimates vary wildly, an indication both of the emotional reaction to the uprising and the political uses to which it was later put. The Irish historian Foster estimates 2,000 to 4,000 deaths. The American Protestant Leyburn offers a range taken from a variety of sources of 8,000 to 200,000, with a ballpark guess of 15,000 dead, "of whom a third lost their lives in the fighting and the rest died of privations."[45]

Whatever the numbers, this was a catastrophic event for the settlers of the Ulster Plantation. The English settlers were hit particularly hard, no doubt because they were the least prepared, contrary to the careful military structure the war-hardened Scots had built into their own settlements. It also came at a time of extreme national vulnerability, with the beginning of the English civil war only months away. Later histories on both sides seem to attribute the motives for the uprising to vitriolic resentment among ordinary Irish toward the Protestant settlements. But the initial attacks were instigated by Ulster's Irish Catholic leadership, and as the rebellion spread southward they were joined by many of the older Anglo-Irish leaders. And these attacks were carried out for complicated reasons that cut even more deeply into the emotional and social fabric of the Ulster Scots.

As the Irish historian Foster comments, "Those who led the revolt . . . were not the dispossessed natives, driven beyond endurance; nor were they fanatically Catholic revanchists. They were the Ulster gentry, of Irish origin but still possessing land: the 'deserving Irish' whose interests had survived the Plantation."[46] Significantly, as Foster points out, "The emphasis fell on threats to land titles, the depredations of the new-style government, and—most importantly—a residual loyalty to the king."[47]

This brutal revolt invited and received a brutal response, but throughout its early stages the rebels did their best to steer clear of the Ulster Scots. There were good reasons for this approach. First, they knew the Scottish settlers were organized to fight and were

able fighters. Second, they feared that Scotland itself, then positioned with a strong army across the North Channel of the Irish
Sea in Cumberland, could send a portion of that army to protect
fellow Presbyterians and decimate the rebellion. And third, in
many ways the Covenanters in Scotland had actually inspired this
Irish rebellion, and the Irish leaders wished to narrow the scope of
their attacks to the English-dominated governing forces in Ulster.
"Catholics or not, they had been inspired by Scottish pressure tactics. 'The Scots have taught us our ABC's.' "[48]

Their approach failed horribly. The rebellion itself quickly
spread beyond the intent of its originators until it did take on
a heavily anti-Protestant tone, designed to attempt to drive the
Ulster Plantation's settlers back across the sea. Predictably, the
Scottish settlements retaliated with ferocity. Many of the terrorized
English did return home, particularly those of the less warlike mercantile classes who had come from London and the southern areas
of England. And the end result of the uprising was a thorough
hardening of the Protestant elements of Ulster, with a pronounced
Scottish flavor and military approach.

"By mid-1644," Foster writes, "the Scots army in Ulster was
effectively a Covenanting force, in arms for Parliament, against
whom any royalist elements grudgingly stood down. . . . The vital
importance of Scottish influences was further emphasized by the
overspill of Scots refugees from the western Highlands to Ulster,
many of whom stayed on. The events of the 1640s, which began
with a threat to the Ulster Plantation, ended by solidifying the
Scottish nature of the province."[49] Indeed, an Irish state paper in
1660 indicated that by then there were "not above 5,000 English in
the whole province besides the army."[50]

English migrations to Ulster did pick up again in the late 1600s,
particularly from the northern border areas next to Scotland,
where many of the English emigrants shared the predominantly
Celtic heritage of the Scots.[51] Others, such as Puritans and
Quakers, who, like the Scots, were "dissenting" Protestants in con-

flict with the "reformed" English Episcopacy and the Catholics, also trickled into Ulster during this period. They frequently joined the Presbyterian congregations, intermarried, and thus became part of the Scottish communities.[52] As a consequence, despite their English antecedents, both of these groups tended to reinforce rather than detract from Scottish dominance of Ulster. In large measure they also account for the many English-origin surnames that show up among Americans of Scots-Irish descent. The "notion of Celtic kinship" was again well served, as the Scots characteristically absorbed the new immigrants.

In the following decades this "solidifying the Scottish nature of the province" proved to be a formula for more rather than less tension in Ulster. While the Royalists during the English civil war had been opposed to the Scottish Calvinists, some forget that Cromwell's Roundheads, whose anti-Irish sentiments are justly remembered for their uncontrolled viciousness, hated the Scottish Presbyterians with an equal passion. Indeed, in 1650, just months after he lopped off the head of Charles I, Cromwell led a notoriously brutal slash-and-burn "pacification" campaign throughout Ireland, putting sword and fire to Catholic and Presbyterian alike. Leyburn's figures, derived from Sir William Petty, a statistician of that period, indicate that "out of a population in Ireland of 1,448,000, three-sevenths, or 616,000, perished by sword, famine and plague." Of this number, 504,000 were Irish, meaning that more than 100,000 were not.[53]

Further, when Charles II returned to the throne after Cromwell's demise, he was convinced by his advisers to pass the first of a series of restrictive laws that eventually became known as the Test Acts. These acts were designed to produce an English government that was closely aligned with the Episcopal Church of England. As Churchill describes it: "Was not the Anglican Church the mainstay of the Throne? . . . The Corporation Act of 1661 required all persons holding municipal office to renounce the Solemn League and Covenant—a test which excluded many of the Presbyterians; to take the oath of non-resistance—which excluded Republicans; and to receive the sacrament according to the rites of the Church of England—which excluded Roman Catholics and some of the Nonconformists. The object of this act was to confine municipal office, closely connected to the election of members of Parliament, to Royalist Anglicans."[54]

Such restrictive laws ebbed and flowed over the following decades, both in their language and in the vigor of their enforcement in Ulster. But a particularly harsh version enacted by the newly crowned Queen Anne's government in 1703 would be a strong catalyst for the Ulster Scots to finally decide that a better future awaited them in the American colonies. The 1703 Test Act was specifically aimed at subduing the dominant Presbyterian culture in Ulster, requiring that all officeholders in Ireland take the sacrament of the Anglican Church. It also eliminated the legitimacy of Presbyterian ministers, thereby removing the legality of marriage ceremonies, baptisms, and even burial rites. Thus, in the eyes of English law, the non-Anglican Ulster Scots had instantly become fornicators for having married outside the Anglican Church, and their children were now regarded as bastards. In many parts of Ulster the Presbyterians could not even conduct a burial ceremony unless an Episcopalian minister performed the service.

In addition, Queen Anne's Test Act forbade dissenting Protestants from teaching school, holding even minor positions in the government, or serving as officers in the militia. It would be more than twenty years, until the beginning of the reign of King George II, before this act was moderated. It would not be until 1755, more than fifty years later, that Presbyterians were allowed to again serve as officers in the militia. And the act would not be repealed until 1782—long after the great Scots-Irish migration to America that saw so many former Ulstermen take up arms willingly and effectively against the English government during the American Revolution.[55]

Such seeds would bear predictable fruit, sown as they were

among a people whose ancestors had never bent a knee to Rome, either in ancient or modern times. The insistence on such restrictive policies by London's Anglican governors not only contributed heavily to the eventual migration from Ulster that began in 1715. It also inflamed the traditional Scottish contempt for central authority and caused the Ulster Scots to be known as the rebellious, argumentative, ever-combative "problem children" of Ulster.

Indeed, a revealing term crept into the Anglican and English lexicon during this period. The Anglicans started to call themselves "conformist" Protestants while the Presbyterians—who were not religious Presbyterians in the modern sense, but rather were the forerunners of the fundamentalist Christian movement in the United States—were referred to as the "nonconformists." And no better word can be found to describe the Scots-Irish political and social contribution in America, for they were to become America's first radicals.

The Presbyterian experiences in the new communities in Ireland made them even more uncompromising than those they had left behind in Scotland. In a less violent but still consistent backlash that mirrored the reaction of the Scots to Edward's torture of William Wallace, Henry VIII's "rough wooing," and Charles I's attempt to force them into Episcopacy, the edicts from above only made the Ulster Scots more intransigent. As Leyburn points out, they were now fully convinced of "the superiority of the Presbyterian Church to any order a king might make that curbed or thwarted it, . . . that there is a justification for revolt against authority . . . [and that] the principle of revolution may also apply to the individual."[56]

Foster agrees, commenting that "the denial of their civil rights and the bitter antipathy felt for them by the Church of Ireland set them in a mould that was firmly antiestablishment in more ways than one. . . . The Presbyterian political culture was always ready to withdraw compliance from authority; their loyalty was conditional. . . . This helps account for the special odium in which

Ulster Presbyterians were held; points could be stretched for Huguenots and Quakers . . . but in the Ulster context, fundamentalism, though attacked in every generation, tended to win out. 'No temporizing' in theology was joined with 'no surrender' in politics. Thus, despite their role in 1688–1691, the Ulster Dissenters' interest remained against the government."[57]

This "role in 1688–1691" was principally military. Without the hard backbone of the Ulster Scots during those years, the preservation of English rule in Ulster would almost certainly have been lost. And further, the military victories of that period thwarted a serious attempt by James II to regain the British throne from William II. That the newly crowned Queen Anne could so cavalierly disregard these contributions barely ten years later when she imposed the draconian restrictions of her Test Acts was a clear—and final— signal to the Ulster Scots that the Episcopal English aristocracy could never be trusted. As in so many other cases when it came to London, their assistance was vital during times of crisis, but a Presbyterian ascendancy on their own terms was viewed as an unacceptable threat.

To fully comprehend why Queen Anne's Test Acts culminated in such overwhelming bitterness and self-imposed cultural isolation, it is crucial to read her decision to impose the acts against the military turmoil that immediately preceded them. And the key symbolic event of the 1688–1691 period was the siege of Londonderry. Although not a great military battle in historical terms, the 105-day siege of Ulster's second-most-important city called upon the courage and tenacity of men, women, and children alike.

The Londonderry siege was not the only successful defensive effort by Protestants in Ulster as Ireland fought out its own battles in the wake of the deposition of James II. Foster writes of "equally successful, if less spectacular resistance" throughout the province during this time.[58] But in it the Ulster Scots found an allegorical microcosm for all the ills and betrayals that had haunted them throughout the turbulent century since they had left lowland Scotland. Many Catholic Irish allied themselves with a great European power in an attempt to expel them. The English rulers in London urged them on and then failed to support them through their most critical hours of need. The Anglican elite in Ireland minimized their contribution once the siege had been lifted. And hardly a decade later, a new English queen sought to cut them away from governmental, educational, military, and even religious power in the very province in which their numbers and culture had become clearly dominant.

In the end the siege reinforced the notion that the Ulster Scots were an isolated people who could depend only on each other. And its aftermath convinced many of them that they no longer belonged in Ireland's increasingly toxic ethnic mix.

4

Londonderry. The Boyne. Exodus.

WHEN WILLIAM OF Orange ascended the British throne in December 1688, it brought a quick reaction from Louis XIV of France. The most powerful ruler in Europe viewed the succession of a Dutch Protestant to the English crown as a dramatic shift in the balance of power and a threat to French influence in overall European affairs. Louis immediately threw his weight behind the exiled King James II, receiving him with great fanfare in France and providing him with extensive military supplies, financing, and a large contingent of French soldiers in an effort to help him regain his throne.

James then left for Ireland, arriving in March 1689 and setting up a regency in Dublin as a first step toward ousting William of Orange. In May, England reacted to this and other provocations by declaring war against France, and sent an eight-thousand-man army to do battle with the French in Flanders. The forces under James were now viewed by the English not only as an army rebelling in Ireland, but also as wartime allies of the French. And in that sense the situation in Ireland became a replay of Hugh O'Neill's rebellion of almost exactly a hundred years before, with the French taking the place of the Spanish in their desires to flank England by creating a second front on the island.

As Churchill wrote, in Ireland, James "was welcomed as a deliverer. He reigned in Dublin, aided by an Irish Parliament, and was soon defended by a Catholic army which may have reached a hundred thousand men. The whole island except the Protestant settlements in the North passed under the control of the Jacobites, as they were henceforth called. While William looked eastward to Flanders and the Rhine the eyes of his Parliament were fixed upon the opposite quarter. When he reminded Parliament of Europe they vehemently drew his attention to Ireland. The King made the time-honoured mistake of meeting both needs inadequately."[59]

Those loyal to James II had been active during his brief reign and had engaged in military pursuits even prior to his arrival in Ireland from France. When James became king, he had appointed Richard Talbot, the earl of Tyrconnell, as his lord deputy in Ireland. Tyrconnell came from long-established Anglo-Irish stock and was charged with bringing Catholics to positions of importance in Ireland. He had focused on the legal system and especially the military, which became the "cutting edge of the policy of Catholicization."[60] This allowed Tyrconnell not only to eliminate Protestants from key positions in the army, but also to station Catholic-dominated troops in almost every key location in Ulster. Unlike the rebellion of 1641, this action was legal, under the imprimatur of the Crown. Thus, even as the English Parliament sought to oust James II from the throne, Catholic military strongholds dominated the cities and towns of the Ulster Plantation.

In late 1688, as William approached from Holland, a nationwide revolt against James had broken out in England. But in the Catholic parts of Ireland, similar revolts had broken out to protest against William. By early 1689, William's usurpation of James was still unaccepted in Catholic Ireland, while the Protestant areas were refusing to support James's regency in Dublin. The province fell into chaos as Tyrconnell declared them rebels and rampaged though the countryside. Protestants "in the line of march of the army pulled down their houses, burnt and destroyed what they could not take with them, and fled to the fortified towns" of Enniskillen, Coleraine, and especially Londonderry. Between the punitive acts of Tyrconnell's army and the scorched earth policies of the colonists themselves, Londonderry County became so desolate that, in the eyes of one French officer, it was "like traveling through the deserts of Arabia."[61]

Wild rumors were flying about Catholic intentions. A widely circulated letter predicting a replay of 1641's massacres created a panic. Soon the city's usual population of 2,000 had burgeoned to 7,000 soldiers and as many as 30,000 refugees. The standoff at Londonderry quickly became the focal point of the revolt, on both sides. As the months passed, a large force of Irish and French troops gathered outside the city's stone walls, calling for its capitulation.

Londonderry—historically and more properly known as Derry, still a sore point among many Irish—was no stranger to conflict. Located in the far north of Ireland where the River Foyle meets a wide, seaworthy Lough of the same name, Derry had been for centuries an accessible safe harbor when ships hit bad weather on the stormy North Atlantic. Founded by the famous missionary St. Columba in A.D. 546, the town was long known for Catholic landmarks that included an ancient cathedral, the Teampul Mor, erected in 1164, a Cistercian nunnery built in 1218, a Dominican abbey and church built in 1274, an Augustinian friary and church, and a Franciscan friary. Its churches and abbeys plus its accessibility from the nearby sea also made Derry an easy target for plunderers. The Danes sacked its churches and burned the city numerous times during the ninth and tenth centuries, followed by the Anglo-Normans, who found it a frequent and choice target throughout the twelfth. For centuries thereafter, Derry became both a favored destination for plundering Irish tribes and a headquarters for others. Between 1560 and 1604 the city was twice laid to ruins during Irish rebellions.

In 1613, with the settlement of the Ulster Plantation, the English renamed the city Londonderry and over the next six years built a redoubtable series of walls around it that exist to this day. During the rebellion of 1641, seven heavily Scottish regiments whose soldiers were taken from nearby farms and townships defended the city. In 1649, as Cromwell closed in on the hapless King Charles I in London, Londonderry endured a partial siege that lasted several months, largely because the Ulster Scots in and around it had been aligned with the Scottish Covenanters against the king. And now, as troops loyal to James II wreaked havoc through Ulster, the thick stone walls of Londonderry were the reason the people of the countryside poured into the city. They were also the reason that the soldiers under James could not forcefully attack it. And thus began the longest and most famous siege in modern British history.

The standoff began on December 7, 1688, with the arrival of a Catholic contingent that had been ordered by Tyrconnell to occupy the city. As the soldiers approached, thirteen young apprentices grabbed the keys of the city from a guard and closed the city gates, locking the army out. The army remained and steadily grew. Those inside the city, recently supplied arms and munitions by an English ship, organized its defense and fought. The resulting standoff would not end until August 1, 1689, nearly nine months later, although heavy fighting did not begin until late April. More than seven thousand men, women, and children would perish, some from the siege guns and others through disease and starvation.

James II elevated the importance of Londonderry in April. Having just arrived in Ireland, the deposed king marched his heavily French army to the city, reinforcing Tyrconnell's contingent. On April 18, during a cease-fire, the king approached the city gates and offered terms of surrender to the besieged Protestants. His answer was a barrage of cannon and musket fire that killed an officer and several soldiers near him, and a chorus that became the battle cry of those inside.

"No surrender."

The full siege had begun. The surprised James fell back beyond range of the city's cannons and sat motionless on his horse in a heavy rain for several hours. Back in Dublin, he ordered a trainload of siege guns to Londonderry. By the end of May the city was surrounded by an estimated twenty thousand French and Irish soldiers, and was under a relentless pounding. The siege guns, actually heavy mortars, lofted hundreds of shells above the stone walls, with great impact on the cramped population and the buildings in the city itself. Inside the walls the Protestants chose their leaders, developed military discipline, and began to carefully ration a dwindling supply of food. They also collectively wrote their battle cry in blood, just as the Scottish Covenanters had done fifty years before when Charles I had ordered them to accept the Anglican faith.

No surrender.

Londonderry's defense was not simply a passive affair. In addition to their individual weapons and the artillery that lined the city walls, Protestant ground forces made frequent raids, patrols, and ambushes outside the gates. Col. Adam Murray, a Scot who commanded the military forces, led several successful cavalry campaigns against the French and Irish besiegers. In late April the French general Maumont was killed in one such attack. In another, Murray made a brief, false attack on Jacobite forces (followers of James II) at Pennyburn Mill and then lured French cavalry forces into a deadly ambush set up by his infantry as he retreated. Other battles were fought over key pieces of terrain, including two at Windmill Hill and one at the Butcher's Gate.

In an effort symbolic of larger issues between England and the Ulster Protestants, the vaunted English navy did not enshrine itself with honor. On June 8 a British warship, the *Greyhound*, attempted to run the Jacobite blockade on the River Foyle and was badly damaged by French and Irish gunfire coming from Fort Culmore, a key spot above the river. Initially running aground, the damaged *Greyhound* soon abandoned the besieged Protestants, limping back to England.

On June 11 a larger naval relief force along with soldiers and provisions arrived within sight of the city's towers at the mouth of the Lough Foyle. Seeing the damage done to the *Greyhound* and learning that the besieging army had laid booms of logs and chains across the mouth of the river, the English commander, Maj. Gen. Percy Kirke, hesitated. The French and Irish guns at Fort Culmore were trained on the booms, prepared for a barrage if the relief ships attempted to break through. As Derry's defenders watched from above, Kirke turned his task force around and sailed off to the Lough Swilly, on the other side of a peninsula a few miles west of the city. And there he stayed. For six weeks, during the worst part of the siege, the English relief force remained encamped on Inch Island in Lough Swilly while the city's defenders absorbed a heavy pounding from the siege guns and began dying in droves from starvation.

Anger and bitterness filled the city. Their only hope for survival rested a few miles away as they continued to die from enemy fire and began eating dogs and rats to survive. This anger was matched by many of the soldiers and sailors in the relief force itself, some of whom were Ulster natives.

Finally the duke of Schomberg, King William's military commander in Ireland, sent a harsh note to General Kirke, ordering him to lift the siege. On the evening of July 28 the relief force pushed forward toward the city. Darkness was falling as they entered Lough Foyle. The tide was running with them. Three supply ships, covered by the heavy guns of the British warship HMS *Dartmouth*, moved against the boom. The lead ship, the *Mountjoy*, stalled as it tried to ram the booms and was taken under heavy fire by the guns at Fort Culmore. Swaying in the current, the *Mountjoy* ran aground, but as it returned fire the recoil from its guns dislodged it from the riverbank, floating it again. Its commander, Londonderry native Capt. Michael Browning, was killed while commanding the guns on the main deck. But soon a party of sailors on a longboat cut the chains and broke the booms. And finally, under cover of darkness, the three supply ships made their way to the city's walls.

The siege was lifted. Two days later the French and Irish soldiers, themselves exhausted, began to withdraw. James had been defeated in a symbolic standoff that he had personally initiated. But ironically, the victory only widened the rift between the predominantly English Anglicans and the principally Scottish Presbyterians who had fought alongside them.

The Reverend George Walker, an Anglican minister widely hailed as one of the heroes of the siege, was, if not the major reason, certainly the flash point of this rupture. Walker was the son of an Anglican minister who had migrated to Ulster from Yorkshire. He had married the daughter of Sir John Stanhope of Melwood and through her influence had been appointed chancellor of the diocese of Armagh, near Londonderry. Following his father into the clergy, Walker himself was seventy years old when the siege began. Despite his age and his being, as the Anglicans put it, "in Holy Orders," Walker reportedly had raised a regiment in the months before the siege began and was commanding it in the towns of Dungannon and Strabane when the French and Irish forces began surrounding Londonderry. He and other army commanders had briefly fought the advancing soldiers and then retreated to the city in the final days before the deposed King James II arrived at its gates.

Although accounts vary, Walker was apparently one of two joint governors inside the city during the siege, commanding fifteen companies and also supervising the commissariat, a vital job given the starvation-level rationing that went into effect. He also was known to have given many simply worded but inspirational sermons during the hard days of the siege, Londonderry's cathedral being divided on Sundays with the Anglicans offering morning services and the Presbyterians using it in the afternoon. Indeed,

Walker is said to have given the last of the sermons in the besieged city, on July 30, just before its final relief.

Within days after the siege ended, Walker was on a ship to England, where he was greeted by the admiring court of William and Mary. William awarded him five thousand pounds for his services, a truly princely sum for the time. Soon thereafter he was named bishop of Londonderry, a position he never actually occupied because he was killed the next year at the Battle of the Boyne. In September he published his narrative *A True Account of the Siege of Londonderry*, obsequiously dedicated to the king. In October he was granted an honorary degree at Cambridge. A few months after that he was given one by Oxford.

Walker's *True Account*, and the personal glory he brought unto himself in England at the expense of others, created immediate anger in Ulster, particularly among the Scottish Presbyterians. His memoir failed to mention the services of even one Presbyterian minister during the siege. Nor did it credit the audacious combat leadership of such fighters as Col. Adam Murray, who had led so many excursions outside the city walls and had been the first to coin the phrase "No Surrender." Walker's book was soon followed by a rebuttal called *Narrative*, written by John Mackenzie, a Presbyterian minister who also was at the siege. Mackenzie claimed among other things that Walker had exaggerated his military credentials and that he had never even held the post of joint governor at all.

This rift fell rather cleanly along both ethnic and religious lines. For the Presbyterian Scots who stayed in Ulster, the insults at the hands of the principally English Anglicans would burn for more than a century.[62] For those who eventually left Northern Ireland to settle in America, the slighting of their contributions at the Londonderry siege would become simply one more piece of evidence that it was time to move on. And they brought with them a far greater antipathy toward the English hierarchy than they ever could have felt toward the ordinary Irish.

The reason, in both cases, was the same. Although ethnic labels overlapped here and there, the predominantly English Anglicans in Ireland intended to remain politically and culturally superior, regardless of whether the Irish Catholics and the principally Scottish "dissenters" outnumbered them. As Foster succinctly put it, the Presbyterian position in Ireland "was not much more enviable than that of the Catholics; the Established Church remained the fountain of privilege in Ireland, more closely linked than ever to the Church of England and the possessors of land. In return, membership gave exclusive rights to political power."[63]

Although defeated—or, more accurately, outlasted—at Derry, James II continued his campaigns in Ireland. At the same time, William III focused on fighting the French on the European mainland. As winter passed, bickering broke out between James and his French advisers. But in the spring of 1690 the French provided James with significant reinforcements, forcing William to pay closer attention to the Irish flank. Belatedly—and dangerously—William decided to personally face James in Ireland. In a reflection of Europe's complicated loyalties of this period, William assembled an eclectic army of 36,000 Ulster Scots, Irish, English, Dutch, French Huguenots, Germans, and Danes to fight against James's equally diverse army of about 30,000 Irish, French Catholics, Germans, and Walloons. William then crossed the Irish Sea with his force, bringing with him forty pieces of heavy artillery, some so large they required a pulling team of a dozen horses. He landed at Carrickfergus, east of Belfast, on June 14, and after a brief ceremony there and another in the Ulster capital, he and his soldiers headed south.

William was taking a great military risk by dividing his forces so completely between Ireland to England's west and the Continent to its east, placing him at the very strategic disadvantage that Louis XIV had longed for when first deciding to help James. Further, by deploying so much of his army outside of England, William had left the country vulnerable to direct invasion from France. This possibility was not out of the question. On the Continent, the French soon attacked a depleted English army at Fleurus, defeating it. At sea the French navy soundly defeated a combined British and Dutch fleet at Beachy Head, giving the French at least temporary control of the English Channel.

William needed a quick and decisive battle in his effort to face down James. He would not be disappointed. And he would be heading back to England less than a month after he landed at Carrickfergus.

From Belfast, William's army moved southward toward Newry. James, positioned a dozen miles farther south on key terrain at Dundalk, sent a reconnaissance patrol of mounted dragoons forward to gain information on the strength of the English. The patrol clashed with an advance guard of several hundred English infantrymen and dragoons, losing a number of soldiers as well as their commanding officer. The returning soldiers warned the deposed king of the large size of the advancing force. James immediately withdrew from Dundalk and set up defensive positions twenty miles farther south, on the southern bank of the River Boyne near Drogheda. Now William would have to cross the river with an entire army in order to attack.

William's forces, hot in pursuit, closed on Drogheda. As they positioned themselves along the northern bank of the Boyne, they learned that James's army was spread along a front of several miles between Drogheda and Slane Bridge to its west. Surveying their positions, William himself decided on the battle plan, frustrating his field marshal, the vastly experienced, eighty-year-old duke of Schomberg. But the king was also battle tested, having fought many campaigns in Europe. Indeed, although he was known as grim and humorless and had been sickly all his life, William seemed to come alive on the battlefield.

Never viewed as a battlefield genius, William's evenness under fire nonetheless inspired loyalty. He was also a man largely without bias. In matters of government he aligned himself with Catholic and Protestant alike, and did not care to dawdle in the usual royal schemes of jealousies and petty revenge. Many of his soldiers, including the crack Dutch Blue Guards, who would carry much of the fight at the Boyne, were Catholic. Other Dutch units were heavily manned by exiled French Huguenots. Their service in the battle would cause William to allow many Huguenots to migrate to Ulster, where in the following decades they became active in the linen industry. His composure in the face of death became apparent soon after arriving at the Boyne, when an Irish marksman saw him riding in front of his men in full regalia and shot him in the shoulder. The undeterred William had his wound treated, then remounted his horse and continued to prepare his battle plan.

It was historic irony that these two accidental kings would meet in this remote place called the Boyne. James had been crowned because his brother left no direct heirs and was flawed by his obsession with returning all things Catholic to a nation that had abandoned Catholicism. William was a casual Calvinist at best, never very concerned about the domestic politics of the nation he now ruled, who himself would die childless and whose great passion was to deny Louis XIV his dream of French dominance of Europe. And neither of them cared, really, about things Irish—James wishing eventually to do away with Irish traditions and replace them with English teachings, the Dutch-born William obsessed with continental Europe. And yet each of them had bet his right to the throne on this showdown.

William's scheme of maneuver was simple. His main forces would pound James's positions with his heavy artillery, then conduct a frontal assault, crossing the river and marching directly into them. At the same time, a cavalry unit under Marshal Schomberg's son Meinhard would move upstream to the west and turn the left flank of James's army at Slane Bridge, creating so much chaos behind James's front lines that his army would be forced to retreat in disarray.

Just before dawn the English heavy artillery began firing on

James's positions, and after several barrages the assault began. As the Dutch Blue Guards waded up to their armpits directly into the heart of James's defenses, an Irish cavalry unit under Richard Hamilton forced them back in some of the heaviest fighting of the day. The battle ebbed and flowed along the riverbank and in the water. The duke of Schomberg, seeing the Blue Guards stagger, decided to rally them. Moving forward from the riverbank, the duke took charge of the assault and was soon killed, later found with a bullet in his throat and two saber gashes on his head.

The enigmatic Reverend George Walker, whose presence at the Boyne has never been fully explained—whether soldier, minister, or observer—was also killed during the assault. King William, upon hearing that Walker had fallen, is reported to have asked incredulously, "What took him there?" Others reported that Walker had been coming to the aid of the wounded Schomberg. Some maintained that he had raised troops for the battle, but there are no records supporting that claim.

As the frontal assault ebbed and flowed, Meinhard Schomberg's cavalry force managed to turn James's left flank, guaranteeing William's victory. James had anticipated the move and sent an Irish regiment of dragoons under Neill O'Neill, a nephew of Tyrconnell, to stop them. But O'Neill was quickly killed, causing the Irish under his command to retreat. Lauzun, the French commander, tried to fill the gap with a fresh contingent of French troops and Irish cavalry, but this left only Irish foot soldiers along the riverbank to defend against William's persistent frontal assault. The assault broke through the lines, and soon James and his army were in full retreat.

Victory assured, William made no effort to pursue James's army or to capture James himself. Instead, he made a triumphal march into Dublin, establishing the validity of his own regency, and then immediately returned to England. James, humiliated, left for France three days after the battle, complaining bitterly of Irish cowardice at the Boyne. He would never return. And although the

Irish continued their rebellion for another year, the matter of William III's succession to the British throne was forever settled.

In modern-day Ireland, the siege of Londonderry and William's victory at the Boyne are still well celebrated among the Protestants in ceremonies that never fail to draw bile from the Catholics. But the centuries have brought with them a simplified, two-sided depiction of the fights—a view that did not exist in the decades immediately following these key events.

Those who choose to remember James's Irish campaign and William's response in simple religious terms ignore the complexities of the issues. James was hardly in Ireland as the champion of either Irish or Catholic causes, which is the reason the pope himself celebrated William's victory at the Boyne as a repudiation of Louis XIV's international ambitions.[64] And the Orangemen who march in their parades on the anniversary of the Boyne as a celebration of Protestant unity against the Catholics ignore the deep divisions among Protestants themselves during this era. Ulster's famous Orange Order was not even created until more than a hundred years later, in 1795, after the great Scots-Irish migration to America was completed.[65]

Unfortunately for the Ulster Scots, the victory over James did nothing to change Anglican dominance of Irish affairs. As Foster writes, Ireland remained "a kingdom containing a Protestant elite who had intermarried, established dynasties, stored up fortunes, built houses, colonized both the polite society and the political institutions of the capital, and defined themselves against the cultures of Catholicism and Dissent."[66] And the succession of Queen Anne not only continued this preeminence, but also through the Test Acts hardened it.

The eighteenth century dawned quietly in Europe and America, giving no hint of the political turbulence that would overtake its final twenty-five years. A steady evolution of democratic institutions would mark its decades, led principally by English, French, and colonial American theorists. What no one could have guessed in 1703 as Queen Anne's government passed her Test Acts was that the hard-nosed, unyielding Presbyterian Scots of Ulster would themselves provide the denouement of this march toward individual freedoms—in America. For by 1828 their culture would have shaped the direction of a unique frontier-style democracy and also have given the new nation its first populist president.

After a hundred years of struggle, Ulster was no longer the swamp-laden wilderness that had greeted the first settlers when the Irish earls had fled to Spain. But the province still remained the ugly adopted stepchild of the British Isles. Ireland itself did not enjoy Scotland's legal status as a kingdom and was headed for more turmoil as the Catholic Irish resisted further domination. Ulster had England's eye, but it was not a formal colony in the sense of those now beginning to flourish in America. Its woolen and linen industries were frequently subjected to tariffs and restrictions placed on them from London. Few Ulster Scots owned land, and a Byzantine policy of "rack-renting" brought exponential increases in their payments to absentee landlords. Rack-renting caused a vicious circle where improvements they themselves made on the land raised the value of the property and thus their own rent. Additionally, a cycle of drought and deadly famine seemed endemic to the island's geography.

Most important, the impact of Queen Anne's Test Acts hit the "nonconformist" Protestant community even harder than it did the Catholics. Catholic priests were at least viewed by the government as "lawfully ordained, whereas dissenting ministers were 'mere upstarts' not in the line of apostolic succession." In addition to negating the legal effect of their ministers, the acts' removal of Presbyterians from local government caused both embarrassment and political chaos. As two examples, the entire Corporation of Belfast had to be immediately dismissed once the acts were passed, as were ten of Londonderry's twelve aldermen.[67]

These realities urged upon the Ulster Scots a special kind of restlessness, and with it a pull toward the American colonies. Small groups had begun to migrate across the treacherous Atlantic Ocean from the time James II ascended the throne in 1685, scattering themselves from New Hampshire to South Carolina. But after 1715 the migrations assumed a powerful dynamic, growing in intensity and concentrating almost exclusively on the mountainous areas from central Pennsylvania to the Georgia border.

These later migrations were not the scattered, small-scale immigrations of the past. Rather, they became the movement and relocation of virtually an entire people. From their inception after 1715 until the American Revolution, at least 200,000 and as many as 400,000 would leave Ulster for America, almost all of them Dissenters and the great majority of them Presbyterians.[68] Commentators who insist that economics played the principal role in this mass migration should ask themselves why, at this point in Ireland's history, so few Anglicans and Catholics joined the exodus.

Who were these people? The English mixed among them, as did the Irish and a smattering of Huguenots. But principally these were the same lowland Scots who had left the thin-soiled and embattled border areas, hoping for a better life in Ireland. Many of these families had spent more than a hundred years in Ireland. Almost all had spent more than a generation there, so that their children had no direct memory of Scotland. Some observers claim that they were at this point neither Scottish nor Irish. The truth is that they were both, having gleaned from the culture of one people and the land of another until they were a unique hybrid mix. They were Protestants but could not coexist peacefully with the Anglican English. They were Irish but had brought with them from Scotland a view that Catholic religious leaders had veered away from God. They were Scottish in their history and traditions but had lost their physical connection to their homeland and thus had become Irish in many aspects of their daily lives.

Whatever one may have wished to call them, they had had enough of Ireland. They were a new people, strong and unfulfilled, and they were ready for a new land. The "nonconformists" who had given the Anglicans such continual fits were aptly named. And they would take with them from Ireland a greater sense of injustice at the hands of the English governing class than any sort of anger toward the Irish.

Unfortunately, even as they began their second great migration within the span of a century, as a culture the Ulster Scots were missing out, both on the dawning era of educational enlightenment and on the benefits of the Industrial Revolution.

In the early 1700s, Scotland's economic and educational systems would begin to change dramatically. By the 1780s the country would be in an intellectual and commercial "takeoff," still rural but having passed a turning point fed by the Industrial Revolution and the advent of the cotton textile industry. Indeed, the country would be entering a "golden age, the likes of which had never been seen before or since."[69] Some have compared this "explosion of creative energy" to "the great periods of Athens or Florence. It included the philosophy of David Hume, the poetry of Robert Burns and the architecture of Robert Adam. The study of economics was transformed by Adam Smith, of physics by Black, of geology by Hutton and of sociology by Adam Ferguson."[70] Those who had moved on to Ireland and then to America were long-gone from the treeless lowlands by the time this renaissance occurred.

In Ireland, the Anglicans of the Church of Ireland and the Catholics who were benefiting from a Jesuit emphasis on education would press the importance of academic learning on their parishioners. The Kirks of the Calvinist Ulster Scots would continue to lecture more about discipline and self-reliance than on book-fed philosophy. In America, the settlers of New England and to a lesser extent those Cavalier societies along the Southern coast had already created many of the great universities that survive even to this day. But the Ulster Scots would head into the mountains with few texts other than the Bible in their canvas sacks, beginning a century of educational regression even as others saw the New World as a land of enlightenment.

The world that they would inherit was harsh and unforgiving. No towns had been platted out to await their arrival. No London municipal corporation was financing their venture. No merchants traveled among them. No schools would welcome their children. The threat of Cherokee and Shawnee war parties would be the reality that filled their long nights in the dark woods behind the log walls of their fresh-built cabins. And no government other than that which they agreed upon among themselves would control their daily interactions.

In such a wild, uncharted place the book of God was vital, for it nourished their spirit and laid boundaries for their conduct. Other subjects simply had no relevance. Trigonometry and calculus would not help them find their way along the mountain trails. Adam Smith's economics were of no consequence in the matter of planting corn and breeding cattle. Nor did they need the essays of Plato or the plays of Shakespeare to teach them how to shoot a rifle, or to make clothes from animal skins, or to clear away the wilderness with their own bare hands.

They would not go to America as Scots or as Irishmen, nor would they go as tradesmen or plantation owners. A century of turmoil in the beautiful but tormented hills and waterlines of Ulster had changed them. They were, as always, farmers and fighters, these two callings inseparable in their history and in their culture. But they now were a different people. Their blood and traditions had been shaped by centuries in Scotland, then both hardened and sentimentalized by Ireland. And yet neither land would ever again fully claim them. They were the unsung orphans of both.

In Ireland, they would always be remembered as a hybrid, the Ulster Scots. In America, they would gain a new hyphen, becoming known as the Scotch-Irish, and also by the more ethnically proper term, the Scots-Irish. Although the term Scotch-Irish is still frequently used inside the United States, in other countries and especially in Scotland itself it is considered rude to refer to a person as being Scotch. "Scotch," as they say, is a whiskey. "Scots" are people whose roots go back to Scotland. This book honors that judgment.

PART FOUR

The Spirit of a Revolution

Call this war by whatever name you may, only call it not an American rebellion; it is nothing more or less than a Scotch Irish Presbyterian rebellion.

—A HESSIAN OFFICER,
writing home during the War of the American Revolution

1

Roots

SOME MIGHT THINK it morbid, but I find solace and even affirmation among old graves.

And here I stand on a sloping hill in a remote cemetery two miles east of Natural Bridge, Virginia, staring at a marker that rises above the remains of my five-times-great-grandfather. Thomas Lackey was born in Ulster in 1732, a member of a family—variously spelled Lecky, Leckie, and Lackey, even among the stones in the small confines of this cemetery—that for centuries in Scotland before their journey to Ireland had been part of the McGregor clan. Relocating in Ireland and then shipping out to America from Londonderry in 1748, the family lived first in Lancaster, Pennsylvania, then later moved south to this solitary and thickly wooded section of the Blue Ridge Mountains not far from the Appalachian Trail.

And here old Thomas died. It is an eerie feeling thinking of the bones that are buried just beneath my feet, a corpse who braved the harsh Atlantic and later walked the long trails through the mountains to just this spot, and whose blood still courses in my veins. And old Thomas Lackey is not alone. Looking around this small cemetery, I see numerous other family names that still dot its hills. In fact, I'm having a pretty jolly family reunion as I stand among the gravestones in the sweet spring grass, recognizing this long-remembered person and that—except of course that everybody else is dead. But, no matter, I'm happy to find them, after all the bedtime stories and front-porch chronicles of my youth. Their journey in many ways defined me. And just as important, by placing their families in what was then an isolated wilderness, these old souls dared to make a nation.

Actually I'm living out a ritual, for an irony abounds in the Scots-Irish mind-set. On the one hand, for a variety of reasons Americans of Scots-Irish heritage seldom refer to themselves by a specific ethnic identity. And yet on the other, they probably boast a higher percentage of ardent genealogists than any other cultural group in the country. This paradox is instructive, for it is a millennial rather than a recent phenomenon. It reaches back to the distinctions in ancient Scotland that encouraged strong family pride and even patriotism while at the same time dismissing notions that nationalism needed to be wrapped up in a specific racial or ethnic identity or even in a larger loyalty to king and crown.

The Scots-Irish, like other cultures, have always had their group prejudices as well as their fiercely held internal codes. But on the whole they are an embracive people who have tended to focus more on shared concepts such as family loyalty and personal honor than on simple ethnic similarities. Historian Ned Landsman writes of "the emphasis on collateral rather than lineal descent" in the clan structure and points out that "when a Scottish man or woman took a spouse who was not of Scottish descent, the whole family [of the new spouse] could be absorbed into the 'Scottish' community."[1] The long history of family feuds that marks this culture, from the border areas of western Scotland to the hills of West Virginia, is testimony that local and personal loyalties drive their passions far more deeply than any contrived notion of larger ethnic differences. The Hatfields and McCoys were hardly different in their ethnic origins, but they killed each other for generations.

Just as the notion of Celtic kinship was defined from the bottom up even a thousand years ago by clan allegiance rather than a mandatory fealty to some distant king, in modern times studying the movement of family members over the generations has provided the clearest way to tell the story of the Scots-Irish journey. Of the communities on the American frontier, Professor Landsman observes that "the patterned dispersal of the Scots, rather than isolating individual settlers from their homes and families, served instead to bind together the scattered settlements through a system of interlocking family networks."[2] David Hackett Fischer amplifies this thought by pointing out that in America, "[A]s time passed, clans became stronger rather than weaker in the southern highlands. . . . These clans fostered an exceptionally strong sense of loyalty . . . which recognized a special sense of obligation to kin."[3]

Couple this with the near-biblical storytelling tradition of the culture, and the journey of an extended family can be the most logical way for those who came in the first great migration out of Ireland to relate the history of the frontier writ large. The personal becomes history, and history becomes personal. Names introduce themselves on the well-worn pages of family Bibles, some of those books carried from Ulster into the wilderness and treasured through the centuries, births and marriages and deaths entered carefully as the book itself was passed down over the generations into the present day. Others show up in faded letters sent from faraway relatives recalling places and events, pooling information that might reconstruct a family's journey. Still others appear in the handwritten notes of people like my maternal grandmother, who when I was twelve years old finally wrote out an amazingly accurate eleven-page summary of her family's movement from Virginia through Tennessee, then down into Mississippi and finally into Arkansas, replete with the dates of births and deaths, marriages, and military enlistments. Granny Doyle had been carrying all of this in her head, passed down from mother to daughter through each generation in singsong verses on the narrow front porch of some latest cabin as the hot summer sun gave way to a sultry, bug-filled evening, or huddled next to the fireplace before there ever was such a thing as radio to fill the boredom of a winter night.

My Daddy was Francis Adolphus Doyle. His great grand daddy Zachariah Thomas Doyle was in the War of 1812 in Hicks Ford, Virginia, a town that later became known as Emporia. My Mama was Louella Marsh, the only member of her family except for her Daddy to survive the cholera epidemic that swept the Memphis area in 1873. My Mama's Daddy was Samuel Jasper Marsh, whose family came to Tennessee from North Carolina and who himself helped settle Woodruff County Arkansas. Samuel Marsh enlisted in the Eighth Arkansas Infantry in July 1861, then later on returned to Tipton County, Tennessee and served in the Confederate army over there. My Mama's Mama was Parmelia Long Marsh, whose brother Alec Long was a Confederate soldier and died of smallpox in a Federal prisoner of war camp in Alton Illinois. My Grandpa Samuel caught the cholera when he took a mule run of cotton into Memphis during the epidemic, and came on home to die. Then the whole family caught it, and only Samuel and my Mama Louella survived. When Parmelia died of the cholera, before Samuel buried her he cut off a lock of her hair and a piece of her dress and wrapped it in her wedding glove. He kept it with him, along with her wedding ring, until the day he died. Your great aunt Lena still has those things, and since she has no natural children maybe she'll pass them on to you when she dies. . . .

And here, as I sort through reams of family genealogy, is a note written to me by my father nearly thirty years ago. Along with the note, he sent me dozens of pages copied from a book called *History of the House of Ochiltree*. Written in 1916 and published by a remote press in a small Kansas town, the book traced a group of families that had their beginnings in the Ochil Hills of Ayrshire, Scotland, just west of Stirling, where William Wallace turned back Proud Edward's army and not far from the battlefield of Bannockburn. These were Braveheart's people. The families included many of my father's direct ancestors such as the McKnights (also known as McNaught and McNaughton), the Leckeys, the Leeches, the Johnsons, and the Millers. All of them made the long trek from western Scotland to Northern Ireland and then later to the Pennsylvania and Virginia colonies and beyond. The book was never intended to be great literature, but like so many similar works of family genealogy, it was a means of capturing vital family information before it became lost in the frenzy of America's obsession with the future rather than the past. And in that sense its author, Clementine Brown Railey, succeeded quite well.

As was his fashion, my father had marked a few sections of the book for my perusal. Along with it he also sent me a dozen typewritten pages, worn and faded with age, filled with amplifications and personal observations about different family members mentioned in the *House of Ochiltree* book. I do not know their origins, but the typed pages appear to be the transcript of a personal letter sent more than fifty years ago by one of my father's aunts. And across the first page he had written, "Have you ever heard of the Battle of the Boyne? See page 9."

The dozen typed pages focus on one branch, the Millers, revealing a mere trickle of our own family's journey and only a drop or two in the stream of the great Scots-Irish migration. But they give us human faces and comment on personal tendencies, thus allowing an honest window into the distant past. Henry Miller, born in Londonderry in 1726, came to Lancaster County, Pennsylvania, in 1745, where he married Rebecca Boggs, also a native of Ireland. In 1770 they migrated to Rockbridge County, Virginia, along with a group of closely knit Northern Irish families that included the Lackeys, the Leeches, and the McKnights, with whom the Millers intermarried. The family cemetery at which I found Thomas Lackey's and others' graves is near the old Miller homestead, as is a church that was reportedly built on land donated in part by Henry Miller.

Other details abound in these simple pages, showing us a people impelled by the inescapable momentum of a larger political history that finds its way so dryly into little-read textbooks, living the hardships that we objectively describe through footnotes and excerpts from the speeches of great statesmen, affected by political events rather than controlling them. We are reminded that even in colonial Virginia "no churches except the Church of England were allowed by law, but in order to make the Presbyterian frontier settlers contented to live there and be a buffer between the Indians and the coast towns, they were allowed to build their churches—but only in the country." There is mention of the "horrible Indian massacres" that broke out in the settlements along the mountain regions of Pennsylvania and Virginia after 1754 and continued for years thereafter.

We learn little things about long-dead people. That John Miller loved fine horses, priding himself in a silver-mounted harness, and eventually left Virginia by himself, disappearing into Kentucky. That William Miller, my four-times-great-grandfather, fought as a soldier in the Revolutionary War, including at the famous Battle of Cowpens. That every farm had its own distillery, and that Samuel Miller, another ancestor, "was inclined to drink more than he should." And that his wife "saw that it was an evil in their house, so she closed the distillery."

And on page 9 of the typed version of a letter written long, long ago, my father's aunt introduces us to her mother—my great-great-grandmother—Rebecca Miller. Born in the remote wilderness of Virginia's Blue Ridge Mountains in 1825, Rebecca had filled her daughter with stories of her own grandmother, Margaret Lackey. *The House of Ochiltree* mentions the Millers as having "distinguished themselves in the terrible siege of Londonderry," a high honor to be singled out among so many courageous people, and the aunt's letter confirms how deeply those memories had burned into the progeny of those who had survived. "Their ancestors had been in the Siege of Londonderry, and my Mother said she had often heard her grandmother Margaret Lackey Miller tell the stories of that time, and sing the song of 'The Battle of the Boyne' in a most dramatic and thrilling manner. She would sometimes get quite excited in describing the sufferings and courage of her people in the Siege of Londonderry."

All this written no doubt from an obscure farm in Missouri by a woman in her later years, now reflecting on the memories of her mother telling the stories she herself had learned from a grandmother while sitting before the fireplace in the near-dark of a Virginia cabin within a few miles of what we now call the Appalachian Trail. Voice to voice, before my eyes I am transferred back six generations and am looking back several generations further, to the remembered tragedies in Northern Ireland that both shaped these people and helped spur them on into a new and sometimes fearsome wilderness.

In their words, I can sense them looking coolly at the pretenses and attempted restrictions placed upon them by yet another branch of an Anglican establishment that they imagined they had left behind in Ulster, a pervasive aristocracy that in America controlled most of the "flatlands" along the colonial coast. They were told that they could practice their religion in the mountains even if it was not "lawful," so long as they did not seek to infect the more ordered societies along the coast. And they were expected to reciprocate by both staying in the mountains and keeping the Indians at bay. These memories burned like fire among people who knew, even nearly three centuries ago, that the Eastern Establishment looked down on them, openly demeaning their religion and their cultural ways, and at bottom sought to use them toward its own ends.

Their answer, then as now, was to tell the Eastern Establishment to go to hell. A deal was a deal—they would fight the Indians, although many of them would also trade with them and even intermarry. But at bottom they would not forget the duplicity that followed Londonderry, or the Test Acts that fell on the heels of their contributions at the Boyne. Nonconformity as well as a mistrust of central power was now in their blood. America was a far larger place than Ireland, a land in which they could live as they wished and move as freely as they dared whether or not the established government liked what they were doing and were about to do, so long as they did not move too conspicuously toward the east.

So they made their own world in the mountains. And most of them knew that their future was not along the coast anyway, but ever westward, where they might meet fierce challenges, but where they also could create a new kind of society more akin to their own traditions.

2

Pioneers and Radicals

THE SCOTS-IRISH PRESBYTERIANS began trickling out of Ulster soon after the 1704 Test Acts came into force. In the next two decades a rather small assortment of families, typically traveling in "parcels" of 600 to 800 people, ventured across the Atlantic to test America's promise as well as its receptivity to their religion and their cultural ways. They traveled in tiny, crowded, disease-ridden two-masted ships that sailed from the ports of Londonderry, Belfast, Newry, Larne, and Portrush, taking on the average about two months to cross the treacherous Atlantic. In this first experimental wave of emigration the Ulster emigrants scattered their arrivals among the major ports of Boston, New York, Philadelphia, Annapolis, and Charleston, South Carolina.

But by the early 1720s, when the large-scale migrations from Northern Ireland began, the port of choice had become Philadelphia. Over the next five decades the overwhelming majority of Scots-Irish settlers entered the American colonies through either Philadelphia or the nearby cities of Chester, Pennsylvania, and New Castle, Delaware, which were just south of Philadelphia along the Delaware River.[4] From these locations the Scots-Irish settlers first spread westward into the vicinity of Lancaster, Pennsylvania, and then later followed the mountain roads southward into Virginia, North and South Carolina, and points beyond.

From the early 1720s to the beginning of the American Revolution in 1775, there were four great surges of Scots-Irish migration. Each was brought about not only by events in Ireland, but also by a series of incidents and incentives in different American colonies that affected both the pace of their migration and the locations they chose for settlement. The first large migration, from 1720 to about 1730, brought them heavily to Pennsylvania. The second, concentrated in the years 1740 and 1741, drew them to the Shenandoah Valley of Virginia and brought with them many of those who had already settled in Pennsylvania. The third, beginning in the mid-1750s, saw a heavy influx farther down the Appalachian and Allegheny Mountains into southwest Virginia and then into North and South Carolina. This influx included many Scottish highlanders—although they generally arrived in Wilmington, North Carolina, rather than in Philadelphia and settled in the Piedmont rather than in the mountains—as well as Scottish and English borderers, these three groups having been uprooted by political events that followed the Battle of Culloden in 1746. The final surge, in the years just before the beginning of the American Revolution in 1775, saw large numbers of new settlers from Northern Ireland move into the communities that had already been established, especially in southwest Virginia and the Carolinas.

By the time this migration was complete, as many as a half million Scots-Irish immigrants and their American-born descendants were living in a cohesive geographic area in the mountainous areas of modern-day Pennsylvania, Virginia, West Virginia, Kentucky, Tennessee, North Carolina, and South Carolina.[5] It has been estimated that as much as one-third of the entire Protestant population of Ireland left for America between the years 1731 and 1768 alone, and this ratio was much higher for the Scots-Irish since few Anglicans were leaving Ulster.[6]

Once in America, this was a highly reproductive cultural

group—early studies showed its fertility ratios to be 40 percent higher compared to those who remained in the Delaware Valley, and higher also than on the northern frontier.[7] Within a few decades they would spill farther west into the southern regions of Ohio, Indiana, and Illinois as well as the northern regions of Georgia, Alabama, Mississippi, and Louisiana. Within another generation they would move farther west, becoming the dominant culture in the settlements of many parts of Texas, Arkansas, Kansas, Iowa, and Missouri. In the decades following the Civil War, the Scots-Irish would count heavily in populating the Rocky Mountains and the Far West. In these early years, at every step of the way, English, German, and other settlers intermarried and joined these communities, but the sheer numbers and cultural power of the Scots-Irish would shape and define the mores of America's rural heartland, particularly in the South.

Philadelphia became the Ulster Scots' most popular port of entry for two reasons. The first was that the Pennsylvania colony had been created with an eye toward accommodating religious freedom and thus largely welcomed the Ulster dissenters, at least initially. And the second—equally as important—was that the communities in New England and New York wanted nothing to do with them.

The Ulster Presbyterians who migrated to New England in the early 1700s had believed that the Puritan communities would embrace them as fellow Calvinists, but "the Puritans liked neither Scots nor Irish . . . especially because of their illiteracy, their physical dirtiness and slovenliness, and their notable divergence from Puritan customs, habits, and outlook."[8] To make the obvious point, the fact that the Scots-Irish were Calvinists hardly made them Puritans. A quick-tempered but sensual and playful people, they often dressed provocatively, acted with a volatile belligerence, drank to excess, engaged in constant and open competition in every form, and adamantly defied the attempts of outsiders to control them.

This initial, instinctive dislike of the Scots-Irish by the Puritans was a clear harbinger of things to come in future decades and even centuries as the American colonies matured into a nation. The Scots-Irish were the cultural antithesis of those who had founded New England. In the years preceding and following the Civil War, not to mention during the war itself, the predominantly Scots-Irish culture of the South would frequently square off against the descendants of those who were making these judgments in the early 1700s. Suffice it to say that none of the characteristics that defined the Scots-Irish culture warmed the hearts of the rigidly intellectual, rules-oriented, and frequently humorless founders of New England.

As Leyburn put it, the reception of the Scots-Irish who attempted to settle among the Puritans was "grudging in the extreme . . . They were shortly informed that citizenship would not be granted in any Puritan colony except by membership in the established church, which was Congregational." As a result, most of the Scots-Irish moved off to the frontiers, eventually settling in the remote areas of Maine, Vermont, and New Hampshire. In the Puritan areas it was common to refer to them as "these confounded Irish." Feelings against them grew so strong that in 1729 a mob arose to attempt to prevent the landing of one of the ships arriving from Ulster. "Wherever the Scotch-Irish went in New England it was made abundantly clear to them that they were unwelcome." Despite such resistance, the Ulster Scots succeeded very well in New England's mountainous frontier. The town of Londonderry, New Hampshire, was founded by a group that had emigrated from Ulster under the leadership of James McGregor, a minister who had lived through the Londonderry siege as a boy. And to this day many descendants of those early settlers still occupy the rural areas of New England.[9]

The migrations to New York and New Jersey were even smaller than those that went to New England, with much the same consequences. There was "nothing to attract them to New York. Its land policy was not generous; its country regions along the Hudson were taken up in great estates; and no special effort had been made . . . to attract colonists from Northern Ireland . . . only three small colonies of Scotch-Irish settled in New York throughout the eighteenth century."[10]

In Pennsylvania the story was entirely different. Not only had the colony been founded with an emphasis on religious tolerance, but also the provincial secretary during the early years was an Ulsterman who, at least at the outset, actively sought their presence.

James Logan, Pennsylvania's provincial secretary at the beginning of the Scots-Irish migration, was born in 1674 near Belfast, of Scottish parents. His father was an Anglican clergyman who became a Quaker and thereafter worked as a schoolmaster, causing the family to experience firsthand the differences in treatment in Ulster based on religious affiliation. Apprenticed at the age of thirteen to a linen merchant in Dublin (coincidentally, by name of Edward Webb), James fled with his family to Bristol, England, in 1688 during the uprisings that led to the siege of Londonderry and the Battle of the Boyne. Due to his Quaker faith and his involvement with the linen industry, Logan was befriended and then personally recruited by William Penn, who in 1699 appointed him provincial secretary of the Pennsylvania colony.

As provincial secretary, Logan spent the next thirty years alternating between his own business interests and representing William Penn's family in all matters pertaining to Pennsylvania. A self-trained but gifted mathematician who also dabbled in such serious scientific issues as crop hybridization, Logan was best known for inventing the Conestoga wagon, which became the most memorialized vehicle used by the early pioneers as they made their way into the wilderness. He served briefly as mayor of Philadelphia in 1722 and 1723, was chief justice of the Supreme Court of Pennsylvania in the 1730s, and even served a brief term as acting governor of the colony.

Logan's principal role was to act as William Penn's land agent and administrator, and in that capacity he was the agent for all land sales in Pennsylvania. And in a related area that gave him increasing concern, he was responsible for both the burgeoning fur trade, on which he made considerable money, and for relations with the Indian tribes. As the years progressed and tensions with the Indians increased, it became clear to Logan that Penn's dream of forming a government with strictly pacifist principles in this raw frontier was impractical. The Indians were threatening many settlements, and yet the pacifist Quakers who controlled the colony's affairs could not bring themselves even to raise a militia to counter the incidents of violence at the mountainous edges of the colony.[11]

And so Logan, who still retained strong memories of the fighting spirit of the Ulster Scots at Londonderry and elsewhere, decided to import one, convincing the Pennsylvania government to encourage their migration to settlements he would create along the mountains west of Philadelphia. Advancing this idea in 1720, Logan wrote admiringly of his "brave fellow countrymen," pointing out that he and others in Pennsylvania had become "apprehensive from the Northern Indians . . . I therefore thought it might be prudent to plant a settlement of such men as those who formerly had so bravely defended Londonderry and Inniskillen [sic] as a frontier in case of any disturbance. . . . These people if kindly used will be orderly as they have hitherto been and easily dealt with. They will also, I expect, be a leading example to others."[12]

Over the coming years Logan would be more than well rewarded for his faith in the fighting ability of these Ulster immigrants. But the example that they would provide to others was not the one he expected. Ten years later he would be lamenting that "a settlement of five families from the North of Ireland gives me more trouble than fifty of any other people," and that the Scots-Irish were "troublesome settlers to the government and hard neighbors to the Indians."[13]

The problem was as old as the issues that had brought about the creation of the Presbyterian Kirk. The refusal to be intimidated from above was by now in the Scots-Irish DNA. Inclined to obey no one other than their local leaders, they were reluctant to follow any dictate of government that contradicted their individual consciences. Logan wanted a warlike people to fight the Indians, and he got them. But he was naive to have expected them at the same time to be docile in the face of laws and other restrictions that were neither to their benefit nor their liking.

Logan set aside a large tract of land for the Ulster Scots near modern-day Lancaster, Pennsylvania, which the settlers immediately named Donegal in memory of the Northern Irish county near Londonderry from which many of them had migrated. But after settling the land Logan had earmarked for them, they then proceeded to expand in every direction without regard to who owned the properties, causing Logan to lament their "audacious and disorderly habits." Outside Donegal they began building small farms on virgin land owned by absentee landlords, largely inventing the concept of "squatter's rights" that would become famous on the American frontier. Logan and others in the Pennsylvania hierarchy grew furious at this usurpation of their own legal authority. Now and then government officials, accompanied by land surveyors and sheriffs with armed escorts, would tear down the squatters' simple cabins, but once the official party had departed the settlers would simply rebuild them.

Tensions increased, and the Scots-Irish settlers took to their own style of renegade justice—as the modern-day country song goes, "When you've got nothing, you've got nothing to lose." Even though they were legally in the wrong, they believed they were morally in the right, and many of them brought their own weapons into play. The Scots-Irish settlers began facing down government parties sent out to destroy their homes and plow under their crops. In the process, they established a rather disturbing point—that they owed no allegiance to the arbitrary actions of the government and were just as prepared to fight Quakers and English bureaucrats as they were the Indians. A litany arose among the settlers who had braved the fierce Atlantic at the invitation of the good Mr. Logan. "It was against the laws of God and nature that so much land should be idle, while so many Christians wanted it to labor on, and to raise their bread."[14]

This conduct could hardly have surprised anyone who had paid attention to the evolution of Presbyterian nonconformist doctrine in Ulster. Indeed, they might even have expected it. The Ulster experience had hardened the traditional Scottish belief that revolts against authority were morally justifiable, extending that concept into the view—important even in today's America—that the principle of revolution could also apply to the individual in the form of civil disobedience.

Many historians have contrasted this cultural volatility with the more orderly and respectful behavior of a similarly large but much calmer population of German immigrants during this early period, pointing to these and other rebellious acts as evidence of the admittedly fierce temperament of the Ulster Scots. It is also common to point out the Scots-Irish tendency to move three and four times before finally settling into a permanent home. As Leyburn commented, "If impetuosity early proclaimed itself as a dominant trait among many Scotch-Irish, so also did their restlessness. In contrast to the Germans, who once they found a home tended to remain fixed, the Scotch-Irish never seemed satisfied. . . . Long before fertile areas in the Susquehanna and Cumberland valleys had been filled up, scores who had settled here had . . . moved on down the Great Valley into Virginia, and thence into the Carolinas. . . . One result of this mobility was that excellent land in Pennsylvania which had originally belonged to Ulstermen now came into the hands of the Germans."[15]

The Scots-Irish settlers were indeed restless, as if their natural makeup demanded turmoil. They showed no hesitation in pushing into Indian territory and settling on lands claimed by tribal chiefs. In so doing, their aggressiveness actually helped "light the torch of Indian resentment" rather than discouraging uprisings through a forceful defensive presence, as Logan had first imagined.[16] They pressed ever westward across the Pennsylvania mountains and were among the first settlers of Pittsburgh, so that by the mid-1800s the city was viewed as "Scotch-Irish in substantial origin, in complexion and in history—Scotch-Irish in the countenances of the living, and in the records of the dead."[17] Some of them were even lured by Pennsylvania's proprietors into settling along the Maryland border where they might be "happy in constituting the frontier line against encroaching Maryland Catholics."[18] But their greatest push was to the southwest, along the Wilderness Trail that took them into settlements that spanned the spine of Virginia and eventually led to the western reaches of North and South Carolina.

Restlessness to some extent drove this journey, and impetuosity no doubt filled their conduct. But so also did a sense of moral and biblical righteousness coupled with an unrelenting poverty. Land values had increased in Pennsylvania as a consequence of the improvements brought by pioneering, driving many who had made the improvements as well as new arrivals out of the local market because they could no longer afford to pay rent. Some squatted, some headed south. Few had left Ulster with financial assets, and fewer still were destined to own appreciable amounts of land, even in the coming generations. As David Hackett Fischer points out, even in later decades, "A majority of adult males in the southern highlands owned no land at all. . . . One of the most stubborn myths of American history is the idea that the frontier promoted equality of material condition. . . . Inequality was greater in the back country and the southern highlands than in any other rural region of the United States."[19]

Luckily—for them and for those who wished to expand the American frontier—the Scots-Irish and their counterparts from Scotland and the border areas of northern England had brought a special skill with them. That skill was in demand, particularly farther south. It eventually brought them individual and community freedom, but in and of itself it would never make them rich. This skill was their unique ability to combine family homesteads with military expertise and to adapt to a battlefield on which they and their families actually lived. It was not simply that these people made great soldiers, in the sense of the rampaging armies of Europe that paraded in pennant-crested columns and met each other on famous, set-piece battlefields. Many of them were indeed great soldiers, but unlike in most other scenarios, their family unit itself had become part of a warrior culture as well. The entire family structure had been shaped by a millennium that spanned the formation of the Scottish nation, the centuries of border warfare in the regions that ebbed back and forth between England and Scotland, and in the case of the Scots-Irish, the decades of unrelenting tensions in Northern Ireland. The families from the north of Britain accepted—and actually expected—that their lives would at some point include harsh and even bloody conflict.

The men expected to fight, and every able-bodied man was automatically a member of the local militia. The women expected their men to fight, and sometimes their homes to be invaded. Strongly independent, these women understood also that they would be required to run households and farms when their men were away, and to be at risk from raiding parties in their home communities. The children grew up playing constant games of physical challenge, wrestling, racing, and becoming familiar with weapons. Young boys began hunting wild game with their fathers at an early age, knowing that it was only a matter of time before they would be expected not only to hunt but also to fight, or at least to defend their family against attack. And finally, the generations along the war-torn Scottish borders and in the frequently ravaged hamlets of Ulster had taught them to accept simple, expendable living structures, because one never knew when their home might be attacked and burned to the ground.

In the 1730s and beyond, nowhere were these skills more needed than along the long spine of the Appalachian Mountains of Virginia and into North and South Carolina. And nowhere were the economic inequalities between the Scots-Irish and those who controlled government affairs greater than in these colonies. In many ways the reasons that brought the Scots-Irish to Virginia and the Carolinas, and the economic disparities that existed there, provided a microcosm of what was to happen in the entire Southern region after America won her independence. And the pervasive disparities among white cultures, so pronounced along ethnic and religious lines but largely unnoticed outside the region, would foreshadow not only the way the South has been misunderstood in the years following the Civil War and Reconstruction, but also some of the major divisions that linger in American society today.

After the founding of Jamestown in 1607, the Virginia colony had evolved into a rigid, three-tiered society. At the top was a landed English-American aristocracy whose wealth and holdings owed much to the patronage of the ruling royalty in the mother country. Contrary to the prevailing mythology of a ruggedly competitive, rags-to-riches ethos among those who had braved the Atlantic to come to America, the majority of this privileged class was originally granted huge tracts of land by royal decree. Family names and quasi-royal prerogatives were taken seriously, and as the generations unfolded, this "Cavalier aristocracy" took great pains to protect and advance their own interests as well as those of others in their small circle of elites.

As one famous but not exceptional example, Thomas, Lord Fairfax, who was the friend and patron of the young George Washington after Washington's father died, first came to Virginia in 1735 to inspect his hereditary land grant of 5,282,000 acres—an area between the Rappahannock and Potomac Rivers including a vast portion of the Shenandoah Valley that was as large as the entire country of Wales. This private domain had been granted with all the rights of a traditional English baron, including the power to develop, rent, or sell portions of the property. It had its origins in a royal grant in 1649 by Charles II when he was exiled in France, had been renewed in 1673 through a reissue to Thomas, Lord Culpeper and Henry, earl of Arlington, and had descended through marriage to the good Lord Fairfax himself. Lord Fairfax originally settled at Belvoir in 1747 and then moved to an estate in the Shenandoah Valley in 1752. Those who live in or have visited modern-day northern Virginia will find all of these names strikingly familiar, although few will have understood their royal origins.

The power of this elite group of "first families of Virginia" was pervasive and decidedly English in both its bloodlines and its outlook. And in contrast to the more intellectual and cultural "Englishness" of the New England colonies, it was also unapologetically aristocratic—a seminal distinction that would manifest itself again and again in the decades leading up to the Civil War and that still has its implications in today's much more variegated America. This aristocracy kept close ties with England, many of its families wintering in London and many more sending their children to English boarding schools. Its leadership established the Anglican Church as the only formally recognized religion in Virginia. Its members controlled the political and business affairs not only of the colony, but also of the state of Virginia for many years after American independence. And its attitudes creep up here and there in the snobbishness, profligate spending, and excessive behavior that still mark the "upper crust" in many areas throughout the South.

The second tier in early-eighteenth-century Virginia consisted of an almost exclusively white underclass mixed with a small gentry of tradesmen who could never aspire to joining the so-called "Tidewater aristocracy." Until the mid-1700s this underclass was predominantly English and heavily populated by men and women who had come to Virginia either as indentured servants or as convicts "transported" from England in lieu of death or long-term prison sentences. In this group was also a very small percentage of mixed-blood "people of color"—including the descendants of some families that had intermarried among blacks, Indians, and whites in the earlier years of the colony before miscegenation laws came into effect—and small pockets of Indian tribes along Virginia's east coast. But the class lines in early Virginia were clearly calcified. As David Hackett Fischer comments, these were "a degraded rural proletariat who had no hope of rising to the top of their society. Not a single ex-servant or son of a servant became a member of Virginia's House of Burgesses during the late seventeenth century. The mythical figures of Virginia cavaliers and poor whites were solidly founded in historical fact."[20]

The third tier were the slaves imported from Africa, who were overwhelmingly in the hands of the plantation-owning Tidewater aristocracy. As Virginia's agricultural base expanded, driven heavily in the early years by the exportation of tobacco, slaves became an essential commodity of the wealthy class. By 1700 they comprised 20,000 of Virginia's population of 70,000, and by 1740 they actually outnumbered the whites in the colony.[21]

But these numbers would change very quickly as the Scots-Irish and other settlers began pouring out of Pennsylvania into the distant mountains, forming a veritable ring of frontier fortresses around this "flatlander" system.

As the eighteenth century dawned and the Virginia colony moved into its second century, its leadership had a problem: security along its western frontier. The solution to that problem—military protection by the Scots-Irish—would add an unexpected fourth component to this societal makeup, comprising not so much another "tier" as a catalyst that rarely intermixed with the other three but would in many ways change the formula altogether. As evidence of the immediacy of its impact, by 1756 the population of Virginia had jumped to 292,000, more than four times its population only fifty years before, and a firm majority of 172,000 were white, a direct indicator of the magnitude of the Scots-Irish migration to the Appalachian and Allegheny mountains.[22]

The brittle structure of lords, servants, and slaves had been sufficient to establish and control the plantation system along the flatlands of Tidewater Virginia. But as the colony expanded westward into the Piedmont region, the plantation system itself was not suited to the terrain. And as it neared the mountains on the other side of the Piedmont, it was not only unworkable in an economic sense, but it also brought the fragility of the aristocratic plantation system face-to-face with the volatility of the Indian nation, and particularly the warlike Cherokee. The colony's leaders recognized this danger as early as 1701, when they offered generous terms to settlers for land in the mountains if they would establish forts and other means of defense. By 1705, Virginia's leaders were offering fifty acres of land in the mountains for free to any settler who would venture into the "up country." They got few if any takers. As Leyburn points out, "Such offers brought no results, so far as the Valley was concerned, for the Shenandoah was as yet unknown and unexplored, too far away from any available supply of settlers to be practically accessible."[23]

Two farsighted Virginia governors, Alexander Spotswood and William Gooch, would change this situation, and in so doing forever alter the character of the mountain South. Spotswood, an early ally of James Logan, was a former soldier who led one of the first expeditions into the Shenandoah Valley, in 1716. A strong believer in the military necessity of fortifying the mountains against the Indian tribes, his expedition did much to reassure prospective immigrants that the empty but fertile lands in the valley also offered good potential for successful farming. Gooch went further. In 1730 he decided, in the modern parlance, to put the market into play. He granted several huge but remote tracts of land to a few prominent individuals, with the stipulation that they must populate the lands with a minimum number of settlers in order to keep the land grants. And, as an added incentive, in 1738 he guaranteed to the Ulster Presbyterians and other "dissenters" that they would be able to practice their own religions in the mountains despite the restrictions inherent in Virginia's official "state religion."[24]

This structure seemed to be a deal designed in heaven. The flatlander aristocracy got free land as well as the profits from selling it. William Beverly, a man "prominent in colonial affairs," received a "splendid gift" from Governor Gooch of 118,491 acres along the Shenandoah River. Benjamin Borden, an agent of Lord Fairfax, swung a deal for 500,000 acres near Lexington, a parcel on which several of my own father's ancestors settled. Both of these developers were "indefatigable" in their efforts to procure settlers, making fortunes in the process.[25] The leading families of Virginia got the resourceful and pugnacious northern British settlers to protect them, and at the same time were able to maintain a comfortable distance from their strange, combative ways. And the settlers got cheap land—many of them in fact getting land for free, taking up squatter's rights as the migration hit full flow, owning no land but paying no rent, either—as well as the opportunity to live their lives as they saw fit.

The Ulstermen as well as many German settlers were ready to come. And once they began their trek, the road that stepped out into the wilderness from Lancaster became an ever-lengthening highway. Settlers from Pennsylvania immediately poured into the lands made available through Gooch's land grants. The Germans, typically wealthier and more stable, bought good lands in the northernmost areas of Virginia and western Maryland and for the most part remained on them rather than continuing the southward migration. The migration from Germany itself dried up in the early 1750s even as those from the north of Britain, and particularly from Ulster, kept increasing. The odd political situation of the non-Anglican Protestants in Ulster did not abate, and in combination with a series of crop failures and famines in 1740–41, 1744–45, and 1756–57 drove many more families onto the small ships that sailed for Philadelphia. New turmoil enveloped Scotland, brought about by Bonnie Prince Charlie's romantic but absurd attempt to reinstate the Stuart family to the throne, an effort that Winston Churchill termed "one of the most audacious and irresponsible enterprises in British history."[26] His defeat at Culloden in 1746 added a mix of highlanders and border dwellers from northern England and southwestern Scotland to the surge of emigration.

The North and South Carolina governments, representing the interests of a less-refined governing class that was similar to the three-tiered society dominated by Tidewater aristocrats, quickly followed the Virginia pattern. Again the English aristocrats benefited enormously, although the Carolinas were not nearly as tightly structured as the Virginia colony, eventually allowing the Scots-Irish to have far more influence in those governments.

In 1663 a grateful (and possibly inebriated) King Charles II had granted all of what is now North Carolina, South Carolina, and Tennessee to eight English lords in order to thank them for helping him reclaim the British throne after the death of Oliver Cromwell. The equally grateful lords named the territory Carolina (a latinization of Charles), probably as an obsequious gesture to Charles but ostensibly in honor of his father, King Charles I. These eight "lords proprietors" and their heirs controlled the land from their English baronies on the far side of the Atlantic until 1729, when the descendants of seven of them sold the titles back to the Crown so that North Carolina could become a royal colony with the same legal status as Virginia. The one exception was John Carteret, the earl of Granville, who kept his inherited properties—a massive stretch of land that comprised almost the entire upper half of what is now the state of North Carolina, including the modern-day cities of Raleigh, Durham, Greensboro, Winston-Salem, and Asheville.

In truth Lord Granville had taken a gamble, for unlike the Virginia colony, the Carolinas had not prospered. By 1729 there were only some thirty thousand non-Indian inhabitants, mostly English settlers who had inched down along the coast from southeastern Virginia. The land had no navigable rivers for commerce, in contrast to the James, Potomac, and Rappahannock Rivers in Virginia. And other than a marginal port at Wilmington, only Charleston could compare to the many sea-friendly and deepwater ports in

Virginia. But Granville's holdings straddled the Great Wagon Road, and as the unending stream of hard-bitten settlers from the north spilled into North Carolina, he and his agents prospered beyond belief. The movement into the Carolinas was "one of the mightiest migrations of colonial times. So great was the tide pouring in from the north that, by the outbreak of the Revolutionary War, the North Carolina back-country had at least sixty thousand settlers, while that of South Carolina had eighty-three thousand—almost four-fifths of the colony's white population."[27] Some estimates put the number much higher, claiming that the backcountry of North and South Carolina had grown from almost zero in 1750 to a quarter million settlers by 1780.[28]

An interesting distinction revealed itself during the settlement of the Carolinas, which may have given the impetus for the Ulster Scots to begin calling themselves Scotch-Irish, a term that became interchangeable in later years with the more ethnically proper Scots-Irish. Beginning in the late 1740s, a colony of Scottish high-landers fresh from the defeat at Culloden had made their way into North Carolina through the port of Wilmington rather than along the Wagon Trail, settling in the North Carolina Piedmont. Tensions between the Ulster Scots and the highlanders were immediate and strong. On the surface the two groups, although having their origins in the same small country, now had little in common. They dressed differently, used different idiomatic languages, and, most important, had different political beliefs. The Scottish highlanders would overwhelmingly support the loyalists during the Revolution, while the Scotch-Irish were the strongest supporters of the movement to declare independence. Within a few generations these differences would disappear, but in the years just before the American Revolution they were significant and in some ways defining.

Many responsible historians claim that the term "Scotch-Irish" was not used until "the late nineteenth century, when real and imagined descendants of settlers from Ulster embraced it to distin-

guish a Protestant people from Catholic Irish immigrants stream-
ing into the country."[29] But we begin to see a general use of the
term almost from the beginning of the mountain settlements.
James Logan would write as early as 1730, "They are of the Scotch-
Irish (so called here) of whom J. Steel tells me you seem'd to have a
pretty good opinion but it is more than I can have tho' their coun-
tryman."[30] As another example, in 1755, Arthur Dobbs, an Ulster-
born governor of North Carolina, wrote of a group of families that
had settled on land that he owned, "They are a colony from
Pennsylvania of what we call Scotch-Irish Presbyterians."[31] As yet
another, Nathaniel Grubb complained in 1763 to the Pennsylvania
legislature that "a pack of insignificant Scotch-Irish" was responsible for having retaliated too fiercely against a series of Indian attacks.[32]

Leyburn seems to think that Anglicans and Quakers applied the
term to the Ulster Presbyterian immigrants as something of a slur,
to distinguish them from both Anglican Irish and "true Scots."[33] It
is also logical to assume that the reverse was equally true. The
Scots-Irish, not wishing to be associated with the views of many
who had migrated directly from Scotland, may well have begun using the term to distinguish their unique origins and perspectives,
and especially their strongly held views about the English aristocracy, well before there was a need to draw a cultural point of demarcation between them and the Irish Catholics who would
migrate a century later. This probability fits well with Irish historian
R. F. Foster's characterization of the Ulster Scots' "religious and
cultural apartness that enabled communities to emigrate and stay
together . . . The Ulster Scots stood out: possibly because, even in
the New World, they remained ostentatiously separate,"[34] thus allowing their cultural uniqueness to plant itself for generations inside tightly knit communities on the frontier.

This migration into the mountains, especially considering the
thin population of America at that time, was indeed historic. Along
the narrow mud trails that traversed the ridges and disappeared for

miles inside dark forests were Scots, English, Irish, Welsh, French, Swiss, and a good number of Germans who generally kept to their own communities. But mostly, overwhelmingly, the road heading south from Philadelphia was filled with the Scots-Irish Presbyterians who had poured out of Ulster. As the decades of the mid-1700s passed, hardscrabble settlements grew up all along the spine of the Appalachians in places where few Europeans had dared to travel only a few years before. The people came in surges, like an incoming tide. After the Shenandoah Valley met the mountain town of Roanoke, the waves of voyagers split. Some headed farther southwest, down what was called the Wilderness Road, into the gaps and hollows of the difficult mountains and fast-rushing streams where modern-day Tennessee meets the southwestern tip of Virginia. Others pushed directly south, keeping to tamer trails and gentler ridges along what became known as the Great Philadelphia Wagon Trail and ending up in the Carolinas.

From start to finish, this highway of mostly northern British immigration stretched nearly seven hundred miles. Whole families walked hundreds of miles, some of them using cows as pack animals. These were uncommonly tough people, used to hardship. They asked for nothing from the government or anyone else, and nothing is what they usually received. They followed the Wilderness Road into the backcountry and the Wagon Trail into uncharted Piedmont and mountains where only the Indians dwelled, creating a series of log cabin settlements that were little more than small but interconnecting fortresses. Trees were cleared. Cabins were built. Subsistence crops were planted. They built churches, the Scots-Irish first following the Presbyterian faith, but over time becoming more and more inclined to adopt the evangelical Baptist and Methodist denominations, again possibly to draw a line between their communities and the tamer form of Presbyterianism being brought directly from an increasingly enlightened Scotland. By 1906, of the 793,546 members of religious denominations in Virginia, 416,000 would be Baptist, 201,000 would be Methodist, and only 40,000 would still call themselves Presbyterian.[35] In the mountain communities, their principal economic activities were cattle and hog farming, hunting, trapping, and rudimentary trade, especially with the Indians whom the flatlanders so desperately feared. And every male adult automatically became part of a local militia.

The Indians watched them, mingled with them, and sometimes attacked them, as many of them were settling on ancient hunting grounds that the Indians had agreed among themselves to keep unpopulated. The settlers adapted, learning from the Indians and learning how to fight the Indians when necessary. These communities grew and in their own way began to thrive. The Tidewater aristocracy that had allowed such settlements looked askance at these new Americans, often snidely belittling them for their coarseness and their backward, nonintellectual ways. But their ferocious performance against a variety of Indian attacks that began in 1754 and continued even after the seven years of the French and Indian War gained them not only respect but also an enduring legitimacy. They fought and played by their own rules, expecting no quarter from any enemy and giving none in return. And by the eve of the American Revolution in 1775, they had become a political force in their own right.

The emerging power of the expatriate Ulster Scots had become cause for concern back in Britain, especially among the Anglican elites in Ireland. From 1717 forward into the 1770s, the Presbyterian communities in Ulster had steadily dwindled as exodus became the province's most common ritual. Family after family made their way to the port cities of Londonderry, Belfast, Portrush, and Larne, risking—and often losing—their lives on small ships heading across the treacherous Atlantic for America. Statistics for this and other early migrations from Britain are difficult to obtain, but it is clear that those leaving from Ulster numbered in the hundreds of thousands. And the last decade and a half of this huge migration, between the years 1760 and 1775, saw not only an estimated 55,000

Protestant Irish leaving Ulster, but also another 40,000 leaving Scotland and 30,000 departing from England.[36]

These migrations from Britain's north—Scotland, Ireland, and the border areas—involved substantial percentages of the overall local population and caused concerns in London about the economic future of the North. And as this emigration progressed, the English aristocracy and the Anglicans who controlled Ireland became oddly ambivalent about the departure of so many Presbyterian and other "dissenters." On the one hand, many of the governing class understood that their own insistence on dominating this subculture was driving it away. On the other, the structure of favoritism toward Anglicans that had been enforced in the wake of the Protestant Reformation had made the large landowners dependent on revenues generated from the very conditions that these people were seeking to avoid.

The earl of Hillsborough, who became secretary of state for the colonies in 1768, was symbolic of this odd duality. A landowner with vast holdings in County Down, the Anglo-Irish Hillsborough was a staunch opponent of large-scale migration from northern Britain to America. He viewed the Presbyterian Scots-Irish emigration not so much in political or even religious terms, but as an economic risk to the aristocracy. Presuming correctly that the Anglicans would continue to dominate Irish affairs, Hillsborough worried that the massive departure of the Ulster Scots to America was reducing both the tax base and the value of land available for leasing in Ulster. In 1753 he had even argued in Parliament that it would be "for the public good to lay a restraint upon poor people leaving the place of their birth without leave from the magistrates of the place." During this debate he expressed his puzzlement as to why people should be allowed to emigrate "for no other reason but because they hope to live better, or to earn more money in those countries than they can do at home."[37]

The Anglicans needed their revenues. And although the London-ordained Test Acts had protected them from strong political challenges to their local authority, the raw business prospects of the Irish situation became severe during periods when the British economy ebbed and flowed. As the Ulster Scots continued to melt into the far horizons on the dangerous little ships that took them to a new beginning, others joined Hillsborough's camp, searching for the same simple solutions. The secretary to the lord lieutenant of Ireland was typical of the times. He lamented the reduction of excise revenues coming from Ulster, claiming that the loss of revenues was due as much to emigration as to poverty, and warned that the Scots-Irish emigration was threatening the entire future of Ireland. His suggestion was to create a few more economic incentives that might hold the Ulster tenants to their rented lands, reasoning that "if the cow is to be milked, she must be fed."[38]

But the migration to America was raising far more dangerous concerns in political circles. The English ruling class, which had begun the century seeking strong people to settle in the colonies, slowly began to see unintended consequences. The Ulster Scots had brought with them not only a desire for a better life, but also a determination to live life under their own rules. The democracy of the Presbyterian Kirk, an ancient mistrust of higher authority, and a burning resentment of the English hierarchy that had given them so much trouble in Ulster all fueled their interactions with other cultures from their first days in America. Seasoned observers on both sides of the Atlantic began watching the dynamic of the Scots-Irish migration with increasing concern. The out-migration was causing economic difficulties in Ireland, but an even greater problem was percolating across the seas—the very survival of the British colonial system on the new continent. Trouble had almost immediately been set loose in the colonies as a result of the Scots-Irish arrival in America, for although political disagreements had been building in the colonies for some time, the ever-disagreeable Ulster Scots were injecting a new and violent tone to the debate.

In 1775, as the thought of revolution began to dominate colonial American politics, the Anglican bishop of Londonderry wrote a concerned letter to the earl of Dartmouth, who had succeeded Hillsborough as secretary of state for the colonies. This was not the usual lamentation about a dwindling Presbyterian population and its effects on the local economy. In fact, it did not deal with the Irish situation at all. Rather, the bishop outlined "a summary of the political fears of the consequences of emigration that had been circulating since the early seventies. The bishop attributed much of 'the rebellious spirit' in the central colonies in America to the emigration from Ireland 'of nearly three hundred thousand fanatical & hungry republicans in the course of a few years.' "[39]

The bishop may or may not have been prescient, but he certainly was correct. However, by 1775 his argument had also become moot. The first Great Celtic Migration from Ireland was complete, and the people who had traveled to America were now largely positioned in a broad swath of mountains that marked the geographic—and political—boundary between an aristocratic, colonial past and a future so wide and promising that its dimensions were unfathomable. And although it was mainly the English-American aristocracy that framed the intellectual arguments for the movement toward independence, it would be the Scots-Irish who would bring the fire of revolution to the pulpits of almost every frontier church and also would provide a disproportionate share of guns and soldiers to the battlefield once war broke out.

As the eminent English historian James Anthony Froude put it in 1872, "The resentment which they carried with them continued to burn in their new homes; and, in the War of Independence, England had no fiercer enemies than the grandsons and great-grandsons of the Presbyterians who had held Ulster against Tyrconnell."[40]

3

Preachers and Warriors

THE FRONTIER WAS broad and long, marking the boundaries of a country within a budding country, a self-sustaining civilization at the outskirts of a civilization. The woods were deep, heavy with stands of pine, hemlock, white oak, wild cherry, and yellow poplar. Meadows appeared where the Indians had burned back the trees in order to create grazing areas so that the wild buffalo could fatten and be more easily hunted, their high grass lush with blackberry, raspberry, and blueberry. Wild game was plentiful, the birds thick in the meadows, buffalo and elk roaming freely in those early years, deer and bear abounding, useful for rugs and even clothing, squirrel and rabbit nearby for quick meals, wolves and cougars lurking a ridge away, a constant threat to livestock. West of the Shenandoah Valley and everywhere south of Roanoke, the mountains often became impassable except by following a wide circle of winding trails and shallow, rocky streams until a gap revealed the way into the next small valley, and then the next. And in the far woods all along the Appalachians were the Indians, Shawnee and Cherokee the most hostile among them, watching carefully as this steady stream of settlers led wagons and pack animals along narrow buffalo trails into a land that for a thousand years had been theirs alone, reserved by tribal agreement as a common hunting ground.

The valley and nearby mountains were overwhelming in their vastness, desolate in their human emptiness. Small groups of families migrated down the trails together, cut off from the sea and even from the inland towns, the only evidence of civilization that which they carried in their memories or in the Bibles that so many had packed among their scant belongings. They picked homesteads near rushing streams, seeming to prefer the thin, slate-scarred soil of fields that might have reminded them of Ulster or the lowlands of Scotland rather than the rich, limestone pastures that the German settlers had chosen farther north. They scratched out small patches of farms, learning to grow squash, pumpkin, beans, potatoes, and Indian corn, which along with hog meat became a staple at most meals. Usually they would also save a small area for growing flax, which the women wove into homemade linen clothes. Whiskey stills were everywhere; "brown Betty" liquor was as common as water at their meals. And weapons were their birthright, as natural to their daily lives as a television might seem today.

Unlike in New England, where towns and community infrastructures had been carefully plotted out, or in the flatlands along the Southern coast where the plantation system and the waterways fed a class-scarred society based on slave-racked commerce, the Appalachian Mountain settlements grew from nothing a cabin and a vegetable patch at a time. Towns formed almost accidentally, growing outward from a trading post or a trail intersection or a church. Schools were nonexistent. Justice was a fancy legal term used in Williamsburg or Charleston, its mountain equivalent most often based on crude forms of biblical logic and group retaliation rather than formal law.

But it would be wrong to think of those early days as chaos. In contrast to the vast randomness of the wilderness, the first generation of Scots-Irish settlements were carefully nurtured and the people themselves were tightly organized. Two powerful forces bound these pioneers, not only to each other but also to their long traditions. The first was the democratic organization of the Presbyterian Kirk. The second was the military hierarchy that formed the basis of their local militias. These two energies, while seemingly at odds with each other—the bottom-up populism of the Kirk contrasted with the demand for strong leaders inherent in the Celtic military tradition—combined to create a unique form of frontier democracy. And as with the ancient Scottish interactions from which it sprang, this system was at the same time "aristocratic, unconscious of class, and designed for war."[41]

This interdependence among the settlers was essential, for these were not war parties in the mountainous wilderness but transplanted families. As the Irish historian R. F. Foster mentions, in this first migration from Ireland to America "distinctive Ulster Scot communities could evolve because Ulster women emigrated, too."[42] Few families ventured alone into the emptiness of the frontier. From the very beginning, groups of families that had known each other in Ireland or in Pennsylvania traveled together, pooling their energies in everything from "raising" barns and individual cabins to defending themselves from outside attack. In time these families were joined by others, usually with a church meetinghouse as a focal point, thus creating new congregations in the wilderness.

Organized religion led by strong ministers was the backbone of the communities, for without it (as later decades proved), many would simply regress into the decadence and spiritual emptiness of the wilderness. Just as important, the churches became vital centers of religious, social, and even political activity. From those pulpits, decade after decade, strong men preached about the power of the individual, decried the evil of a government that sought to interpose itself between man and God, and reminded parishioners of the two centuries of discrimination by the Anglican English aristocracy against their people, a discrimination that in many ways still existed in America. Even in colonial Virginia, which was slowly inching its way toward religious freedom, those who were not of the Anglican faith were precluded from holding public office, and

marriages were technically legal only if an Anglican minister performed the ceremony. Although the "dissenters" were allowed to
practice their religion in the mountains, they still were required
to pay an annual "parish levy," a tax for the benefit of the Anglican
Church.

Religious discrimination fueled fresh anger and then political
dissent, and that dissent spewed forth with ever-reaching power
from the pulpit. These sermons were not simply well attended. In
the intellectually famished backwoods they became both great en-
tertainment and a weekly staple. One querulous Anglican minister,
Charles Woodmason, wrote after being sent on a missionary visit to
the Carolina backwoods in the 1760s that the congregation in Wax-
haw "was most surprisingly thick settled beyond any Spot in
England . . . Seldom less than 9, 10, 1200 People assemble of a
Sunday."[43] Woodmason was little impressed with the quality of the
parishioners, however, disliking the fact that many of them drank in
church and calling them "Ignorant, mean, worthless, beggarly Irish
Presbyterians, the Scum of the Earth, and Refuse of Mankind."[44]
Such invective is not unheard of in modern days. If a sensitive ear
would substitute "redneck" for "Irish Presbyterians," he might
have a pretty accurate picture of how many modern-day New En-
glanders and European elites still characterize rural Southerners.

The power of numbers and the strength of the rhetoric began to
tell. In the late 1740s and early 1750s a wave of religious tolerance
swept the region, becoming known as the Great Awakening. This
movement was led not so much by the Presbyterians as by the
Baptists, who slowly gained great favor in Scots-Irish communities
by echoing the strongest edicts of John Calvin that no government
had the right to stand between God and His people. Evangelical
revivals filled the backcountry. Governments themselves softened,
slowly allowing religious freedoms. Transitional figures such as the
legendary orator Patrick Henry, whose Scottish father was "properly" Anglican but whose mother was an ardent Presbyterian, took

up the cudgel and worked to remove "established religion" from the realm of government. This issue, forced heavily by Scots-Irish and other "dissenting" mountain communities, was a major factor in the creation of the First Amendment to the Constitution, which begins, "Congress shall make no law respecting an establishment of religion, or prohibiting the free exercise thereof."

As the ministers reinforced the notions of individual freedom, the leaders of the backcountry militias inculcated the reality that every able-bodied male had an obligation to risk his life for the common good. This seeming contradiction would define a culture, as the insistent, bottom-up populism of the Kirk melded seamlessly with the natural warrior aristocracy of the militias.

The new arrivals did not have to wait long to be tested. In the early 1750s, as the Appalachian Mountain settlements were still taking shape, a hard war came to them and their families. Its genesis was a combination of misunderstandings among the French, British, and several Indian tribes regarding ownership of land in the Ohio Valley. The French, desiring to connect their holdings in Canada and Louisiana, claimed vast territories west of the Appalachians based on the explorations of several Frenchmen acting on behalf of their government. The British, seeing that such French holdings would bottle up their settlements on America's East Coast, claimed that the charter of the Virginia territory extended all the way to the Mississippi River, and that several treaties with the Iroquois, Shawnee, and Delaware tribes validated their holdings. The Indian tribal leaders, forced to choose between what they saw as a British population explosion compared to a series of remote French trading posts, sided with the French.

The so-called French and Indian War spanned the years 1756 to 1763, although in the mountains serious and violent conflict with the Indian tribes actually began in 1754 and did not fully end until after the Revolutionary War. A few conventional battles involving British and French forces took place, but the bulk of the fighting was in the Appalachian region, largely between the Indian tribes and pioneer militiamen. The Treaty of Paris in 1763 granted the victorious British virtually all the lands in America east of the Mississippi River, while at the same time Britain's King George III issued a proclamation prohibiting any colonial settlements on Indian territories west of the Allegheny Mountains. The ever-restless and usually landless Scots-Irish settlers could be expected to immediately ignore King George's distant decree, which they did. And their continuous, antlike expansion through the ridges and hollows and then into the Dark and Bloody Ground of Kentucky was the grist for constant warfare, including retaliatory raids by Indian war parties on legal settlements in the Appalachians.

From the very beginning, the Scots-Irish carried few delusions with them into the mountains. The "Indian problem" was the reason James Logan had lured them to Pennsylvania, and it was also why Governor Gooch had sought them in Virginia. From the moment the members of a new settlement began building their first cabin, every man, woman, and child knew they were in a land that could quickly turn into a war zone. A militia had to be formed, with clearly defined responsibilities. Some militia members became scouts, responsible for patrolling the distant woods in order to detect the possible advance of Indian war parties. Others, such as the legendary Daniel Boone, took it further, exploring deep into the lands on the far side of the mountains, even mixing and trading with the Indian tribes during intermittent periods of peace. In many mountain areas, "blockhouse" forts were built on centrally located farms, where the settlers could gather in order to defend themselves from attack. Attacked they were, war parties sometimes carrying away women and children as prizes. Fight they did, learning from the Indians themselves how to use the woods and blend into their surroundings, tossing aside old European ideas of battle and becoming masters of the frontier.

The militia's leaders were in some cases early settlers who had already shown that they were good soldiers and competent leaders. More often, particularly in North and South Carolina, they were prominent leaders from families that had already been established in Northern Ireland before the emigration. David Hackett Fischer gives a long list of dominant Ulster families known "in Ireland and along the borderlands as 'the Ascendancy.' These people were few in numbers among the flood of immigrants. But they quickly established a cultural hegemony in the American backcountry, and kept it for many generations."[45] It was hardly surprising that such an "Ascendancy" would establish itself in the new world. Indeed, it was simply testimony that the notion of Celtic kinship was alive and well. Acts of courageous leadership from the more powerful families were expected because of their status, and the loyalty shown to them was usually rewarded. These were not people who led from the rear or who simply put others at risk when it came to conflict. In 1760 alone, the famous and powerful Calhoun family of South Carolina lost twenty-three of its members in fights against the Cherokees.[46]

The formalized clan leaders who had replaced the ancient Celtic tribal chieftains had been largely left behind on the Old Continent. In their place were now born the Great Captains, around whom the Scots-Irish yeomanry would gather for the battles of the Revolution and the Civil War, and to whom they would listen in the difficult postwar years of occupation, Reconstruction, and denigration that closed out the nineteenth century. Thus continued the odd but effective paradox of this peculiar culture that was on the one hand a warrior aristocracy while on the other adamantly individualistic and strangely unconscious of class. The battlefield courage of its leaders, and in some cases their unapologetic ruthlessness in business and political affairs, would remain the role model for others who aspired to high success. As the years progressed and the migration moved westward, the surest way for an ambitious young man to join their ranks was through military performance or conspicuous acts of bravado, which might also allow the shrewder among them to marry into a powerful family. This emphasis on boldness and raw audacity would also have its drawbacks as America became more sophisticated. By selecting leaders based on military skill and a penchant for action rather than educational or commercial acumen, a dilemma would evolve in later centuries, manifested clearly in the Scots-Irish of today's America.

As the American colonies moved toward declaring independence from Great Britain, the Scots-Irish were all but unanimous in their desire to be free of the English government. Although the trained minds of New England's Puritan culture and Virginia's Cavalier aristocracy had shaped the finer intellectual points of the argument for political disunion, the true passion for individual rights emanated from the radical individualism of the Presbyterian and, increasingly, Baptist pulpits. New political theories of democracy and federal systems were being tested and debated in the learned salons and legislative chambers along the coast. But for the people in the mountains, two centuries of Kirk-dominated Calvinism had already nurtured a raw yet powerful concept—the individual's moral right to rebel against the unjust policies of any government. This concept, which for the moment dovetailed neatly with the aristocratic forces of revolution in the East, would later form the basis for a more inclusive brand of populism first characterized by the presidency of Andrew Jackson.

The noted journalist, historian, and diplomat Whitelaw Reid summed up the differences among these three approaches neatly nearly a century ago in successive papers presented to the Edinburgh Philosophical Institution (1911) and the Presbyterian Historical Society of Belfast (1912). "The Puritan did not seek a new world to establish liberty of conscience—far from it. He only sought a world where he could impose his own conscience on everybody else. The Cavalier did not seek a new world where he could establish universal freedom. He only sought freedom for himself. Even for the early Scottish immigrants sent out to him he had no use save as bond-servants. Later on he found them also useful as Presidents."[47]

The power of this Scots-Irish resistance was not lost on the British and loyalist elites. As Leyburn writes:

> An Episcopalian of Philadelphia said that "a Presbyterian loyalist was a thing unheard of." A Hessian captain wrote in 1778, "Call this war by whatever name you may, only call it not an American rebellion; it is nothing more or less than a Scotch Irish Presbyterian rebellion." It was reported that King George III characterized the Revolution as "a Presbyterian war," and that Horace Walpole remarked in Parliament, "There is no use crying about it. Cousin America has run off with a Presbyterian parson, and that is the end of it." A representative of Lord Dartmouth wrote from New York in November 1776 that "Presbyterianism is really at the Bottom of the whole Conspiracy, has supplied it with Vigour, and will never rest, till something is decided upon." Jonathan D. Sergeant, member of the Continental Congress from New Jersey, said that the Scotch Irish were the main pillar supporting the Revolution in Pennsylvania. A New Englander who opposed the rupture with England declared the Scotch Irish to be, with few exceptions, "the most God-provoking democrats on this side of Hell."[48]

Despite such passions, for practical and ideological reasons the Scots-Irish were at the outset divided in their opinions about how to react to the war itself. Many flocked immediately to the Continental Army. The famous Pennsylvania Line, perhaps the best unit in the regular army, was mainly Scots-Irish. True to form, it is also remembered for angrily (and drunkenly) marching on the Continental Congress on New Year's Day, 1781, after having not been paid for more than a year.[49] Estimates vary, but it is undeniable that the Scots-Irish comprised at least one-third and as many as one-half of the "rebel" soldiers during the Revolutionary War. They became quickly known not only for their battlefield tenacity, but also for their loyalty during the brutal winter of 1777 at Valley Forge, where they remained steadfast while large numbers of soldiers deserted George Washington.[50]

Many others among them, while loyal to the cause of independence (one is tempted to write, with a hint of premonition, the cause of secession), nonetheless remained for several years as members of the militia units in the mountains, fearing that a mass exodus of the militias toward the coastline to fight the British would open up their Appalachian communities to attacks from Indian war parties in the west. And finally, a sizable percentage felt an equally strong dislike of the colonial elites who were pulling all the strings in the war for independence and felt little obligation to fight and die for the English-American aristocrats who for so long had controlled government services without bringing benefits to the communities in the mountains.

In 1780, while the war slid miserably into its fourth year of conflict, these differences would disappear as the British compounded a key political and strategic misjudgment with the grave error of attempting to intimidate an unyielding people. And in the space of a few months the fierce militiamen from the rock-strewn, frequently embattled Appalachian Mountain settlements would show the Redcoat forces a whole new way of fighting, in the process finally forcing an end to the war.

1780 was a pivotal year for the hierarchy in London. An antiwar element had gained favor among many key British political leaders after their defeat in the pivotal Battle of Saratoga in late 1777, which brought the French into the war on the side of the American colonists. Lord North, heading the government of King George III, had then offered his resignation with the observation that "the best we can make of the war is to get out of the dispute as soon as possible," but George had rejected both the resignation and the advice.[51] The king and others in London persisted largely at the urging of a group of "loyalist exiles who had fled from America to spend the duration of the war in Britain. They were loud and positive in asserting that they represented a large, though muffled, body of opinion in the American colonies."[52] With visions that reflect the distorted dreams of exiled elites throughout history, including the recent predictions that the Iraqis would rise up to greet American forces who came to "liberate" them from Saddam Hussein, the "potential of loyalist support in the Southern backcountry became primary 'evidence' in arguments for continued prosecution of the war . . . There was no alternative now. Britain, rent by internal divisions and increasing weakness of its far-flung external resources, increasingly dependent upon a surge of Southern loyalists to win its war, launched the Southern offensive of 1780."[53]

This strategy envisioned a "domino effect" whereby the Southern colonies would be rolled up from Georgia northward, creating enough despair in an already demoralized Continental Army that the "rebel" forces would eventually surrender. It was not wholly without merit, and as long as it was applied along the coastal areas, the strategy had good effect. In February 1780 the British landed at Savannah, Georgia, with 6,000 regulars under the command of Sir Henry Clinton. By May the British, whose forces had swollen to 10,000 with the addition of colonialist Tory soldiers, had put Charleston, South Carolina, in a noose through a combination of naval and ground attacks. The mass surrender of 5,500 Continental soldiers in that city on May 12 would remain the worst embarrassment for American military forces until the defeat of Gen. Douglas MacArthur's army at the hands of Japanese attackers at Bataan in 1942.[54]

Shortly afterward, one of Sir Henry's key officers announced that "the most violent Rebels are candid enough to allow the game is up," and Clinton himself sailed back to New York, leaving his second-in-command Lord Cornwallis in charge.[55] But the most violent rebels were not yet even in the game. The population of the coastal areas of North and South Carolina where the initial battles were fought was dominated by English-Americans and highland Scots, many of whom had already shown allegiance to the Crown. The great majority of the population in the Carolinas was in the mountains, and the bulk of the people in the mountains were Scots-Irish with long memories, deep hatreds, and battle skills that had been continuously honed against the Indians. Blindly—some might say arrogantly—the British ignored that reality as they pressed their campaign farther inland. Having toppled the Continentals so easily along the coastline, their leaders reasoned that a policy of terror and intimidation in the western communities would quickly bring the rest of the Carolinas into the fold.

This misjudgment proved to be perhaps the most costly error of the war. By launching a campaign that in its tone was chillingly reminiscent of Proud Edward's attempt to hammer Scotland and Henry VIII's "rough wooing" of the Scottish lowlands in centuries past, the British and their Tory cohorts provoked the anger of the very people who were capable of smashing their advance. And smash it they would.

The first British mistake, a series of cavalry raids into the Carolina countryside to convince the locals of their overwhelming superiority, oddly mirrored the actions of the Norman conquerors seven hundred years before. What had worked in England had not worked in Scotland, and what worked along the Carolina coastline did not work where the Piedmont began to give way to the mountains. British colonel Banastre Tarleton, the commander of Clinton's light cavalry, was, to be blunt, an avid butcher who had learned the wrong lessons from England's past. A twenty-six-year-old graduate of Oxford, the short, stocky redhead was known as "a hard-riding, high-living dragoon officer who bragged about his triumphal subjugation of sundry women and the victorious conquests of his Legion."[56] Determined to fully intimidate what remained of the Continental Army in the South, on May 29, 1780, Tarleton attacked a retreating column under the command of Col. Abraham Buford. "After the Americans were driven together in a mass, with white flag flying and arms grounded, the Tories fell upon them with sword and bayonet. That was 'Tarleton's Quarter,' a byword for the slaughter of surrendered men."[57]

The British and Tory soldiers, in an attempt to stamp out what they believed to be the last pocket of resistance in the Carolinas, shot or bayoneted every surrendering soldier. In all, 113 were killed "and another 150 so badly maimed that they were left to die on the battlefield. Tarleton lost five men killed and 12 wounded."[58] But instead of quelling the countryside, Tarleton had enraged it, drawing famed guerrilla fighters such as Francis "Swamp Fox" Marion, Thomas Sumter, and Andrew Pickens into fresh retaliation in the lowlands. "Tarleton's quarter" became a rallying cry for colonists bent on revenge. Word of such British atrocities spread quickly into the western mountains as well—even to the remote "over-mountain" communities in eastern Tennessee and in the Clinch River area of southwest Virginia—convincing the hard-bitten militiamen of Appalachia that they could no longer stay out of the fight.

This led to the second, eventually fatal, British mistake. Rather than leaving the backcountry to these mountaineer militiamen or perhaps trying to lure them toward the coast, the British decided to directly challenge them on their own terrain. Worse yet, they boasted that they would soon hang the mountaineer leaders and destroy their homes.

In late summer, his army increasingly harassed by patriot guerrillas and slowed by malaria and yellow fever, Lord Cornwallis decided to sweep through North Carolina from the south in order to wipe out what he viewed to be the last pockets of patriot resistance. The British army would advance on three fronts: the first along the coast, a second, commanded by Cornwallis, moving through the center, and a third to fan out into the mountains and neutralize the principally Scots-Irish militia units. For the movement into the mountain region, Cornwallis chose Maj. Patrick Ferguson, a highly regarded Scottish highlander who at age thirty-six already had served as a soldier for twenty years. Along with Ferguson was a core group of about 300 New York and New Jersey loyalist soldiers called the American Volunteers, who had been handpicked from the King's American Regiment, the Queen's Rangers, and the New Jersey Volunteers, plus a supplementary force of about a thousand local Tory militiamen that Ferguson himself had recruited and extensively trained.

Ferguson was by all accounts an exemplary soldier and a charismatic leader. Raised as the son of Lord Pitfour on an estate in Aberdeenshire, he had entered the army at age fifteen and within the next year had fought with the Royal North British Dragoons in Germany and Flanders. By the time of the American Revolution he had also served in the West Indies and Nova Scotia, and had also invented the first breechloading rifle ever used in the British military. A true campaigner, during the Revolutionary War he had distinguished himself in the Battle of Brandywine, where he was wounded so severely that his elbow was shattered and his right arm permanently crippled, and then returned to the battlefield to fight at Monmouth, Little Egg Harbor, and in the siege of Charleston. His leadership and persuasive skills were the main reason that the loyalist militia forces under his command had been recruited and prepared for battle.

As opposed to the brutal Tarleton, Ferguson was known as a persuader rather than an eager executioner. But even he underestimated the tenacity of the people of the mountains. Lord Cornwallis had issued a clear mandate "that all the inhabitants of this province, who have subscribed and taken part in this revolt, should be punished with the greatest rigor, and their whole property taken away from them or destroyed."[59] Following this cue, Ferguson paroled a prisoner taken from a minor skirmish and sent him across the Blue Ridge Mountains with a message: the mountaineer militias would "desist from their opposition to the British arms, and take protection under his standard," or Ferguson would "march his army over the mountains, hang their leaders, and lay their country waste with fire and sword."[60]

The rhetoric grew more acrid. Maj. George Hanger, an officer briefly attached to Ferguson, derided the backcountry militiamen as "more savage than the Indians, and possess[ing] every one of their vices and not one of their virtues. I have known one of these fellows [to] travel two hundred miles through the woods never keeping any road or path, guided by the sun by day, and the stars by night, to kill a particular person."[61] Ferguson himself wrote a proclamation to the people of the mountains as he prowled the backcountry, challenging local men who did not support him that, "If you choose to be degraded forever and ever by a set of mongrels, say so at once, and let your women turn their backs upon you, and look out for real men to protect you."

As he would soon find out, such taunts and threats were nothing more than an invitation to his own funeral. Hanger labeled the backwoodsmen savages and Ferguson called them mongrels, but they both should have known better. Certainly these new settlers, while retaining their own identities, had begun to mix their blood with German, French, Welsh, Irish, and English, not to mention Cherokee. But that had always been the case. Mountain culture was Celtic culture, and Celtic culture had always been assimilative. The Chinese had assimilated many peoples and made a nation. The Celts assimilated first into families and then into tribes, and the concept of duty, kinship, and personal loyalty always trumped any fanciful notion of racial purity. Tarleton's slaughter of surrendering soldiers and now Ferguson's personal slurs had upped the stakes beyond the issues of politics and Crown. For the fierce men of the far frontier, the British had called into question their courage as well as their personal honor.

The over-mountain men responded, gathering their militia troops and pouring from their settlements in and beyond the Blue Ridge Mountains, its trails covered with an early snow. Four different militia groups descended on Sycamore Shoals, just east of modern-day Johnson City, Tennessee, and no more than twenty miles south of Big Moccasin Gap. Some came down from Virginia.

Some traveled from the far Tennessee settlements near modern-day Knoxville. Some followed the trails out of the North Carolina settlements near modern-day Asheville. Their uniforms were buckskin hunting shirts or homemade linen blouses, belted at the waist and reaching to their knees. In contrast to the Redcoats, who were traveling with a supply train of seventeen wagons, they carried their own bedrolls, rations, and ammunition. And they brought their own well-tended and accurate long rifles, for which many of them were famed.

Under the militia concept their command structure fell somewhere between loose and nonexistent—John Sevier, one of their leaders, "gave his commands as to equals, and, because these orders appealed to his men as being wise and practical, they gave unquestioned obedience."[62] Another commander, Isaac Shelby, told the militiamen that once combat ensued, "don't wait for the word of command. Let each one of you be your own officers . . . availing yourselves of every advantage that chance might throw your way."[63]

From their gathering point at Sycamore Shoals, the overmountain militias headed southeast, toward the North Carolina Piedmont. In early October they picked up the trail of Ferguson's meandering battalion and began tracking him. Shortly, other militia units joined them, one coming up from South Carolina, another traveling down from North Carolina's Piedmont. They now numbered more than 1,000, almost even in size with Ferguson's 1,300 Redcoats. And on October 7, 1780, they found Ferguson on a narrow ridge that the locals called King's Mountain.

Ferguson, learning from two deserters that he was being tracked, had sent vainly for reinforcements and then decided to head toward Cornwallis farther inland. Sensing that it was too late, he finally decided to circle his forces into an impregnable defense. Against a traditional European army, the steep slopes and bare rocks of King's Mountain might have proved effective, as his soldiers could use the rocks for cover and also see clearly down the mountain in order to fire at their attackers. But for mountain men who had now been fighting Cherokee and Shawnee war parties for more than twenty-five years, the Redcoat commander had done little more than offer them their own kind of war. They dismounted, carefully forming into eight attacking sections, and encircled the mountain. And then they fought him Indian-style.

The battlefield was small; the length of six football fields on top of a mountain a few hundred feet high. The numbers involved were not huge; a thousand or so on each side. The battle did not last long; little more than an hour. But the victory was so stunning and the differences in military style so complete that one can say without exaggeration that Colonial America, with all its stylistic dependence on European forms of propriety, began conclusively to die along with Ferguson's soldiers on King's Mountain. And it was being replaced by the raw individualism of an uneducated and testy group that the Europeans, perhaps always, would quizzically view as "mongrels." This was not the carefully replicated English society along the coast that was mangling Ferguson on the mountain. Rather, it was something fresh and new, occasionally even ugly, that could not yet even be defined.

Ferguson put forward a classic defense, calmly—and bravely— controlling his battalion while riding on a horse, using a silver whistle to blast instructions to his soldiers. They followed his commands, firing "in volley" at the advancing frontiersmen and even racing down the slopes three times in time-honored bayonet charges that caused some of the attackers to retreat to the base of the mountain and regroup. The Scottish major seemed to be everywhere along the ridge, shouting instructions, blowing his whistle, commanding a relocation of his besieged soldiers to a tighter perimeter as the backwoodsmen moved forward, and even slashing down several white flags of surrender with his sword.

But while inside the Redcoat perimeter there was a whistle and a determined commander, along the steep slopes of the mountain were a thousand Indian war whoops, every one of them coming from fighting men who knew the battle plan and were their own commanders. Virginian William Campbell, the senior militiaman among them, had simply told his men to "shout like hell and fight like devils," and Ferguson could not keep up with the relentless, decentralized attack that used no "volley" firing and needed no orders from on high. Rock by rock, slope by slope, fighting sometimes so close that a rifle went off into the belly of a Redcoat whose bayonet had pierced the same rifleman's arm, the buckskin and linen-clad militiamen used every skill that a generation of Indian warfare had taught them. The volleys of Ferguson's ever more nervous soldiers went repeatedly high, over their heads, while the individual shots from well-used long rifles were seldom off the mark.

Ferguson fought bravely to the end, at the last moment leading a small group of officers in an attempt to break through the militiamen's lines and escape. His sword snapped in two as he hacked at an attacker. They turned their guns on him, and no fewer than eight bullets hit him. He died in the saddle, head-shot, one foot caught in a stirrup as his body sagged to the ground. And with him died not only the left flank of Cornwallis's vaunted sweep through Carolina, but also the ill-founded fantasy of those loyalists still sitting out the war in London who had intoned that a British sweep through the Southern colonies might somehow bring a revolution to heel.

The over-mountain men had not merely defeated the Redcoats at King's Mountain, they had totally destroyed them. At a cost of 28 killed and 62 wounded, "Ferguson's detachment of 1,100 men was annihilated."[64] Indeed, "only 200 Tories sent out earlier on a foraging expedition were able to escape. Hearing of Ferguson's defeat, Cornwallis began backpedaling into South Carolina."[65]

The victorious mountaineers spent a few days marching Redcoat prisoners to a collection point, growing increasingly restless and violent during the slow, rain-soaked journey. But they were warriors rather than professional soldiers. Their work was done and they did not take well to further discipline. And the anger still ran deep, not only in remembrance of friends killed in the battle, but also of the threats the arrogant British command had sent their way only weeks before. Mindful of Tarleton's butchery and Cornwallis's early promise to hang them, they held court on a number of Red-coats who were recognized as local Tory leaders, sentencing thirty-six to death and hanging nine of them before growing tired of the killing. Other prisoners were shot in individual incidents, and still others were left on the trail to die. And then the militiamen who had changed the course of the Revolutionary War simply went home. There were Indian war parties to worry about, and rough settlements in the crags and hollows of distant mountains where their families needed their help.

But other militiamen soon filled their void. The victory at King's Mountain solidified resistance against the British throughout the South. Three months later, on January 17, 1781, the hated Tarle-ton, commanding 1,100 legion cavalrymen and highlander dra-goons, would get his due at Cowpens, hardly twenty miles away. A small force of Continental soldiers and Virginia militiamen used deception, maneuver, and decentralized command to destroy his army and send him into full retreat. On two separate occasions the Americans lured Tarleton's forces into a devastating crossfire by feigning withdrawals while other units laid in ambush, in one instance driving his vaunted cavalry from the battle with fifteen empty horses after one volley, where it refused to reengage. Cow-pens, "the glittering gem of the Revolution, was brought off by an American backwoodsman [Daniel Morgan] who, like the great Hannibal himself, was merely adapting himself to men and ter-rain." At a cost of 12 Americans killed and 60 wounded, the British lost nine-tenths of their force killed or captured.[66]

Two months later the Americans met Cornwallis in a larger fight at Guilford Courthouse in North Carolina, using tactics similar to those at Cowpens. Fighting the determined British commander to a tactical draw, they nonetheless forced him to withdraw and re-group. And by the end of that year the British would be defeated at Yorktown, finally forcing an end to the Revolutionary War.

One who is descended from these acts of courage inevitably must remember them with a special emotion. Samuel Cochran of the 14th Virginia Regiment crossed the Delaware with Washington and fought at Brandywine, Germantown, and Monmouth Courthouse, walked with bleeding feet wrapped in rags through the desolate camps at Valley Forge, and then fought again at Guilford Courthouse. Tidence Lane and John Smith and John Condley rode out of the east Tennessee over-mountain settlements and helped finish off Ferguson and his New York, New Jersey, and Carolina Tory Redcoats at King's Mountain. William Miller, a scion of those who stood at Londonderry, made the trek from Natural Bridge, Virginia, to Cowpens and helped deliver Tarleton and the British a deserved and telling blow. These men and others, great-great-great-grandfathers all, fought with purpose on behalf of concepts that were older than the Scottish Kirk, views of human dignity that in time, in many places, became America itself.

History becomes personal. And the personal becomes history.

PART FIVE

Rise and Fall:
The Heart of the South

When I grew tall as the Indian corn,
My father had little to lend me,
But he gave me his great, old powder-horn
And his woodsman's skill to befriend me.

. . .

We cleared our camp where the buffalo feed,
Unheard-of streams were our flagons;
And I sowed my sons like the apple-seed,
On the trail of the western wagons.

—STEPHEN VINCENT BENÉT,
"The Ballad of William Sycamore, 1790–1871"

1

Westward, Ho

A NEW COUNTRY had been formed. Forests were hacked away. Mud trails widened and hardened, becoming packed roads. The wagons poured westward through gaps in the mountains, especially down the Wilderness Road that had been pioneered by the daring Scots-Irish explorer Daniel Boone, funneling thousands of settlers into Kentucky, Tennessee, and beyond. In 1803 the Louisiana Purchase opened up the new nation on the far side of the Mississippi River, although it would take more than another decade for viable settlements to reach Arkansas, Missouri, northern Louisiana, Texas, and areas farther west. In 1814, soldiers led by Gen. Andrew Jackson forced the Treaty of Fort Jackson, moving American territory farther south into lands once held by the Creek Indians, including three-fifths of Alabama, an additional one-fifth of Georgia, and an open road from western Tennessee to the Gulf of Mexico. In early 1815, Jackson humiliated the British in a stunning, brutal defeat at New Orleans, forcing them once and for all to abandon dreams of regaining their hold on American interests. By 1818, Jackson had driven the Spanish out of Florida, opening up further avenues into the Deep South, including the coastal areas of Alabama and Mississippi, which had been in Spanish hands.

As the new land began to fill with fresh settlers, the generation that followed those who had fought the Revolution remembered Cowpens and King's Mountain and even New Orleans more clearly than those old battles at Londonderry or the Boyne, and cared more deeply about whoever wheeled or walked into their latest isolated settlement than they did about arcane and distant national labels. Past ethnic identities were quickly falling away in favor of a new and special word—American.

Some historians, such as James Leyburn, claim that the story of the Scots-Irish ends here. "After independence the Scotch-Irish were integral parts of the American nation, making no distinction between themselves and any other Americans, nor having them made, either for praise or for blame. If a man made his impress on American life he did it as the individual he was."[1] To be sure, if this were merely a story about ethnic purity, focusing on a homogeneous national group, such observations would be at least partially correct. But the impact of the Scots-Irish culture on America was so deep and profound that it transcended its own people. And in many ways the Scots-Irish had no need to distinguish their ethnic heritage from the dominant tenets in the new lands of the South and the Ohio Valley, because in those areas their culture came to define the very essence of what it meant to be American.

The Scots-Irish culture lived on in the mountains of Maine, New Hampshire, and Vermont. It continued to impact heavily in Pennsylvania, especially along the southern boundaries and in the mountains. It was already traveling along with the wagons to Texas, Missouri, and points beyond. But in the mid-South and the Ohio Valley it was clearly dominant. In this part of America, those of Scots-Irish descent still made up the largest numbers of settlers. From the beginning of the Revolution until well into the 1800s, the population of the United States grew primarily through reproduction, with very small rates of immigration. Even in the 1820s, annual immigration never reached 10,000 in a country that now numbered 10 million people, and that small immigrant stream continued to be heavily northern British. In 1820 there were a total of only thirty immigrants from Italy, five from Poland, five from all of Asia, and one from Mexico.[2] Importantly, those who had traveled over several generations from Ulster through the Appalachian Mountains and then westward did so not as individuals but in families, and not merely as families but in groups of families that frequently intermarried, thus extending the center of their culture into the next generation and frequently into the one after that.

The Scots-Irish culture's emphasis on collateral rather than lineal descent bound these groups of families together, both in reality and in emotion, even as those families extended out in different directions. This heightened sense of family affiliation created the tendency cited by Professor Ned Landsman in the previous section to tightly connect many settlements through a system of interlocking family networks, comprising an unconscious but very real "oil slick" theory of cultural expansion. Similarly, Wilbur Cash pointed out in his perennially well-regarded book *The Mind of the South* that "by 1800 any given individual was likely to be cousin, in one degree or another, to practically everybody within a radius of thirty miles about him. And his circle of kin, of course, overlapped more or less with the next, and that in turn with the next beyond, and so on in an endless web, through the whole South."[3] And the culture, like its ancestors before it, was with a few notable exceptions willing to assimilate others into it rather than exclude family members who married men or women who were not Scots-Irish. This brought an ever increasing number of English, ethnic Irish, Welsh, French Huguenots, Germans, Dutch, Swiss, and even Indians (including one of my great-great-grandmothers) into the Scots-Irish community.

And most important, the Scots-Irish, along with their ethnic and historic kin from Scotland and the English border areas, were laying out this cultural tapestry on an empty slate, in frontier settlements devoid of civilization that had no conflicting tenets to be overcome. As David Hackett Fischer points out, "90 percent of the backsettlers were either English, Irish, or Scottish; and an actual majority came from Ulster, the Scottish lowlands, and the north of England." He goes on to point out that, "These emigrants from North Britain established in the southern highlands a cultural hegemony that was even greater than their proportion in the population." This vast area extended "800 miles south from Pennsylvania to Georgia, and several hundred miles west from the Piedmont plateau to the banks of the Mississippi." Fischer indicates that "The borderers were more at home than others in this anarchic environment, which was well suited to their family system, their warrior ethic, their farming and herding economy, their attitudes toward land and wealth and their ideas of work and power. So well adapted was the border culture to this environment that other ethnic groups tended to copy it."[4]

Thus began a trend that would repeat itself over the decades in many other parts of America, particularly among the working classes from a variety of nations that would later come into contact with the Scots-Irish and their converted "kin." True to its Scottish and Irish roots, the culture that dominated this region was openly unafraid of higher authority, intent on personal honor, quick to defend itself against attack of any sort, and deeply patriotic. It was also oddly paradoxical, managing to be at the same time both intensely populist and yet indifferent to wealth. The measure of a man was not how much money he made or how much land he held, but whether he was bold—often to the point of recklessness—whether he would fight, and whether he could lead. Even from the outset it was expected that the Great Captains, just as the clan chieftains of old, would on the one hand own more land, but on the other would put themselves at immediate risk by providing leadership in times of wider crisis.

Physical courage fueled this culture, and an adamant independence marked its daily life. Success itself was usually defined in personal reputation rather than worldly goods. A survey of eight sample counties in Tennessee in 1850 "showed that more than half of all adult males (free and slave together) owned no land at all," and even as recently as 1983 "the top 1 percent of landowners possessed half of the land in Appalachia. The top 5 percent owned nearly two-thirds."[5] One of this culture's great strengths is that it persistently refuses to recognize human worth in terms of personal income and assets. But as the country grew more sophisticated and cosmopolitan, this strength at some level also became a tragic flaw as other individuals and cultures that measured power and influence through the ownership of property would devalue Scots-Irish contributions, and even take advantage of the simplicity of this view as it applied to business and politics.

This formula would also mutate rather harshly where it combined with the false aristocracy that evolved out of the eastern Virginia plantation system in the so-called Black Belt of lower Alabama, Mississippi, Louisiana, western Tennessee, and eastern Arkansas. In this sense, as later pages will address, the South writ large would continue to perpetuate a widely misunderstood but pervasive three-tiered class structure that in many ways still exists to this day. Suffice it to say that from the outset, "poor but proud" was an unapologetic and uncomplaining way of life. Nor, on the other side, did modern liberals invent the term "redneck," although it is only in recent decades that the term has been uttered by American elitists with such an arrogant, condescending sneer. In truth "redneck" is an ethnic slur, however ignorant those who use it may be of that reality. The moniker was used to earmark the rough-hewn Scots-Irish Presbyterians as early as 1830 in North Carolina and had its roots in the north of Britain long before that. Similarly, the term "cracker" was used pejoratively by the English upper classes even before the Revolution in referring to the "lawless set of rascals on the frontiers of Virginia, Maryland, the Carolinas and Georgia."[6]

The difference between this culture and most others is that its members don't particularly care what others think of them. To them, the joke has always been on those who utter the insult. As a country song happily puts it, "It's alright to be a redneck." In recent

years, comedian Jeff Foxworthy has made a prosperous career out
of inventing insulting "redneck" jokes aimed at an audience of his
own people. Not long ago, during a debate in which Native Americans were denouncing the Washington Redskins for the supposedly demeaning nature of their team name, a listener from West
Virginia called into a local radio station. "Screw this," he said. "Let's
call them the Washington Rednecks and we'll ALL come to the
games."

It was indeed alright to be a redneck, even from the beginning.
A tremendous energy percolated inside these remote and fiercely
independent communities. A hypnotic and emotionally powerful
musical style evolved from its Celtic origins until "country music"
became a uniquely American phenomenon. The famed Scottish
talent for inventiveness and adaptability showed itself on the frontier regions again and again. Settlers had long studied the Indian
ways, learning how to hunt, what to eat, and how to turn animal
skins into clothes. They applied modern lessons as well—as one example, within a few miles of each other in Rockbridge County,
Virginia, in the early and mid-1800s, Cyrus McCormick invented
the reaper, thereby revolutionizing American farming techniques,
and James Gibbs invented the Willcox & Gibbs sewing machine.
And the culture's most important contributions during this early
era came from the courage and innovative talents of its soldiers and
pioneers as well as the evolution of an adamantly independent style
of democracy that forever changed the face of American politics.

The power—and ultimately the attractiveness—of the Scots-
Irish culture stemmed from its insistence on the dignity of the individual in the face of power, regardless of one's place or rank in
society. This infectious egalitarianism had bound its people together from the earliest days after the Romans built a different sort
of nation on the southern side of Hadrian's Wall. The ideas that fueled the concept had been adapted into its religious base through
the Scottish Kirk and were then further refined in Ireland as the
notions of nonconformity evolved, asserting that every individual

had the moral right to resist any government that did not respect his beliefs. This was not a concept that had to be learned in a book or taught in a classroom. It emanated directly and viscerally from the daily functioning of the culture itself. In America, and particularly in the mountain South, this streak of independence transcended narrow definitions of ethnicity and religion, extending to concepts of individualism and then to political philosophies that provided the roots of a powerful and unrelenting populism.

To most of the American political elite of the early 1800s, the thought of empowering a mass of uneducated, seemingly half-wild backwoodsmen was not simply preposterous; the economic implications of watering down a system built on the privileges that attended the ownership of property were nothing short of alarming. The seeds of this political shift were sown in 1791 and 1792 when Vermont and Kentucky were granted statehood, both of them having eliminated the requirement that one own property or pay taxes in order to vote. But a true widening of the electorate and a fairer distribution of the benefits of government would not become a part of the American political process without the benefit of an unusual leader, one whose political instincts were adept enough to face down the entrenched political machines and whose leadership credentials were relevant enough to hold great sway with the common man.

There was, in truth, only one such leader. His name was Andrew Jackson. This combative, self-made lawyer and military commander, whose parents had emigrated from Ulster, became the first president who was neither a product of the landed English-American aristocracy of Virginia nor of the intellectual English-American elite of New England. "Irish Andy" changed the chemistry of American politics more profoundly than any other president. And—which is difficult to even comprehend in this age of preening, blow-dried, self-important career politicians—he did so with no other motivation than a passion for the common good. The oft-overlooked Jackson was the quintessential "tribal chieftain" Scots-Irish leader, melding together the two ancient concepts of the warrior aristocracy and populist egalitarianism that had always earmarked Celtic culture as it had evolved in the north of Britain. And, more than any other president in Ameran history, he was indeed a self-made man of the people.

2

Old Hickory

⸻

MODERN-DAY HISTORIANS and political scientists often minimize the Jackson presidency by claiming that there were no remarkable leaps forward—no Louisiana Purchases, no great statements equal to the intellect of Adams and Jefferson, no wars—while Jackson stoically marched the Indian tribes off to Oklahoma on the Trail of Tears and the nation seemed obsessed with internal bickering. They neglect to consider that this very internal conflict and the changes it brought to the American political structure comprised one of the most fundamental shifts in the nation's history, and also that Andrew Jackson rewrote the book on American political leaders just as surely as Nobel laureate Ernest Hemingway remade the narrative form of the novel. Lots of people could write like Hemingway—although not as well—once he showed them how. And the same thing could be said for the political talent of Andrew Jackson: Lots of politicians could approach the voters in the home-spun style of Andrew Jackson—although rarely as authentically—once he showed them how.

The Scots-Irish culture has to date produced at least a dozen other presidents, some of them pretty fine leaders, but Old Hickory remains in a class by himself. Andrew Jackson was an original, an unusual and fearless leader who dominated the American political process more fully than any president before or since. And he did so not through the tedious, secretly sneering Machiavellian half-truths that pervade so much of today's carefully scripted American politics. Jackson gained power, and also governed, through the force of his personality, fueled by a directness that came from an entire lifetime of overcoming obstacles that most politicians either manage to evade or have been spared through the circumstances of their birth and upbringing.

By the age of fourteen, Andrew Jackson was an orphan in the wilderness of the Carolina mountains, having lost his entire family. He was also a scarred combat veteran.

His father, for whom he was named, died a month before he was born, having migrated from Ulster with enough money to purchase two hundred acres of farmland in the mountainous Waxhaws settlement where North and South Carolina came together. Both of his older brothers died as teenage soldiers in the Revolution, one from exhaustion after the Battle of Stono Ferry and the other from smallpox after being held as a prisoner of war. Captured along with his brother while serving as a thirteen-year-old soldier, Jackson also caught smallpox, somehow surviving a forty-mile journey on foot after a prisoner exchange and arriving home "a raving maniac" from the fever.[7] Earlier, a British officer had slashed him with a sword deep on the hand and across his head when he refused to clean the man's boots, leaving scars that would remind him for the remainder of his life that tyranny and human denigration were more than words. His mother, Elizabeth, a fiercely anti-British Presbyterian, had nursed many of the mangled survivors after the infamous Col. Banastre Tarleton massacred Buford's surrendering regiment, and then left for Charleston to tend to American prisoners of war kept aboard ships in the city's harbor. She herself caught cholera while on the ships and died there, to be buried in an unmarked grave.

Though left motherless, fatherless, and without siblings, the young boy-man still carried with him the social status of his family. His grandfather was a reasonably well-to-do weaver and merchant in Carrickfergus, on the northern Irish coast just outside Belfast. His father had held a good piece of property near the town of Castlereagh and had been the leader of a large group of Presbyterians who migrated to the Carolinas in 1765.[8] This family status, while not one of great wealth, was still significant in the backwoods communities and would open doors for him during his early life. At the same time he was a wild daredevil who in his youth loved "gambling, drinking, cockfighting and horse racing—mostly horse racing, a sport he could never resist," and at the age of fifteen blew a three- or four-hundred-pound inheritance from his grandfather in one wild and glorious spree.[9]

Scarcely schooled, Jackson worked odd jobs while living with different aunts, uncles, and cousins, until at the age of seventeen a lawyer in Salisbury, North Carolina, named Spruce McCay hired him so that he might "read the law" and become an attorney. After two years with McCay, he moved on to study under Col. John Stokes, a powerful attorney who had lost a hand at Tarleton's massacre and no doubt already knew of the young Jackson's wartime service as well as his family heritage. Six months later he was admitted to the North Carolina bar. A year after that, in the spring of 1788, he and a few friends set out for the wild unknown of middle Tennessee. "Each man was equipped with a horse, a few belongings, a gun, and a wallet containing letters from distinguished citizens of the old community to the settlers of the new."[10]

He was heading for Nashville, and the letters were probably more important than the horse or even the gun since they allowed Jackson to transfer his social status to the new frontier. And a raw frontier it was. At this time "the Nashville community consisted of a courthouse, two stores, two taverns, a distillery, and a number of cabins, tents, houses, and other nondescript shelters."[11] Arriving in Nashville in 1788, he was immediately taken in as a boarder by the widow of Col. John Donelson, who eight years before had led a group of about 120 settlers to this remote outpost, including his wife and eleven children. Donelson, a patriarch of the settlement, had recently been murdered, either by a white robber or an Indian. Most of his children were now grown, although his youngest daughter, Rachel, now twenty-one, was living at home. Rachel had married a prominent Kentuckian, but the couple was having continuing marital difficulties. Three years later Jackson would marry Rachel, under the false impression that her first husband had obtained a divorce in Virginia. He had not, and their legal maneuverings, which required them to remarry a few years later, would haunt the honor of his wife for the rest of her life.

Jackson's energies, his legal profession, and his affiliation with the leading families of the new territory allowed him to move quickly to the forefront of Tennessee's still-emerging political establishment. He was a delegate to the state's first constitutional convention, became Tennessee's first congressman in 1796, and soon thereafter moved to the U.S. Senate after William Blount was expelled for misconduct. But by 1798 he had grown tired of Washington and resigned from the Senate in order to serve as a judge on Tennessee's Superior Court. Then in 1802, at the age of thirty-five, he achieved a long-held goal by winning election as major general of the Tennessee militia.

Jackson had made his way to the top of Tennessee's oftenraucous political hierarchy not only through shrewdness, but also by a reputation for audacious conduct. Naturally combative, he also knew that his frequent acts of boldness were the coin of the realm in American frontier society, the surest way to gain him entrance into the ruling circle, just as centuries before they would have earmarked him as a future tribal chief. Andrew Jackson knew the game, both viscerally and from having studied it. He was well read on the ways of the ancient Scottish chieftains and also required his subordinates to study those histories.[12]

But one cannot simply invent courage for political gain. Jackson was a true fighter, and not merely on the battlefield. He fought his first duel at the age of twenty-one. While seeking election to head the militia, he gained a reputation for unshakable boldness when he physically faced down Tennessee's most famous war hero, John Sevier, who had been one of the commanders at the Battle of King's Mountain. A few years later he took a bullet in the chest that he would carry for the rest of his life, said to be too close to his heart for any doctor to extract. This bullet was the result of a duel with Charles Dickinson, the best shot in Tennessee. Ostensibly over an argument about a horse race, the dislike ran far deeper, as Dickinson had repeatedly implied that Jackson's wife, Rachel, was a bigamist. Dickinson fared worse. After taking the hit, in very un-gentlemanly fashion Jackson had coldly and deliberately shot Dickinson dead. He took another slug in the shoulder in 1813 at the age of forty-six, nearly losing his arm, from the brother of a much younger man he was busily caning for having publicly insulted him. Within a few months he was out of his sickbed, leading a war party against the Creek Indians. The bullet would not be extracted until 1832. The man he caned, Thomas Benton, found it necessary to hurriedly leave Nashville after the incident, later resurfacing as an influential senator from Missouri and becoming one of Jackson's staunchest political allies.

On the battlefield he was unbeatable, making up for his lack of formal military training through audacity and personal example. He had a leadership style that combined praise and discipline in order to get the most out of every soldier, an ability to out-think his enemies, and a ruthless ferocity once combat began. His toughness was matched by the special kind of humility before his troops that would impress any modern-day soldier or Marine. In the tradition of the great warrior chieftains from William Wallace forward, Jackson made no distinction between himself and his men other than the authority that came from command. At one point early in 1813, he ordered his officers to give their horses to sick soldiers, turning over all three of his own in order to march alongside his men. It was his soldiers who first began calling him by the famous sobriquet Old Hickory, because of the unbreakable resoluteness of their far-older general.

He was a firm believer in both discipline and forgiveness. Not unlike the legendary George Patton, another general of Scots-Irish heritage, cowardice repulsed him while courage in the face of great danger overwhelmed his emotions. On two different occasions during the harrowing Indian wars he allowed soldiers under his command to be summarily shot for mutiny and disobedience. On another, when rations were running low and a company of volunteers had decided to return to Tennessee, Jackson rode his horse in front of them to block them and personally threatened to shoot the first man who took a step toward home. No one called his bluff.[13]

And yet when the great Creek warrior Chief Red Eagle defied almost impossible odds of survival by riding directly into Jackson's camp and personally surrendering, Jackson let him go. Red Eagle, bold and intelligent, was also known as William Weatherford, as he was seven-eighths white. In terms that by themselves might otherwise have endeared him to his Jackson-led enemies, Red Eagle used to boast that he had French, Scottish, Spanish, and Creek ancestors, "but not one drop of Yankee blood."[14] Many Indian tribes had sided with the British during the War of 1812, the Creeks among them. In August 1813, Red Eagle had led a raiding party of 800 braves against a settlement at Fort Mims, Alabama, killing and scalping more than 400 settlers. As war historian Robert Leckie observed, of the entire garrison of 550 "whites, half-breeds, Indians and Negroes . . . fifteen persons escaped, and most of the Negroes were spared for slaves, but everyone else in Fort Mims was cut down."[15]

Jackson, his arm still in a sling from the slug that had smashed his shoulder while caning Thomas Benton, had tracked the "Red Stick" warriors for months, slaughtering thousands of Indians in retaliations just as brutal as the Creek attack, and also soundly defeating Red Eagle's warriors in several major battles. Notably, among his able lieutenants in this first major incursion (both of Scots-Irish descent) were Sam Houston, who would gain great fame during the campaigns against the Mexicans in Texas, and legendary frontiersman Davy Crockett, who would later die at the Alamo. Jackson had at first been livid when Red Eagle rode into his camp, but his calculated ranting failed to intimidate the Indian leader, who told him simply, "I am not afraid of you. I fear no man, for I am a Creek warrior. . . . You may kill me if you wish." Jackson held back his soldiers, who wished to do just that, and let Red Eagle depart, claiming, "Any man who would kill as brave a man as this would rob the dead."[16]

Such empathy did not extend to warriors alone. In the aftermath of a particularly bloody attack on the Creek village of Talluschatches, "a dead Indian mother was found on the field still clutching her living infant. Jackson asked other Indian women to care for the child, but they refused. 'All his relations are dead,' they said. 'Kill him, too.' The General rejected this solution and afterward took the boy, named Lincoyer, back to the Hermitage and provided him with every advantage, including a good education. Unfortunately Lincoyer died of tuberculosis before reaching the age of seventeen."[17] And so the general who would lay fire to whole Indian villages during war, who as president is most remembered in modern times for enforcing the legislation that sent the Indian tribes westward from their historic lands to the arid reservations of Oklahoma, had the instinctive compassion to bring an orphaned Indian baby into his own home. The man who himself had been orphaned by war and who would never father children of his own was clearly not so much an "Indian hater" as he was a determined warrior.

He proved that at New Orleans. Jackson's victory over the British in January 1815 was a tactical gem, as one-sided a defensive victory as King's Mountain had been in the offense, but on a much larger scale. Even more, these were British regulars backed by a naval armada and commanded by Sir Edward Pakenham. Paken-

ham had fought superbly in Europe against the French. Five
months after the New Orleans battle, his brother-in-law the Duke
of Wellington would defeat Napoleon at Waterloo. In campaigns
farther to the north and east the battle-hardened British regulars
had made quick work of most of the American militia units they
had faced. In August 1814 they had sailed up the Patuxent River to
the outskirts of Washington, DC, marching through the area for
five days before they found a unit that would even fight them.
Finally at Bladensburg, Maryland, they caught up with an American force, and the skirmish lasted for about fifteen minutes before
the U.S. soldiers dropped their guns and fled.

Only a small group of sailors and Marines had stood their
ground as the British advanced toward Washington. As a reciprocal
gesture, when the Redcoats entered the city, the only official building they declined to burn was the house of the Marine Corps com-
mandant, which to this day is known as the oldest continuously
standing building in Washington. Reaching the White House, the
British found it abandoned with a full meal having been prepared
in the kitchen. They delightedly ate the meal and then burned the
president's house while other Redcoats torched the War and Trea-
sury buildings as well as the Navy Yard, where they also burned all
the naval vessels on the eastern side of the river.[18]

And so, with a false optimism eerily similar to that of the long-
dead Maj. Patrick Ferguson at King's Mountain a generation before, the British hardly expected the supposedly ragtag Indian
fighters of the frontier militia awaiting them at New Orleans to
have the staying power to resist their attack. And the capture of
New Orleans would be a valuable strategic prize. Sitting as it did at
the mouth of the Mississippi River, British military control of the
city would choke off the vital river traffic that fed America's newly
formed Western territories along a host of Mississippi river towns
that stretched from New Orleans to Memphis and St. Louis, as well
as the Ohio River towns in Indiana and northern Kentucky. But
Old Hickory out-thought and out-prepared the invading British.

And as the backwoods militia had done at King's Mountain, he fought them frontier-style, with highly accurate sharpshooters firing from behind concealed positions—in this case, bulletproof cotton bales.

During the main battle, the British, 8,000 strong, used fifty barges to ferry troops toward their attack on the American positions. Jackson's 5,700 soldiers were mostly Tennessee and Kentucky riflemen bolstered by New Orleans locals—a mix of Creoles, Frenchmen, pirates, and a unit of free blacks that Jackson had armed and brought to the battlefield despite the protests of local leaders. The Redcoats, many of them veterans of campaigns against the French and more recently the burning of Washington, advanced in traditional European style. Their scarlet tunics were marked by white cross-belts, leading Jackson to order his men to simply hold their fire until the Redcoats came within range, and then aim their bullets just above the cross-belts. Fire discipline and pinpoint accuracy were the key. The British soldiers had never before faced frontier long rifles or the coolheaded men who fired them, and it was a brutal slaughter in front of the cotton bales. At one point an entire regiment of kilted Scottish highlanders died in the advance, only a few dozen of them even reaching the parapets where they would have engaged the Americans hand to hand. Pakenham was wounded three times before he finally fell. In all the British lost more than 2,000 soldiers dead and another 500 as prisoners, at an American cost of only eight dead and 13 wounded.[19]

In handing this invasion force one of the most devastating and humiliating defeats in the history of British arms, Jackson became an immediate national hero, symbolizing the very ascendancy of the new nation. Even nearly 150 years later, the battle was still being celebrated in popular song—Johnny Horton's "Battle of New Orleans" was a huge hit in the summer of 1959, selling 2 million copies and topping the *Billboard* charts six weeks in a row. The legend-makers usually omit the tales of Jackson's autocratic martial rule in New Orleans leading up to the battle, when he happily offended the city's feckless, pleasure-loving elite by throwing a leg-islator into jail for writing a newspaper article that defied his au-thority, and then arresting a federal judge who released the legislator. The Louisiana Senate deliberately omitted his name from a list of officers it thanked for saving the city.[20] But such con-frontations with America's elites had become commonplace for Old Hickory, who no doubt consoled himself through the adulation of the people and the gold medal issued to him by a grateful Congress.

The military campaigns continued, as did his popular adulation and his delight in provoking those he viewed as aristocracy. Now commanding the entire Southern division of the United States Army, he entered the Spanish territory of Florida, from which the Seminole Indians were conducting raids on American soil, and largely on his own initiative seized Pensacola from the Spanish on May 24, 1818. When the Spanish governor protested the legality of his takeover and demanded that Jackson remove his forces from Florida, Jackson captured the governor, his staff, and his soldiers and had them all transported to Cuba "until the transaction could be amicably adjusted between the two governments."[21] The "trans-action" was in fact resolved in February 1819 when Spain decided it had no choice but to sell its Florida territory to the United States for $5 million.

With the takeover of Florida, Jackson's military career reached its natural conclusion. Old Hickory was now in his mid-fifties. He had lived a hard life and his health was beginning to fail. Addition-ally, due in great part to his own efforts, the entire Southern region east of the Mississippi River was now under American governance. Now, after twenty years away from government, Jackson was turn-ing his eyes again to politics, deciding to run for the presidency. And he brought with him a list of accomplishments that would make a frontiersman's heart swim with admiration.

But to the American political elite, then as well as now, Jackson's personal history was nauseatingly crude and violent while his populist beliefs were a threat to the existing order. As Arthur Schlesinger points out in his Pulitzer Prize–winning book *The Age of Jackson*, when Old Hickory decided to run for president he was "specifically opposed by the guardians of Virginia orthodoxy. Jefferson himself is supposed to have told Daniel Webster, 'he is one of the most unfit men I know of for such a place. . . . He is a dangerous man.' "[22] Alexis de Tocqueville would write shortly after his arrival in America, "All the enlightened classes are opposed to General Jackson."[23] Indeed, when Jackson was elected, his predecessor, New England political scion and former president John Quincy Adams, refused to attend the inauguration, and when Harvard awarded Jackson an honorary Doctor of Laws in 1833, Adams wrote to his alma mater that it was a "disgrace in conferring her highest literary honors upon a barbarian who could not write a sentence of grammar and hardly could spell his own name."[24]

Jackson had expected such resistance and had built his political base on a natural constituency of frontiersmen from what was then called the West and the simple wage earners of the cities in the North, in the process founding the modern Democratic Party. As the eminent historian Vernon Louis Parrington wrote in his Pulitzer Prize–winning classic *Main Currents in American Thought*, "In the person of Old Hickory they saw the visible embodiment of their vague aspirations, and they turned to him with an unquestioning loyalty that nothing could weaken. He was our first great popular leader, our first man of the people. . . . He was one of our few Presidents whose heart and sympathy were with the plain people, and who clung to the simple faith that government must deal as justly with the poor as with the rich. . . . In short, General Jackson represented the best which the new West could breed in the way of capable and self-reliant individualism, and the backwoodsmen loved him for the enemies he made, and backed him loudly in his fight against the aristocratic East."[25]

As Jackson ran for president, these aristocratic forces were adept at using the press in attempts to savage his reputation and persistently question the honor of his wife. When he first ran for President in 1824, the *London Times* sardonically observed, "The journals in the interest of the President [John Quincy Adams] teem with the most violent abuse of General Jackson. They prove too much; for if Jackson has been guilty of one half of the atrocities ascribed, it should not be a question of whether he is to be the next President, but whether he ought not to be hanged. They accuse him of adultery, treason, and repeated murders, and yet, till he pretended to the chief place, he was hailed as the American hero."[26] His wife, Rachel, herself was deeply affected by such calumnies and after he won the election four years later, she died of a sudden heart attack shortly before he took office. For the rest of his own life Jackson believed that her death was caused by these intense assaults on her character.

These forces succeeded in denying Jackson the presidency in 1824 when he received a clear plurality over John Quincy Adams and two other candidates in both the popular and Electoral College votes, causing him to lose decisively to Adams when the election was thrown into the partisan House of Representatives. Undeterred, Jackson and his supporters used this setback to widen his popular base even further as he traveled extensively over the next four years, running on an adamantly populist platform. In 1828 "Jackson won 647,276 popular votes to Adams's 508,064. The number of voters who participated in this election nearly quadrupled the 1824 figure, and of these Jackson took approximately 56 percent—a smashing victory that remained unequaled in the nineteenth century."[27]

For eight years Andrew Jackson dominated American politics, bringing a coarse but refreshing openness to the country's governing process. Founded on intense patriotism and the dignity of the common man, his presidency was notable for two remarkable achievements, both of which reflected not only his courage but also his political acumen and the strength of his core political beliefs. The first involved his passion for ridding the government of policies and practices that unduly favored the aristocracy. The second, which would eventually play itself out on the battlefields of the Civil War, reflected his equally strong passion that the Union of the states was permanent and must never be allowed to dissolve.

On July 10, 1830, Jackson vetoed legislation that renewed the charter of the Second National Bank, knowing full well that it would at least briefly send the nation into financial and political turmoil. Contemporary Americans who are accustomed to seeing a "national bank" on every street corner frequently misunderstand the power that had been given to this one central bank. Nor is it easy in modern days to comprehend the stakes for the American political system that were in play with Jackson's veto. Historian Robert Remini writes that Jackson's veto of the bank charter "was the most important presidential veto in American history."[28] Vernon Louis Parrington went further, calling it "the most courageous act in our political history."[29] The political establishment was firmly against Jackson on the issue, as was two-thirds of the press. Most predicted that he would find a convenient way to avoid the veto. What they failed to understand was that Jackson, in the words of Schlesinger, "cared less for his popularity than for his program."[30]

Why did he feel so strongly when other powerful people did not? The arguments for and against the bank charter were complex, but Jackson's conclusion was simple, concerned with the very soul of a new nation. Whatever its economic merits, the bank as it was legally constructed represented the raw power to intimidate and control a whole nation. Many newspapers feared the prospect of diminished advertising revenues if they failed to support the bank. Powerful politicians worried correctly that they would lose lucrative retainers and personal profit flows if they did so. But Andrew Jackson saw the need to confront a system that threatened to corrupt the state at the hands of a growing aristocracy who were benefiting merely from personal influence in ways that completely eluded the ordinary citizen.

The Second National Bank was in reality a private monopoly, insulated from competition by federal law. It had been given extraordinary powers by a Congress that in the aggregate accepted the notion that government policies might openly favor—and insulate from public scrutiny—the wealthy. Indeed, many members of Congress who supported the bank were also on its payroll through a system of blatant payoffs. One can do no better here than to allow Schlesinger to explain. The bank "served as a repository of the public funds, which it could use for its own banking purposes without payment of interest . . . [It] was not to be taxed by the states and no similar institution was to be chartered by the Congress. . . . It enjoyed a virtual monopoly of the currency and practically complete control over credit and the price level. . . . [Its President Nicholas] Biddle not only suppressed all internal dissent but insisted flatly that the Bank was not accountable to the government or the people. [Biddle had written in 1824 that] 'no officer of the government, from the President downwards, has the least right, the least authority, the least pretence, for interference in the concerns of the bank.' In Biddle's eyes the Bank was thus an independent corporation, on a level with the state, . . . the keystone in the alliance between government and the business community."[31]

Nicholas Biddle, headstrong and self-assured to the point of arrogance, was from a wealthy Philadelphia family. He had powerful allies, including the respected and famed orator Sen. Henry Clay of Kentucky, who was a longtime political adversary of Jackson, and New England political giant Sen. Daniel Webster, who made no secret that the retainer he received from the bank had become "a dependable source of private revenue." Biddle also controlled a passel of effective lobbyists. As they moved the legislation through Congress, Clay famously promised his colleagues that, "should Jackson veto it, I shall veto him!"[32]

Jackson vetoed it, and when they tried to veto him in 1832, he was reelected with 687,502 votes against a combined total of 566,297 from two other opponents, one of whom was Clay. His electoral college majority was even stronger—219 to a combined total of 67 for his opponents, including 11 that South Carolina's electors had cast for a Virginian who had not been on the original ballot. Although these numbers were overwhelming, historians such as Robert Remini nonetheless point out that the issue did indeed hurt Jackson, as he became "the only President in American history whose reelection to a second term registered a decline in the percentage of popular votes."[33] In short, although Clay and Biddle took their best shot, Old Hickory, as with so many other battles in his life, was left bloody but unbowed when the duel was done.

He survived because he took the issue to the people rather than allowing it to remain simply in the press or in the back rooms of old-style politics. And his veto message was perhaps the strongest enunciation of Jacksonian democracy ever captured. As Parrington points out, Jackson "had come to associate aristocracy with the control of the economics of society. He was learning how aristocracies are built up through the instrumentality of the state; and as that lesson sank into his mind his opposition to class favoritism hardened into adamant. He would put a stop to such practices, cost what it might."[34]

Jackson's veto message could well have emanated from a meeting of the Scottish Kirk two hundred years before. Its impact on ordinary Americans was so strong that the Congress did not dare overturn the veto. His summation is memorable and might apply to many aspects of American society today. "Equality of talents, of education or of wealth can not be produced by human institutions. In the full enjoyment of the gifts of Heaven and the fruits of superior industry, economy, and virtue, every man is equally entitled to protection by law; but when the laws undertake to add to these natural and just advantages artificial distinctions . . . to make the rich richer and the potent more powerful, the humble members of our society—the farmers, mechanics and laborers—who have neither the time nor the means of securing favors to themselves, have the right to complain of the injustice of their Government. There are no necessary evils in government. Its evils exist only in its abuses."[35]

The second issue, although notionally over the introduction of legislation to extend tariff protection to industries in the North, pitted Jackson against many of his natural supporters. It was also a harbinger of the coming Civil War, which through the force of his leadership Jackson himself managed to avert. The debate that ensued was no more about a tariff than *Moby-Dick* was a story about a whale. At stake was the very definition of the role of government in modern societies as well as the distribution of powers in the new American federal system. Jackson's political opponent was the legendary John C. Calhoun, another powerful Scots-Irish leader who in many ways represented the flip side of Andrew Jackson's own personal journey. And the reduction in Jackson's popular vote during the election of 1832 probably reflected the price of this essential victory more than it did his veto of the Bank Act.

As the nineteenth century progressed, the Northern and Southern regions of the United States had steadily grown apart, not only in their ethnic and cultural makeup but also in their economic systems. The South, slave-based along its fringes and populated by small farms throughout its center, was thoroughly agrarian. The North had become steadily industrial, marked by heavier immigration patterns and increasingly large urban centers. A series of tariff acts, and particularly one in 1828 that became known as the Tariff of Abominations, had protected the emerging Northern industries from foreign competition by placing steep taxes on the importation of finished products, thus allowing Northern industries to charge more for those products at home. Sectional tensions were increasing as the Southern states felt doubly penalized. First, protection of Northern industries meant that Southern farmers had to pay artificially high prices for the manufactured goods that came out of

Northern markets. Second, they themselves had to sell raw agricultural products in a competitive market both at home and overseas, particularly with respect to the growing cotton trade. The protective tariff, in the words of Schlesinger, "exasperated the Southern planters, who regarded it as a tribute levied upon them by Northern bankers and manufacturers."[36]

Jackson was no fan of tariff legislation, regarding tariffs as the "right arm" of America's emerging "nobility system," whose head had been the bank itself.[37] In early 1832 he fashioned and shepherded through Congress a modified tariff bill that reduced many of the inequities of the 1828 law. But to Calhoun and his followers, this was not enough. Calhoun, who Vernon Parrington described as "the one outstanding political thinker in a period singularly barren and uncreative,"[38] was seizing on the issue in an attempt to completely redefine the relationships between the federal government and the states. The lean, brooding South Carolinian, who had been John Quincy Adams' vice president and had continued in the post during Jackson's first term, had taken a long look at wealth flow and immigration patterns, and had seen that the South's future in an age of pure democracy was bleak. A passionate advocate of the slave system, Calhoun sought to protect the region from future dominance through a political concept he termed "nullification." The premise of this doctrine was that each state should have the power to veto any federal law that it deemed inappropriate. In Calhoun's view, the principle of majority rule at a national level was dangerous to local justice, where a majority of the people in a state or region might strongly, and fairly, disagree with prevailing national majority sentiments.

Calhoun was a formidable opponent. Parrington characterized him in terms of his family origins: "It was a hard, stern race—that Scotch-Irish—little responsive to humanitarian appeal; and Calhoun was harder and sterner than most. He held his emotions in strict subjection to his reason."[39] Although he agreed with Jackson that no government was capable of creating a true equality of con-

ditions among its citizens, Calhoun was Jackson's strongest opponent on the principle that all people are entitled to personal liberty,
especially as Jackson himself was interpreting that concept. No
doubt driven by his adamant support of slavery, Calhoun maintained that liberty, even among free whites, "is a reward to be
earned, not a blessing to be gratuitously lavished on all alike;—a reward reserved for the intelligent, the patriotic, the virtuous and deserving;—and not a boon to be bestowed on a people too ignorant,
degraded and vicious to be capable either of appreciating it or of
enjoying it."[40]

Calhoun had supported Jackson's election in 1828 in the mis-
taken belief that he might be able to control Old Hickory's politics,
but the two had quickly fallen apart. The Yale-educated South
Carolinian was known as an intellectual descendant of John Adams,
both of them believing in "the fundamental principle that property
will rule by reason of its inherent power, and that political justice is
attainable only by a nicely calculated system of checks and bal-
ances, which provides each important group with a defensive
veto."[41] At the same time, in his nullification concept one cannot
help but see the legacy of the Scottish Kirk, and especially of the
Presbyterian nonconformism that evolved during the bitter decades in Ulster. But nonconformism was based on the principle
that the individual had the right to rebel against a policy that he
viewed to be immoral. While one might buy its logic when arguing the inequities of tariff acts, it is difficult to imagine those old
Scottish Calvinists, fearsome though they were, supporting its us-
age when it applied to the continued enslavement of another human being.

And even with the issue of unfair tariffs, Calhoun pushed Jackson too far. Under his leadership, in November 1832, South Carolina adopted an Ordinance of Nullification, "declaring the Tariff
Acts of 1828 and 1832 null and void and forbidding the collection
of duties required by these laws within the state of South Carolina.

Also it warned the federal government that if force were used to coerce the state, South Carolina would secede from the Union."[42]

The issue had been boiling for years, and Jackson was ready for the fight, both politically and literally. He had not backed down from John Sevier, the great war hero of King's Mountain. He had not backed down from Charles Dickinson, even after the best shot in Tennessee had put a bullet near his heart. And he was not going to back down from the fierce brilliance of John C. Calhoun. He quickly positioned a strong federal military force in and around South Carolina, quietly letting it be known that he could have fifty thousand troops inside the state within forty days and another fifty thousand shortly after that. He sent trusted advisers into South Carolina to bolster the support of community leaders who did not agree with Calhoun. He then pushed a bill through Congress that authorized him to use force in South Carolina it if became necessary to enforce the tariff laws.

And finally, as with his veto of the bank charter, Jackson issued a proclamation directly to the people of South Carolina, at the same time circulating its language throughout the country. "The laws of the United States must be executed. I have no discretionary power on the subject. . . . Those who told you that you might peaceably prevent their execution deceived you. . . . Their object is disunion. . . . Disunion by armed force is treason. Are you really ready to incur its guilt?"[43]

As with the veto of the bank charter, Jackson's proclamation stirred up strong emotions throughout the country, serving clear notice to Calhoun and his group that if they continued, they would see war, with wide support even in the South. South Carolina's leadership backed down, at least for the moment. Within a few weeks of Jackson's message, Calhoun resigned from the vice presidency, taking a seat in the Senate, where he would remain his generation's most forceful champion of local and states' rights. But Andrew Jackson had set a clear precedent through his insistence that the Union of the states was inviolable and that if necessary its integrity would be preserved through the use of force. And his eminent military record left no doubt that he would follow through if Calhoun called his bluff.

In 1837 an unprecedented twenty thousand devoted followers traveled to Washington to say good-bye when Jackson yielded his presidency to Martin Van Buren. But those who had opposed him were ecstatic, for although Van Buren was Jackson's personal choice to succeed him, the success of Old Hickory's presidency was measured more by the force of his personality than by the popularity of any specific agenda. Jacksonianism was intensely personal, built around the force of one man's leadership and personality. Its negative legacy was the centralization of power into the hands of lesser men who did not deserve it and who did not wish to use the power of the central government in such an altruistic manner. And the governing class had now learned well the political tactics of mass appeal without needing to adopt the honesty of his personal connection to the common American.

As Parrington put it, in terms that again echo into our own era, "The evils entailed on America by the Jacksonian revolution . . . came in spite of him, not because of him, and they came as a result of the great object lesson in the manipulation of the majority will that his popularity laid bare. . . . The later Whigs . . . had discovered that business has little to fear from a skillfully guided electorate; that quite the safest way, indeed, to reach into the public purse is to do it in the sacred name of the majority will. Perhaps the rarest bit of irony in American history is the later custodianship of democracy by the middle class, who while . . . exploiting the state and outlawing all political theories but their own, denounce all class consciousness as unpatriotic, and agrarian or proletarian programs as undemocratic."[44]

Old Hickory had brought the core values of the Scots-Irish culture to the center of American politics, never losing the confidence of the previously powerless people whom he championed. In the process, he forever changed the face of the American system. Many later presidents would attempt to emulate both his direct approach to the voters and his boldness, with mixed success. The emphasis on—and sometimes an exaggeration of—one's humble origins became a staple of political campaigns. Forceful solutions to crises, both domestic and foreign, appealed to the "Jacksonian" sense of honor and combativeness.

Indeed, a close look at Theodore Roosevelt's more highly celebrated political career could lead one to conclude that the cerebral "TR" had assiduously studied the keys to Andrew Jackson's success and then deliberately followed in Old Hickory's path. Roosevelt's Georgia-born mother was principally of Scots-Irish descent, mixed with a bit of English and Huguenot French, and he frequently praised the contributions of that "bold and hearty race." His self-invented obsession with physical challenge, his flamboyant "trust-busting" battles against powerful corporations, a messianic nationalism characterized by his single-minded pursuit of war with Spain during his time as assistant secretary of the navy, and his obsession with categorizing his own military exploits all hint at what might be called a derivative Jacksonianism.

When Andrew Jackson died in 1845 at the age of seventy-eight, it was still difficult for either critics or supporters to categorize him, for his life had been an uncharted and unguided study in contrasts. The orphaned teenage soldier had literally fought his way to the highest office in the land and had used that office for the common good. The Indian-fighter (and supposed Indian-hater) had rescued an orphaned Indian child from the battlefield and raised him in his own home. The slave-owner (and supposed racist) had defied the aristocrats and welcomed free blacks as soldiers during the defense of New Orleans. The supposedly unsophisticated and hot-tempered backwoods duelist had smashed the power of a monopolistic banking system and then smoothly guided several competing political factions through the nullification debate, in the process both preserving the Union and preventing the outbreak of civil war.

The issues that marked Andrew Jackson's presidency survived him, with sectional rivalry and antagonistic philosophies of governance continuing to divide the country. The "emerging nobility" persisted in its view that property ownership rather than simple suffrage should define political power. The slave states grew more restless in the Union. And with Jackson gone from the helm, there was no Great Captain with the force of personality to keep the ship of state from cracking up against the shoals.

3

The Winds of War

DURING THE FIFTEEN years that followed Andrew Jackson's death the nation was on an unstoppable path to war. Historians have spent entire careers characterizing the divisions that led to this national tragedy, for in truth an astounding mix of emotions and rationales has always fed the whole. The eminent Civil War historian Henry Steele Commager's words of more than fifty years ago still ring true today: "No other war started so many controversies and for no other do they flourish so vigorously. Every step in the conflict, every major political decision, every campaign, almost every battle, has its own proud set of controversies, and of all the military figures only Lee stands above argument and debate."[45]

Recent years, however, have seen a new kind of nastiness emerge in these disputes. Even the venerable Robert E. Lee has taken some vicious hits, as dishonest or misinformed advocates among political interest groups and in academia attempt to twist yesterday's America into a fantasy that might better serve the political issues of today. The greatest disservice on this count has been the attempt by these revisionist politicians and academics to defame the entire Confederate Army in a move that can only be termed the Nazification of the Confederacy. Often cloaked in the argument over the public display of the Confederate battle flag, the syllogism goes something like this: Slavery was evil. The soldiers of the Confederacy fought for a system that wished to preserve it. Therefore they were evil as well, and any attempt to honor their service is a veiled effort to glorify the cause of slavery.

This blatant use of the "race card" in order to inflame their political and academic constituencies is a tired, seemingly endless game that is itself perhaps the greatest legacy of the Civil War's aftermath. But in this case it dishonors hundreds of thousands of men who can defend themselves only through the voices of their descendants. It goes without saying—but unfortunately it must be said—that morality and decency were traits shared by both sides in this war, to an extent that was uncommon in almost any other war America has fought. It was "a curious war," as Commager pointed out, "one in which amenities were preserved." Commager went on to mark the essential truth that, "The men in blue and gray . . . had character. They knew what they were fighting for, as well as men ever know this, and they fought with a courage and tenacity rarely equaled in history. . . . Both peoples subscribed to the same moral values and observed the same standards of conduct. Both were convinced that the cause for which they fought was just—and their descendants still are."[46]

At the same time, the path that led to this war was more complicated than any other in the nation's history. This is one reason that the war and the era that surrounded it is the subject of such constant reinterpretation.

Some see the controversy leading up to the Civil War as a continuation of the old English conflict between King Charles's Cavaliers, whose descendants had been granted large tracts of land in Virginia, and the Puritan forces of Oliver Cromwell, whose religious and intellectual descendants had settled New England. Some see the war, and particularly how it was fought, as going back in time even further, to the great fights between the top-down, plodding Norman English and the bottom-up, rebellious Celtic Scots. Some see it in economic and sectional terms, the result of an in-

evitable split between an increasingly industrial and more populous North and a persistently agrarian, rural South that did not wish
to be economically dominated but had lost its political options.
Some see it in constitutional terms, a war that eventually became
necessary in order to resolve once and for all the issue of whether
the Tenth Amendment allowed a state to secede once it entered
the Union. And some—in modern times, probably most—view it in
a purely moral context, with the slavery issue so compelling in and
of itself that it justified both enormous bloodshed and the conquest
of the Southern territories.

The whole truth was in all of these things mixed together, considered at different levels of importance among differing constituencies, so that even today, more than 140 years after the fact,
intelligent and well-meaning people might still argue over the motivations and conduct of the leaders on both sides. Any effort to
reach a consensus on the war is made even more difficult by the reality that certain portions of these truths burned more brightly than
others in different ethnic and regional groupings, depending on
the nature of their involvement. And no one camp held a monopoly
on strong views or in the sincerity of their beliefs, even though they
were in deep moral disagreement.

Similarly, a historian's point of reference automatically shapes
the focus and priorities of the issues that were in conflict. Political
histories that analyze the drift toward Civil War primarily as a study
of governmental leaders in conflict must ineluctably conclude that
the war was about slavery, because slavery as an institution became
the nexus of every single governmental question that caused the
South eventually to secede. Slavery drove the Southern economy,
at least for its planter elites. The debate over slavery's preservation
or elimination was so defined by geography that it trumped the
Tenth Amendment issue of whether states had reserved the right
to secede when they delegated other specific powers to the federal
government, no matter whether the constitutional arguments in favor of secession were valid or not.[47] And in the buildup to war as

well as its aftermath, positions on the slavery issue caused America's sense of itself as a nation of differing social classes and variegated regions to shift instead into the simple sectionalism of North and South.

During the 1832 tariff debate, Andrew Jackson had left no doubt that he opposed any breakup of the Union. But even though he himself had owned slaves, it is not clear where he would have come down on the issue of slavery as it presented itself in the years just before the Civil War. Arthur Schlesinger hints that Jackson would have turned against slavery because it came to be the driving engine of the Southern elites, positing that the Jacksonian antagonism toward unbridled aristocracies "made it imperative for the radical democracy to combat the slave power with all its will." Indeed, Francis Preston Blair, a Virginia-born Kentuckian who had been a key member of Jackson's Kitchen Cabinet, later became one of Abraham Lincoln's important advisers, and in 1858 his son, Missouri congressman Frank Blair, Jr., argued that the slavery issue should be viewed in terms of class rather than region: "This is no question of North and South. It is a question between those who contend for caste and privilege, and those who neither have nor desire to have privileges beyond their fellows." However, the Jacksonians had steadily lost their influence against the "emerging nobility" after the great man's passing, and "as the conflict deepened, the sectional theory gained status and authority, . . . partly because the class theory had to be soft-pedaled in the interest of national unity, and because many conservative Northerners, fearing the explosive possibilities of the class theory, did their best to destroy it."[48]

This left the moral issue predominant in the public sentiment, with the largely slaveless North pointing its finger southward, and the South as a whole coalescing against what many, regardless of class, viewed to be the calumnies of the North's attacks. In this context it is hardly surprising that in 1862, when Abraham Lincoln first met Harriet Beecher Stowe, the author of Uncle Tom's Cabin, he quipped, "So this is the little lady who made the big war." Her novel, which when published in 1852 was the first ever to sell a million copies, had brought the moral issue of slavery to the forefront in many Northern living rooms, creating a wave of revulsion in the North and a backlash of dozens of books in the South defending the practice.[49]

But what many historians miss—and what those who react so strongly to seeing Confederate battle flags on car bumpers and in the yards of descendants of Confederate veterans do not understand—is that slavery was emphatically not the reason that most individual Southerners fought so long and hard, and at such overwhelming cost. Slavery may have been the catalytic issue from a governmental perspective, and its moral dimensions may have motivated many Northerners, but other factors, some cultural and some historical, brought most of the Confederate soldiers to the battlefield. And that was particularly true among the communities in the Scots-Irish heartland that provided the bulk of the Confederate Army's manpower.

From its very beginning the South was never a monolithic cultural entity, and nothing divided its white population in economic and social terms so clearly as the institution of slavery. Slavery's stronghold at its inception had been in the plantations of Virginia's Tidewater "Cavalier" aristocracy. This early ruling class of well-appointed English immigrants had consciously created the royalist, three-tiered society that dominated Virginia's eastern reaches. But most Scots-Irish had rejected this structure. From the first days that the Ulster Presbyterians were allowed to settle in their quasi-military mountain outposts in exchange for the right to practice a religion that had not been tolerated elsewhere in the colony, they had chosen to live outside of it. This separatism largely continued. As the Scots-Irish settlers moved down into the Carolinas and then westward into the mid-South and the Ohio Valley, the Tidewater aristocracy's plantation system had swung like a wheel along the Atlantic seaboard, then into the coastal areas of the Deep South, and finally upward along the Mississippi River basin, not only bringing new legions of slaves with it, but growing ever more cruel along the way. Thus the core of the South was a large mass of heavily Scots-Irish farms and small communities dominating the center, from which their family networks extended northward into southern Pennsylvania and the Ohio Valley, southward into the fringes of the plantation aristocracy along the waterways, and ever westward toward Colorado, California, and Oregon as the country continued to grow.

Some members of the Scots-Irish ascendancy became large-scale slaveholders in the Carolinas, Georgia, and the Deep South, but the slave system was not a part of the usual Scots-Irish way of life, and in truth was in the hands of a very small percentage of the Southern population. As John Hope Franklin points out in his landmark work *From Slavery To Freedom*, by 1860 Virginia was still the greatest slaveholding state, while regionwide less than 5 percent of the whites in the South owned slaves. Franklin goes on to say that, "Fully three-fourths of the white people of the South had neither slaves nor an immediate economic interest in the maintenance of slavery or the plantation system."[50] Further, of the 385,000 who did own slaves, more than 200,000 had five slaves or less, and "fully 338,000 owners, or 88 percent of all the owners of slaves in 1860, held less than twenty slaves."[51]

More emphatically, Wilbur Cash points out in *The Mind of the South* that the South's ruling class in 1860 "ought actually to include only some four or five thousand of the great planters," and that of those the number who could truly "be reckoned as proper aristocrats came to less than five hundred—and maybe not more than half that figure."[52] Ominously and correctly, Cash goes on to point out that despite the typical white Southerner's tendency to be swept up in the rhetoric and debate of politics, the "only real interest involved in [politics] was that of the planter," and that for the nonslaveholding yeoman, his instinctive support of issues that benefited the slaveholding elites would eventually "bear him outside the orbit of his true interest [and] would swing him headlong, perhaps against his own more sober judgment, into the disaster of the Civil War."[53]

Slavery had flourished rather than dying a natural death after Eli Whitney's invention of the cotton gin in 1792 dramatically improved the ability to process cotton and thus made this crop the staple of the South's economy. As Vernon Parrington points out, "In 1791, three years after Andrew Jackson settled in Nashville, the total export of cotton was only 200,000 pounds. In 1803, it had risen to 40,000,000 pounds, and by 1860 the export for the year was of the value of two hundred millions of dollars. Such figures provide a sufficient explanation of the militant spirit of the slave economy. . . . This peculiar institution, which a generation before was commonly believed to be in the way of natural extinction, had the South by the throat."[54] More properly, it had the Southern elites by the throat.

The slave system had become crueler as it expanded for a number of interconnected reasons that affected not only the slaves but also the entire ethical and socioeconomic structure of white society in the South. In 1808, Congress had outlawed the legal importation of slaves, assuming that slavery itself would eventually disappear as the human pipeline from Africa ran dry. Instead, as cotton became king and the plantation system expanded into what became known as the Black Belt in the Deep South, the slave trade became ruthless and even more dehumanizing. Slave runners—many, as Parrington points out, "respectable New England church members"[55]—made fortunes as the price of human bondage reached a premium. Slaves were further degraded through a busy speculative market, uprooted and moved to new locations for the right price as if they were horses or barley, and in some cases made to endure the practice of forced breeding.

As the institution dehumanized the slaves, so also did it corrupt the Great Captains. Again, Parrington: "The generous culture of Virginia failed to take root in the Black Belt. The development of the plantation system under hired overseers infected the masters, few in numbers and absolute in power, with an exaggerated sense of their own greatness. . . . In the frontier Gulf states the rapid expansion of the plantation system created an aristocracy given to swaggering, *bourgeois* in spirit, arrogant in manners. Republican simplicity was losing vogue and there was much loose talk about the superiority of the classes."[56]

What had been created through the extension of the plantation system into the Deep South and Mississippi River basin was not the idyllic, Tara-like antebellum gentility that one finds in wistful novels such as *Gone With the Wind*, but instead a rapacious system based on a false sense of entitlement that looked condescendingly on white and black alike. This system was separate and apart from the daily lives of most Southern whites and especially those in the mountain and backcountry regions. In many ways it represented the creation of a new "hybrid royalty" of the sort brought to Scotland by the Anglo-Normans who intermarried with the Scottish royal families in the era of William Wallace and Robert the Bruce. Remnants of this exclusivity and arrogance remained for generations after the Civil War and still persist in many parts of the South today. That the Scots-Irish yeomen could live alongside such a system is as much a comment on their long-held indifference to wealth and power as it is on their views on slavery, or even of their own diminishment as a result of the slave system.

And they were clearly diminished by it. Benjamin Franklin had predicted as much nearly a century before, commenting that with the introduction of slavery, "the Poor are by this Means deprived of Employment, while a few Families acquire vast Estates; which they spend on Foreign Luxuries, and educating their Children in the Habits of those Luxuries; the same Income is needed for the Support of one that might have maintain'd 100."[57] Wilbur Cash confirmed this prophecy, pointing out that the plantation system had kept ordinary white families on the poorer lands, "walled them up and locked them in there—had blocked them off from escape

or any considerable economic and social advance as a body . . .
Moreover, having driven these people back there, it thereafter left
them virtually out of account. . . . Worse yet, it concerned itself but
little if at all about making use of them as economic auxiliaries. . . .
Following its own interests alone, it always preferred to buy a great
part of its hay and corn and beef and wool from the North or the
Middle West rather than go to the trouble and expense of opening
up the backcountry properly. Roads, railroads, transportation facilities generally, were provided mainly with regard to the movement
of cotton. . . . The slaveless yeomen . . . were left more or less to
stagnate at a level but a step or two above the pioneers."[58]

This remoteness accentuated the historic independence of the
Scots-Irish culture, and not wholly in ways that would benefit its
people in future generations. The hardscrabble lifestyle of the
backcountry was almost wholly lacking in infrastructure such as
schools and libraries that would allow intellectual growth. Governmental functions were minimal, leaving most problems to be
solved through violent personal confrontations or by a rough system of vigilante justice. And contrary to popular mythology, in the
twenty years before the Civil War, more than 90 percent of those
hanged or burned by lynch mobs in the South were white.[59]

The practice of religion took on a harder tone as well. The
democracy of the Presbyterian Kirk had eliminated both the formal
sacraments and the overarching power of a central church authority, but the transformation of this concept into the Baptist and
Methodist backcountry often found whole congregations in the
hands of half-educated preachers and traveling evangelists who
held every word in the Bible to be absolute and claimed that their
voices echoed the lips of God. This fearsome fundamentalism,
which sowed the seeds of today's Bible Belt, was countered on a
daily basis by the heavy drinking that had come, along with the
stills, from the glens of Ireland and Scotland, and by an equally
long addiction to devilish music, sensual pleasures, constant physical challenge, and an inbred defiance of authority.

As was their tradition, the yeoman farmers of the mountains and the Southern backcountry asked for nothing from the propertied, slaveholding class, and as has been their historic fate, nothing is what they received. Left to their own devices by the ravishing plantation owners who controlled the political process and who themselves were addicted to King Cotton, the backcountry folk had grown even tougher and in some degrees poorer than their ancestors. And they had also grown—well, more than a little bit wild. They could hunt. They could fish. They could drink all night and howl at the moon. If you wanted to get past them you had to fight your way through them. And on Sunday they'd stop for a while and let the preacher remind them that there'd be hell to pay "on the other side."

Economically, except for those who benefited from the slave system, the region had fallen into hard times, even before the Civil War. As David Hackett Fischer points out, "By the mid-nineteenth century, the proportion of farm workers in the north was only 40 percent; in the south it was 84 percent. . . . By 1860 . . . the value of farmland per acre was 2.6 times greater in the north than in the south; the amount of manufacturing capital per capita was nearly four times as great. . . . With only one-third of the white population, the south had nearly two-thirds of its richest men and a large proportion of the very poor. . . . In 1860 seven-eighths of [foreign] immigrants came to the north. . . . In the north, 94 percent of the population was found to be literate by the census of 1860; in the south, barely 54 percent could read and write. Roughly 72 percent of northern children were enrolled in school compared with 35 percent of the same age in the south. The average length of the school year was 135 days in the north and 80 days in the south."[60]

But the debate had turned so lividly along sectional lines that even the poorer whites in the South circled their wagons. A quintessential unease hit the key chord in the Scots-Irish experience. In their eyes, an outside force was not only telling them how to live their lives, but also threatening to force solutions on them if they disagreed. They would solve their own problems, if problems there were. The debate over slavery was becoming a threat to how they perceived their very independence. To the leaders of the North and the ever-emerging West, the issues were more clear-cut: slavery was an evil that needed to be done away with, and during the 1850s the new Republican Party was formed with the elimination of slavery as a key plank in its platform. To the leaders of the South, the Northern-dominated federal system promised in due time to simply outvote their way of life and, through the force of a collective national majority, change their entire existence. John C. Calhoun had predicted as much when he attempted to establish the principle of nullification during the debates over the tariff acts.

In 1856 the Republicans "swept every state in the northern tier from New England to upstate New York, Ohio, Michigan, Wisconsin and Iowa. This pattern of Republican support . . . was a map of greater New England. Every state that voted Republican had been colonized by the descendants of the Puritan migration." In 1860 they nominated Abraham Lincoln, who although born in Kentucky and reared in Illinois was the descendant of New England Puritans and Pennsylvania Quakers. He won "every New England county, most of the northern tier, all but three electoral votes in the middle tier from the Delaware Valley west to the Pacific. And at the same time he lost every electoral vote in the southern states."[61]

The Southern states, led predictably by South Carolina, were prepared for this possibility. On December 20, 1860, the South Carolina legislature voted out an Ordinance of Secession, followed four days later by a Declaration of Causes. That document assailed "the frequent violations of the Constitution of the United States by the Federal Government, and its encroachments on the reserved rights of the States," asserting that the nonslaveholding states "have assumed the right of deciding upon the propriety of our domestic institutions, and have denied the rights of property established in fifteen of the States and recognized by the Constitution; they have denounced as sinful the institution of Slavery." It pointed out that,

"A geographical line has been drawn across the Union, and all the States north of that line have united in the election of a man to the high office of President of the United States whose opinions and purposes are hostile to Slavery." It condemned the Republican Party as having announced in its platform that "a war must be waged against Slavery until it shall cease throughout the United States. The guarantees of the Constitution will then no longer exist; the equal rights of the States will be lost. The Slaveholding States will no longer have the power of self-government." It then concluded that "South Carolina has resumed her position among the nations of the world, as a separate and independent state."[62]

On February 4, 1861, representatives of six Southern states met in Montgomery, Alabama, to organize the government of the Confederacy, estimating that once war began they would number thirteen seceded states—thus, the thirteen stars on the Confederate battle flag, although only eleven states eventually seceded. As this was happening, the Confederacy took over all but four of the federal forts, arsenals, and military posts in the South. The Union Army's Maj. Robert Anderson, commander of the federal forces in Charleston, moved his headquarters to the small island of Fort Sumter and declined to turn the fort over to the Confederates. On April 11, Confederate general Pierre G. T. Beauregard, a native Louisianan, opened fire on Fort Sumter. Anderson, a native Kentuckian married to a Georgian, had been Beauregard's artillery instructor many years before at West Point.[63]

Fort Sumter folded, instructor surrendering to student. With this act of odd familiarity that would be repeated a thousand times over the course of four horrific years, the bloodiest war in American history was on.

4

Attack and Die

Not for fame or reward,
not for place or for rank,
not lured by ambition or goaded by necessity,
but in simple obedience to duty as they understood it,
these men suffered all,
sacrificed all,
dared all,
and died.
*—Inscription on the Confederate Memorial
in Arlington National Cemetery, written by a Confederate veteran
who later became a minister*

THE WAR, AS David Hackett Fischer put it, "was not a contest of equals. In 1861, the Union outnumbered the Confederacy in total population by 2.5 to 1, and in free males of military age by 4.4 to 1. So different had been the pattern of economic growth in the two sections that the north exceeded the south in railroad mileage by 2.4 to 1, in total wealth by 3 to 1, in merchant ships by 9 to 1, in industrial output by 10 to 1. A much smaller proportion of the northern workers were farmers, but the Union outreached the Confederacy in farm acreage by 3 to 1, in livestock by 1.5 to 1, in corn production by 2 to 1, and in wheat production by 4 to 1.

"But the south was superior to the north in the intensity of its warrior ethic."[64]

That warrior ethic, which would carry the outnumbered and outgunned Confederacy a very long way, came from the long traditions of service that had begun so many centuries before in Scotland and the north of Britain. The Confederate battle flag itself was drawn from the St. Andrew's Cross of Scotland, and the unbending spirit of the Southern soldier found its energies in the deeds of the past just as strongly as it looked up to the leaders of the present. These were the direct descendants of William Wallace's loyal followers of five centuries before, Winston Churchill's "hard, unyielding spear men who feared nought [sic] and, once set in position, had to be killed."

As noted Civil War historian Douglas Southall Freeman put it, "Good cheer was not unnatural in the union regiments after July 1863, but its persistence until the autumn of 1864 in most of the Southern forces . . . is a phenomenon of morale. . . . The graycoats laughed at their wagons and their harness, their tatters and their gaping shoes. . . . They laughed their way from Manassas to Appomattox and even through the hospitals. . . . These Confederate soldiers and nurses and citizens of beleaguered towns had one inspiration that twentieth-century America has not credited to them—the vigorous Revolutionary tradition. . . . Many in the ranks, North and South, had seen old soldiers of the Continental Army; thousands had heard the stories of the sacrifices of 1777 and of the hunger and nakedness at Valley Forge. . . . Many another Southern soldier told himself the road was no more stony than the one that had carried his father and his grandfather at last to Yorktown. If independence was to be the reward, patience, good cheer and the tonic of laughter would bring it all the sooner."[65]

But not only the Revolutionary War spirit drove them. As I wrote of the Scots-Irish tradition in my novel *Fields of Fire*, the culture even to this day is viscerally fired by "that one continuous linking that had bound father to son from the first wild resolute angry beaten Celt who tromped into the hills rather than bend a knee to Rome two thousand years ago, who would . . . chew the bark off a tree, fill his belly with wood rather than surrender from starvation and admit defeat to an advancing civilization. That same emotion passing with the blood: a fierce resoluteness that found itself always in a pitch against death, that somehow, over the centuries came to accept the fight as birthright, even as some kind of proof of life."[66]

True to the historic militia concept that itself had evolved from the legacy of clan loyalty, the Confederate Army rose like a sudden wind out of the little towns and scattered farms of a still unconquered wilderness, drawing 750,000 soldiers from a population base, male and female, of only 8 million. By contrast, the Northern states drew 2 million soldiers from a population of 22 million, which also benefited from constant immigration throughout the war, including a steady inflow of hardfighting potato-famine Irishmen. In the South the Great Captains called, as they had at Bannockburn and King's Mountain, and the able-bodied men were quick to answer. This army fought with squirrel rifles and cold steel against a much larger and more modern force. It saw 90 percent of its adult male population serve as soldiers and 70 percent of these become casualties, some 256,000 of them dead, including, astoundingly, 77 of the 425 generals who led them. The North by contrast lost 365,000 soldiers and 47 of its 583 generals, a casualty rate in each case less than half that of the South.[67] The men of the Confederate Army gave every ounce of courage and loyalty to a leadership they trusted and respected, then laid down their arms in an instant—declining to fight a guerrilla war—when that leadership decided that enough was enough. And (we shall see later) they returned to a devastated land and a military occupation, enduring the bitter humiliation of Reconstruction and an economic alienation from the rest of this country that continued for a full century, affecting white and black alike.

History has a way of boiling itself down into generalities. The farther away we move from an event, the more we tend to condense its lessons. In recent decades the reasons for the Civil War have been reduced in the minds of most Americans into a simple sentence or two. The Civil War, we are taught, was about slavery, an institution that at the same time both nurtured and corrupted the South. The Union, we are now told, was on the side of God and the angels, its soldiers dedicated to eliminating this dark stain on the human spirit. The Union Army, we are reminded again and again even in these modern times, marched to a "Battle Hymn," one that still inundates political and patriotic ceremonies.

> *As He died to make men holy*
> *Let us fight to make men free*
> *His truth is marching on . . .*

By implication, the soldiers of the Confederacy were with the forces of darkness and evil, fighting to preserve a system that denigrated the human spirit and made mules out of men. But the truth is, as always, far more turgid, and to understand it one must go to the individual soldier. Why did he fight? What loyalties propelled him? What issues, political and otherwise, demanded that loyalty? Those are the key questions, and as they say in the law, all else is *dicta*. The debates in Washington and in the state capitals during the years leading up to the Civil War were clearly dominated by the issue of slavery, but when one looks at the breakup of the Union and the rallying of both the Confederate and Federal armies, a paradox immediately emerges.

How did all of this confusion present itself inside the mind of a typical young man called into action to fight for the Confederacy? First, the odds are overwhelming that he did not own slaves at all. Was he then merely a pawn, a simple agent of those who did? These were loyal and uncomplicated people, but their history could never mark them as either stupid or passive. Civil War historian Henry Steele Commager commented that, "The war required the subordination of the individual to the mass . . . but both Federals and Confederates indulged their individualism in the army and out, rejected military standards and discipline, selected officers for almost any but military reasons, pursued local and state interest at the expense of the national."[68] Wilbur Cash amplifies this point, reminding us that the Confederate soldiers came from a culture that had produced "the most intense individualism the world has seen since the Italian Renaissance."[69] As Cash points out, "To the end of his service this soldier could not be disciplined. He slouched. He would never learn to salute in the brisk fashion so dear to the hearts of the professors of mass murder. His 'Cap'n' and his 'Gin'ral' were likely to pass his lips with a grin. . . . And down to the final day at Appomattox his officers knew that the way to get him to execute an order without malingering was to flatter and to jest, never to command too brusquely and forthrightly. And yet— and yet—and by virtue of precisely these unsoldierly qualities, he was, as no one will care to deny, one of the world's very finest fighting men."[70]

It is impossible to believe that such men would have continued to fight against unnatural odds—and take casualties beyond the level of virtually any other modern army—simply so that the 5 percent of their population who owned slaves could keep them or because they held to a form of racism so virulent that they would rather die than allow the slaves to leave the plantations. Something deeper was motivating them, something that appealed to their self-interest as well.

Second, the Confederate soldier knew that slave-owners in Delaware, Maryland, Missouri, and Kentucky, the slaveholding states that remained in the Union, were allowed to keep their slaves when the war began. This was also true of West Virginia when it broke off from Virginia in 1862 and became a separate state. The consequence of this reality was that in virtually every major battle of the Civil War, Confederate soldiers who did not own slaves were fighting against a proportion of Union Army soldiers who had not been asked to give theirs up. So, what did this say to the individual soldier about the importance of the slavery issue to President Lincoln and the Union government itself?

Third, this soldier was aware that when President Abraham Lincoln ostensibly ended slavery on January 1, 1863, through the Emancipation Proclamation, his order specifically exempted all the slaves in the North as well as those slaves in areas of the South that had previously been conquered. This included vast stretches of Louisiana and eastern Virginia—ironically, the birthplace of the American slave system.[71] Thus, all the slaves on Union territory as of that date remained slaves for the duration of the war, and the only slaves who were freed by this proclamation were those residing in areas of the South subsequently conquered by the Union Army. It does not take a cynical mind to conclude that President Lincoln, having suffered numerous defeats as well as serious morale problems to this point in the war, needed a mission for his soldiers beyond the original goal of forcing the Southern states to rejoin the Union.

And fourth, the more learned among these Confederate soldiers, like their political leaders, believed strongly that the Constitution was on their side when they chose to dissolve their relations with the Union. This does not imply that America would have been a better place a hundred years on if they had succeeded. Nor does it suggest that the South's leaders might not have decided to end slavery and even rejoin the Union in later years. But the states that had joined the Union after the Revolution considered themselves independent political entities, much like the countries of Europe do today. The Tenth Amendment to the Constitution reserved to the states all rights not specifically granted to the federal government, and in their view the states had thus retained their right to dissolve the federal relationship.

This argument was best articulated by Alexander B. Stephens, vice president of the Confederacy. Vernon Louis Parrington, whose views on this matter were hardly rejected by the intellectual paragons of his time,[72] actually supported the constitutional validity of Stephens's views. Parrington begins by pointing out the greatest irony of the Civil War—that "Love of the Union, and of the Constitution as a guarantee of that Union, was far stronger in the South before the Civil War than in the North."[73] He then summarizes Stephens's argument: "that state government existed prior to the Union, that it was jealously guarded at the making of the Constitution, that it had never been surrendered, and hence was the constitutional order until destroyed by the Civil War."[74]

In a fourteen-hundred-page document that the Illinois-born, Kansas-raised, Harvard-educated Parrington characterized as "wholly convincing," Stephens laid out the South's view that the constitutional compact was terminable.[75] Parrington went on to comment that, "Stephens rightly insisted that slavery was only the immediate *casus belli*. The deeper cause was the antagonistic conceptions of the theory and functions of the political state that emerged from antagonistic economic systems."[76]

Importantly, Parrington laments that Stephens as well as other Southern slaveholders gave no consideration to the argument that slavery as a system was economically ruinous to the poor white.[77] But to tar the sacrifices of the Confederate soldier as simple acts of racism, and reduce the battle flag under which he fought to nothing more than the symbol of a racist heritage, is one of the great blasphemies of our modern age.

Why, then, did he fight?

It might seem odd in these modern times, but the Confederate soldier fought because, on the one hand, in his view he was provoked, intimidated, and ultimately invaded, and, on the other, his leaders had convinced him that this was a war of independence in the same sense as the Revolutionary War. For those who can remove themselves from the slavery issue and examine the traits that characterize the Scots-Irish culture, the unbending ferocity of the Confederate soldier is little more than a continuum. This was not so much a learned response to historical events as it was a cultural approach that had been refined by centuries of similar experiences.

The tendency to resist outside aggression was bred deeply into every heart—and still is today.

Rome conquered Britain and tried to subjugate its people, but the "brave and proud" fell back into the mountains of what later became Cornwall, Wales, and especially Scotland. King Edward marched into Scotland to subjugate its people, but he was resisted and ultimately expelled. The Jacobite Irish and the French laid siege to Derry and tried to starve a people into submission, but as the death toll mounted, those same people, men, women, and children alike, wrote their vow in blood: *No Surrender.* The British sent an expedition into the Appalachian Mountains to punish and lay waste to whole communities for not supporting the Crown, and their predictable reward was to be stalked, surrounded, and slaughtered. And now a federal government, whose leadership and economic systems were dominated by English-American businessmen and intellectuals, was sending armies into the sovereign territory of the Southern states in order to compel them to remain inside a political system that their leaders had told them they had every right to reject.

On this point it is interesting to note that when the South fired on Fort Sumter, beginning the war, there were eight slave states in the Union and only seven in the Confederacy. But when Lincoln called for an invasion of the South, North Carolina, Virginia, Tennessee, and Arkansas left the Union.[78] Even the states with Scots-Irish heritage that remained in the Union reacted to this call with outrage. The governor of Kentucky contemptuously replied that his state would furnish no troops "for the wicked purpose of subduing her sister Southern States."[79] Claiborne Fox Jackson, Missouri's governor, sent a wire claiming that such an idea was "illegal, unconstitutional, and revolutionary in its object, inhuman and diabolical, and cannot be complied with."[80]

Perhaps the best proof of this rather idiosyncratic truth is to examine what happened when it was applied in reverse. At the outset of the Civil War, Kentucky's sympathies were with the South, but when Lincoln guaranteed the continuation of slavery in the Union, the state decided to remain neutral. In the early months of 1861 the governor and both houses of the state legislature announced that Kentucky would defend her borders against invasion by either side.[81] Then on September 4 of that year the Confederates occupied the Mississippi River town of Columbus, Kentucky, in a move actually designed to prevent a Union force under Ulysses S. Grant from moving into the town. Although the Union followed suit by occupying Paducah, forty miles farther north along the Ohio River, the Confederates had moved into Kentucky first, and the political reaction was immediate. On September 11, the Kentucky legislature demanded that the Confederates withdraw. When they had not done so by September 18, Kentucky tossed aside its neutrality, joined the Union, and authorized the creation of a military force to expel the Confederates.[82]

Even the arrival of famed Confederate general Albert Sidney Johnston in mid-September to take over the Army of Tennessee failed to sway most Kentuckians. With the war now on in Kentucky, Johnston pushed his forces along a line in the southern part of the state, reasoning that he would provoke an upsurge of support for the Confederate cause. Johnston's logic was well considered and his credentials were beyond question. A native Kentuckian who had later settled in Texas (and is thus claimed by both as a favored son), at the outset of the Civil War, Johnston was ranked above even Robert E. Lee as the greatest general to align himself with the Confederate cause. Confederate president Jefferson Davis, two years behind Johnston at West Point, idolized him. Mexican War hero (and later president) Zachary Taylor called him the finest soldier he had ever commanded.

Johnston's skills as a combat leader were so valued by the South and so feared in the North that when he decided to leave the Union Army and join the Confederacy, the Union attempted to hold him in confinement in California. His escape and two-thousand-mile journey over the desert to link up with the Confederates is the stuff

of legend, and ended with a train ride from New Orleans to Rich-
mond where thousands cheered his passing along the way. His
death while commanding the Confederate attack at Shiloh in April
1862 turned that battle to the benefit of the Union forces led by another general of Scots-Irish descent, Ulysses S. Grant, and in many
eyes changed the complexion of the entire war in the "Southwest
theater."

Johnston was growing an army from scratch in Tennessee, and
he needed soldiers. He gambled that his personal charisma would
swell the ranks in his native state and possibly even pull Kentucky
into the Confederacy. Indeed, one of the thirteen stars on the Confederate battle flag had been reserved for Kentucky. In the months
before Shiloh, Johnston made his move into southern Kentucky.
But the reaction to his invasion was again the opposite, as many
Kentuckians considered the Confederate presence to be a further
violation of their sovereignty.

Kentucky remained in the Union, and eventually two-thirds of
its soldiers fought for the North. Among these Union soldiers was
one of my great-grandfathers, Asa William Hodges, who enlisted in
Company B, 12th Kentucky Cavalry, on August 22, 1862, and fought
as a sergeant continuously for three years, including at the battles
of Resaca, Lookout Mountain, Missionary Ridge, Kennesaw, and
ultimately, Atlanta. Indeed, the only time his military records show
him away from his unit was when he returned home briefly in 1863
to bury his wife.

Asa Hodges was the great-grandson of Samuel Cochran, who as
a soldier in the Virginia Line during the Revolutionary War had
crossed the Delaware with George Washington, spent the infamous winter at Valley Forge, and fought in many key battles of that
war. A typical Scots-Irish Southerner, he was born in Sumner
County, Tennessee, north of Nashville, where his father's family
had moved from the Blue Ridge Mountain region of southwest Virginia. The family of his mother, Mary Ann Murphy, had migrated to

Sumner County from the mountains of western North Carolina. World War II hero Audie Murphy's family also originated in this region of North Carolina, and given the paucity of traditionally Irish Catholic names in those communities, it is likely that they were collateral kin.

And so Asa Hodges should by all logic have fought for the South. But his farm was near Beaver Dam in Ohio County, just up the road from the town of Bowling Green where Albert Sidney Johnston had sent several regiments. This put Asa Hodges' home flush in the middle of the Confederate lines that extended westward from Bowling Green to Columbus. One can never reconstruct the full story for human motivations, but it is not difficult to assume that Asa Hodges fought against the Confederate Army for the same reason that many Confederates fought against the "Federals"—because they had crossed over from another state and invaded his home.

Or—just as compellingly—one might examine the concept from the perspective of those who probably had never even met a slave, but who fought bravely and well for the Confederacy. As one whose family by this time had been "sown like the apple seeds" along the ridges and hollows of Virginia, Kentucky, and Tennessee, and even into the fat river delta lands just north of Memphis, I could offer up a number of examples. But let us return, just for a while, to the harsh and unforgiving soil of Big Moccasin Gap. My great-great-grandfather David Webb could neither read nor write. The 1880 census, taken when he was sixty-three years old, indicates that he owned no land and that his total net worth in personal property was ten dollars. Although he had four children and was in his mid-forties, David enlisted and served as a private in the Confederate Army. In 1871 at the age of fifty-four he fathered his seventh child—back in Alley Hollow they still like to call this capacity the "Webb drive"—and named the boy Robert Lee Webb. And every generation from that point has followed suit. My great-

grandfather named my grandfather Robert Lee Webb. My grandfather named one son Thomas Lee. My brother became Gary Lee.
And my son is James Robert.

Do we honor slavery? No, we honor courage, as well as loss.
And let us now speak of both.

William John Jewell, my great-great-grandmother's brother, did
not live long enough to father children of his own, so let me claim
him. Another Big Moccasin Gap native who probably had never
seen a slave, Jewell served in Company D of the Davis Rifles of the
37th Regiment, Virginia Infantry, under the leadership of the incomparable Gen. Stonewall Jackson. This regiment was drawn exclusively from Scott, Lee, Russell, and Washington Counties in the
southwest corner of the state. The percentage of mountaineers
who were slaveholders was approximately zero. Many of them were
not even property owners. Few had a desire to leave the Union.
But when Virginia seceded, the mountaineers followed Robert E.
Lee into the Confederate Army.

Official records show that 1,490 men volunteered to join the
37th Regiment and that by the end of the war only 39 were left.
Company D, which was drawn from Scott County, began with 112
men. The records of eight of these cannot be found. Five others
deserted over the years, taking the oath of allegiance to the Union.
Two were transferred to other units. Of the 97 remaining men, 29
were killed, 48 were wounded, 11 were discharged due to disease,
and 31 were captured by the enemy on the battlefield, becoming
prisoners of war. If one adds those numbers up they come to more
than 97, because many of those taken prisoner were already
wounded. A few were wounded more than once, including William
Jewell, who was wounded at Cedar Mountain on August 9, 1862,
wounded again at Sharpsburg (Antietam) on September 17, 1862,
and finally killed in action at Chancellorsville on May 3, 1863.

The end result of all this was that, of the 39 men who stood in
the ranks of the 37th Regiment when General Lee surrendered at
Appomattox—meaning that only 3 percent of the original regiment

survived—none belonged to Company D, which had no soldiers left.[83]

The Davis Rifles were not unique in this fate. Such tragedies were played out repeatedly across the landscape of the South. To my knowledge, no modern army has exceeded the percentage of losses the Confederate Army endured, and only the Scottish regiments in World War I and the Germans in World War II come close. A generation of young men was destroyed. One is reminded of the inscription so often present on the graves of that era: "How many dreams died here?"

The lesson regarding William John Jewell's death, plus the hundreds of thousands of others in this war, is far more complex than those who simplify his service into racial slogans wish to make it. He and his fellow soldiers took an oath and then honored the judgment of their leaders, often at great cost. Intellectual analyses of national policy are subject to constant reevaluation by historians as the decades roll by, but duty is a constant, frozen in the context of the moment it is performed. Duty is action, taken after listening to one's leaders and weighing risk and fear against the powerful draw of obligation to family, community, nation, and the unknown future. We, the progeny who live in that future, were among the intended beneficiaries of those frightful decisions made so long ago. As such, we are also the caretakers of the memory, and the reputation, of those who performed their duty—as they understood it— under circumstances too difficult for us ever to fully comprehend. No one but a fool—or a bigot in their own right—would call on the descendants of those Confederate veterans to forget the sacrifices of those who went before them or argue that they should not be remembered with honor.

And that notion extends to the soldiers of both sides in this peculiar and tragic war. The two great defining characteristics of the Scots-Irish culture—a loyalty to strong leaders and an immediate fierceness when invaded from the outside—brought odd battlefield combinations that sometimes defy logic. The far-western counties of Virginia, which eventually became West Virginia, were heavily Scots-Irish, but they listened to their leaders and went with the Union, as did pockets of eastern Kentucky and even Tennessee. The northern counties of Missouri, which had been heavily settled by Scots-Irish migrations from Virginia and eastern Tennessee, saw many soldiers fight for the Confederacy. The Scots-Irish population of Pennsylvania largely honored its own leaders and provided thousands of soldiers to the Union. Indeed, the war became a jumble, with the raw, recent immigrants of the Irish brigades fighting alongside Scots-Irish Pennsylvanians whose ancestors might have faced theirs at Derry or the Boyne, and against Confederate soldiers whose grandfathers might well have suffered through Valley Forge alongside the ancestors of the Pennsylvanians.

But the bulk of the Confederate Army, including most of its leaders, was Scots-Irish while the bulk of the Union Army and its leadership was not. Even here an irony abounds, however, when one considers that President Lincoln finally found "his general" in the hard-drinking Ulysses S. Grant, who was indeed of Scots-Irish descent. Confederate generals of Scots-Irish descent totally dominated the battlefield. Among others they included the doomed Albert Sidney Johnston; the famed raider Jeb Stuart; the unparalleled Nathan Bedford Forrest, a semiliterate who proved to be a master of maneuver and improvisation, and who defeated every West Point general he faced; and the brilliant Stonewall Jackson, whose death at Chancellorsville—the same battle in which William John Jewell, who served in Jackson's brigade, finally perished—deprived Robert E. Lee of his most adept battlefield innovator. And although Robert E. Lee himself was a scion of Virginia's lowland Cavalier aristocracy, his mother was of Scottish ancestry, and it was widely reported that he was a direct descendant of Robert the Bruce, the victor at Bannockburn.[84]

The end result was that on the battlefield the Confederacy, whose culture had been shaped by the clannish, leader-worshiping, militaristic Scots-Irish, fought a Celtic war while the Union, whose culture had been most affected by intellectual, mercantile English settlers, fought in an entirely different manner. At bottom the Northern army was driven from the top like a machine—plodding, systematic, drawing from a far larger manpower pool and bleeding out the South in a brutal and unending war of attrition. By contrast, the Southern army was a living thing emanating from the spirit of its soldiers—daring, frequently impatient, always outnumbered, often innovative, relying on the unexpected and counting on the boldness of its leaders and the personal loyalties of those who followed. The Northern army was most often run like a business, solving a problem. The Southern army was run like a family, confronting a human crisis.

One learned commentator professed that "Southerners lost the war because they were too Celtic and their opponents were too English."[85] But in actuality the reverse was true. The South lasted for four horrific years with far fewer men, far less equipment, far inferior weapons, and a countryside that was persistently devastated as the Leviathan army worked its way like a steamroller across its landscape. It is fair to say that the Confederate Army endured as long as it did against such enormous odds because it was so wildly and recklessly Celtic that it did not know when to stop fighting. And its opponents pressed steadily on to win, and in its aftermath sowed the seeds for a century of hatred and resistance, because in a sense they were so English that they thought victory on the battlefield was the equivalent of conquering a region—and, more important, a culture.

They were wrong, of course. The end result of this war was not to conquer a culture, although the South as a region would suffer enormously for another seventy years. Instead, the war's horrendous aftermath drove so many people of Scots-Irish descent outward, to the north and west, that their core values became the very spirit of a large portion of working-class America.

PART SIX

Reconstruction. Diaspora. Reeducation?

Daddy was a veteran, a Southern Democrat,
They ought to get a rich man to vote like that.

Somebody told us Wall Street fell,
But we were so poor that we couldn't tell.
Cotton was short and the weeds were tall,
But Mr. Roosevelt was gonna save us all.

Gone, gone with the wind,
There ain't nobody looking back again.

— ALABAMA,
"Song of the South"

1

The Mess the Yankees Made

LITERATURE, DESPITE ITS emotional honesty, often thrives in the realm of imagination, histrionics, and deliberate exaggeration. But there are few lies that one could write about the South that would be any more interesting or compelling than its own odd and haunting truths. More than any other region in America, the South's ethnic base has remained surprisingly constant. Although a continuous outflow of dispossessed Southerners has percolated through the other regions of America, particularly the Midwest, the North-Central factory belt, the Rocky Mountains, and along the Pacific Coast, until very recently only a small trickle of new blood has found its way back in. Thus its history still rings true to its inhabitants as a thing literally alive, not as an academic subject to be studied in order to understand the growth of a nation, but as a vivid reminder of the journey of one's ancestors. As I wrote of the Appalachian Mountain region in my novel *Fields of Fire*, "Jackson's people fought those rocks. Here they struggled still. Those sole places where a man could still walk where great-great-great-grandfather walked, still sleep where he died. Not because they were the first and seized it. Because they were the last and no one wanted it."[1] Or, as Nobel laureate novelist William Faulkner so famously put it, "In the South the past is not dead; it isn't even past."

For more than two hundred years before the Civil War, the
South was a variegated, ever-growing laboratory of truly odd social
experimentation, a land of vast economic extremes, of romanticism
unfazed by primitive reality, a place of clashing cultures whose
barons somehow justified the outright ownership of hundreds of
human beings as Athenian in its dignity as well as biblically proper.
During that war, the region paid its dues to history, losing or scar-
ring virtually a full generation of its young manhood, seeing its
towns and cities besieged and leveled, and being forced through
military occupation to rejoin a political compact that its leaders had
rejected. And for nearly a hundred years after war and occupation,
the South along with former slave states such as Kentucky, West
Virginia, and even parts of Missouri that had not officially joined
the rebellion were denigrated, attacked repeatedly through the instruments of the federal government, and economically colonized
while at the same time their leaders defiantly resisted all pressures
from the outside.

A form of self-protection eventually arrived through the Solid
South's power in the Congress, gained by the sort of bloc voting
now used by ethnic groups such as blacks and Jews, except that in
this case the voting was both regional and ethnic, with the deliberate exclusion of blacks after the turmoil of Reconstruction. Sadly,
this solidarity against external manipulation came with quite an internal bill. For decades, fresh or even divergent opinions were sti-
fled from above, sometimes violently, through the vehicle of a
near-mandatory loyalty to the Democratic Party's powerful monopoly. This control of the Southern political process extended from
the local sheriff all the way to the Congress and the Senate, and resulted in the eventual diminishment not only of blacks but also of
many whites.

Contrary to the usual talk among the nation's intellectual elites
about a troublesome "white trash" fringe that circled a larger middle class, in the South of the late nineteenth and early-to-mid-
twentieth centuries, a significant percentage of whites—one is

tempted to say a plurality—were living in economic conditions no different than most blacks. And, contrary to a great deal of current mythology, much of it fed by Hollywood, the diminishment of blacks has always been less a "redneck" phenomenon than a device for maintaining social and economic control ordered from above at the threat of losing one's place—or job—in the white community. The three-tiered power structure that had begun in Virginia from its earliest colonial days seemed actually to gain new momentum in the war-scarred postbellum South. Even on the eve of World War II, eight states of the old Confederacy still used a poll tax, preventing poorer citizens, white and black, from voting, although in many places blacks were further excluded by a series of cleverly administered "literacy tests" specifically designed to prevent their participation.

But before this admitted overreaction by the region's white leadership came the unreasoned and ill-advised onslaught from the North that lit the fires of a permanent and vitriolic resentment.

The legacy of the years immediately following the Civil War is so divisive that it comprises a vast Rorschach test for anyone attempting to neatly assign blame or responsibility for the racial and sectional animosities that followed. The amorphous inkblot that all are asked to interpret is the plight of millions of former slaves who, in abrupt fashion, needed assistance in their voyage toward full freedom. In a nutshell, the victorious Northerners who came south with the military and Reconstruction government viewed the moral justification for the war purely in terms of empowering those who had been enslaved. This goal absorbed their postwar energies above all others, often at the deliberate expense of the "rebels" who had attempted to secede and who in their view had brought such blood and chaos to the country. Not surprisingly their intended and frequent targets, the Southern whites, saw instead a military occupation and the deliberate vilification of their leaders, and also the cynical manipulation of illiterate and pliable former slaves as a weapon to politically destabilize the region.

In the middle, as they would be for more than a hundred years, were the blacks themselves. And by virtue of a whole passel of Northern policies that on the one hand were filled with retribution and on the other ended in halfhearted resignation, they were doomed. As Wilbur Cash put it, "Had there been no Reconstruction the result would have been unhappy. . . . But mark how the Yankee was heaping up the odds. In his manipulation of the unfortunate black man he was of course generating a terrible new hatred for him. Worse, he was inevitably extending this hate to the quarter where there had been no hate before: to the master class."[2]

And the yeomen would stand by their Captains. Again, Cash: "Reconstruction was, for our purposes, simply an extension of [the] War. . . . During those thirty years the South was like nothing so much as a veteran army." But the South itself had come together and was in its emotions a different place than during those years before the war. "If in that long-ago, already half-fabulous time before rebellion roared at Sumter, this South they had cheered had still perhaps seemed to them a little nebulous, it was not so any longer. . . . Four years of fighting for the preservation of their world and their heritage, four years of measuring themselves against the Yankee in the intimate and searching contact of battle, had left these Southerners far more self-conscious than they had been before, far more aware of their differences and of the line which divided what was Southern from what was not."[3]

To the amazement—and the continual consternation—of the outside forces that came south to reap the benefits of conquest and to "reconstruct" the basis of its society, during more than a decade of military occupation and radical political policies, very few whites in the region broke ranks. The warrior aristocracy whose roots were in the long-ago lowlands of Scotland was still in place in the South of the late 1800s. Indeed, the trampled South would surprise the nation with the number of soldiers it provided to the otherwise hated Yankee Blue when war broke out against Spain in 1898. The Scots-Irish culture was resilient, while for better or for worse its core values remained constant. It had hardened and adapted to the changes brought about by long journeys to Ireland, to the Appalachian Mountains, and to all the westward destinations where the informal family ties had melded into an interlocking network in what appeared to be a chaotic wilderness, until its mores had become the very backbone of the South. The Civil War had only strengthened these links of "Celtic kinship," galvanizing them with remembered acts of courage and horrendous loss. If in 1861 a soldier had marched off to battle remembering the sacrifices of Londonderry, Valley Forge, King's Mountain, New Orleans, and the Indian wars, by 1865 he and his extended family—a kinship that stretched throughout the region—knew that no army in modern history had fought harder and at such cost as his own. And in their view, during Reconstruction every piece of the fabric of their existence was still under attack.

The North, under the umbrella of the Republican Party, did indeed come south to free the slaves and improve their lot. But many of its soldiers, government hacks, and businessmen also came for more sinister reasons; to celebrate their conquest, to exact revenge for the war, and to sink their capital assets deeply and permanently inside a devastated economy. David Hackett Fischer mentions that the Civil War "radically transformed northern attitudes toward southern folkways. As casualty lists grew longer northern aims changed from an intention merely to resist the expansion of southern culture to a determination to transform it. As this attitude spread through the northern states the Civil War became a cultural revolution. . . . Radical Reconstruction was an attempt to impose by force the cultures of New England and the midlands upon the coastal and highland south."[4]

And thus the goals of Reconstruction, involving far more than bringing new peace to a nation whose heart had been torn in two by war, became a matter of perspective. To the typical Scots-Irish Southerner, this attempt to impose the culture of New England was little different than the perpetual English invasions of Scotland

or the Anglican attempts at political hegemony in Ulster. The
Northern dominance of all manner of economic systems brought
by Reconstruction laws and policies could not be stopped by the
South's defeated leaders, and in many cases was not even understood by the average Southern yeoman. But assaults on personal
dignity and an attempt to change their way of life were, as always in
this culture, a different thing.

For the most well-intentioned advocates of eliminating slavery,
Reconstruction involved grand ideals, and the cold reality that in
the short term, true equality for former slaves could only be accomplished by the heavy hand of outside force. The clearest and most
honest voice on their behalf came from former slave and noted
abolitionist Frederick Douglass, perhaps the most famous African-
American of the nineteenth century. In 1866, Douglass was calling
for a Reconstructive effort "to bring under Federal authority States
into which no loyal man from the North may safely enter, and
to bring men into the national councils who . . . do not even con-
ceal their deadly hate of the country that conquered them . . .
Slavery . . . today is so strong that it could exist, not only without
law, but even against law. Custom, manners, morals, religion, are all
on its side everywhere in the South. . . . The people . . . want a reconstruction such as will protect loyal men, black and white, in
their persons and property. . . . The plain, common-sense way of
doing this work is simply to establish in the South one law, one government, one administration of justice, one condition to the exercise of the elective franchise, for men of all races and colors alike."[5]

But even Abraham Lincoln himself had favored a gradual
emancipation, with financial compensation given to former slave
owners,[6] while the Reconstruction government attempted to accomplish the new world they envisioned through immediate assimilation and outright confiscation. The result was a predictably fierce
resistance, followed by failure and, ultimately, retribution. By the
end of Reconstruction, Douglass was writing, "You say you have
emancipated us. You have; and I thank you for it. But what is your

emancipation? . . . When you turned us loose, you gave us no acres. You turned us loose to the sky, to the storm, to the whirlwind, and, worst of all, you turned us loose to the wrath of our infuriated masters."[7]

The backlash became inevitable because the pressure from the North was openly hateful, infuriating the whites, and yet at the same time temporary, abandoning the blacks as the Northern occupiers went home without ever having broken the will of those they had conquered. During their stay, the occupation and Reconstruction governments did exact a heavy price in the face of this resistance. These governments were more than military; they had attempted to take over every point of control inside Southern society, from the courts to the educational system to the economy itself. Again, Cash: "For ten years the courts of the South were in such hands that no loyal white man could hope to find justice in them as against any Negro or any white-creature of the Yankee policy. . . . The level of education fell tragically in these decades. Actual illiteracy increased among the millions. But what was worse was that the state universities ceased in effect to exist for loyal whites in the Thorough period and went for long years thereafter with empty halls and skeleton facilities. . . . If the leadership of the Old South in its palmiest days had too often been only half-educated, even by American standards, the leadership of the land in 1890 would be scarcely better instructed and scarcely less simple in outlook than that of the first generation to emerge from the frontier."[8]

And worse. Rights of citizenship were denied many former Confederates, including a provision in the Fourteenth Amendment to the Constitution, which in one passage famously directed that "No State shall make or enforce any law which shall abridge the privileges or immunities of citizens of the United States," while in its very next section it denied many former Confederates the right to vote or hold public office. Since they were labeled rebels and "insurrectionists," Confederate veterans were not allowed federal benefits for their wartime service, reinforcing the concept of states' rights as local governments did their best to assist the legions of men who had become disabled during the war. Tales are rife from this period of the Northern occupiers actively encouraging public ridicule of and personal attacks upon former Confederate soldiers by freed slaves. Predictably, such actions were met with brutal retaliatory attacks in the dead of night designed to intimidate both the hated Yankees and the African-American instruments of their revenge.

Violence in defense of one's honor had always been the moniker of this culture, and the region now exploded with it. At the eventual but then unknown price of a continuing inequality on the inside—among both whites and blacks—the hard people in the mountains and the backcountry again locked their elbows against the invaders, the occupiers, the political reeducators who this time around called themselves Radical Reconstructionists, the philosophical fairies, the carpetbagger businesspeople with their grand plans and special deals, the ridiculers and the laughers, the moralists, and especially the scalawags from their own midst who would genuflect to the altar of Yankee power in order to live in a better house and make an extra dollar. Most of those who came south eventually left, although they did so with their ownership of the Southern economy firmly in place so that their businesses could be controlled from outside the region, thereby sucking generations of profits out of the South and into their own communities. But those who had cooperated with them and the recently freed slaves who had benefited from their presence would reap the whirlwind of their arrogance.

This last phenomenon—revenge on the powerless—had no historical precedent among the Scots-Irish, no real basis in the now-ancient teachings of the Kirk, and the decades of retaliation against those of African descent would prove to be a monstrous mousetrap that cracked their own necks as well. With a combination of cynicism and romanticism, the Northern occupiers had freely used their treatment of the former slaves as a cudgel to again and again extract a form of retaliation against their Civil War enemies. And now the white people of the South, urged on and even directed by their leaders—claiming to be the spiritual descendants of the vaunted Great Captains whom their traditions had forever taught them to respect and obey—took their vengeance on the beneficiaries of Yankee power, the very symbols of their own humiliation.

The motivating force behind this massive retribution was the rawest form of power mixed at the top with a bit of nostalgia. These were no longer the Great Captains of old, leading an ascendant culture out of the wilderness into the Promised Land. They had their dignity and their bearing, but many were at bottom reacting rather than leading, trying to re-create what they perceived to have been an idyllic antebellum existence that the war and outside intervention had destroyed—and to regain their financial status. Others were awash in an overwhelming confusion that the war and its aftermath had created, particularly when it came to defining the social and legal status of millions of former slaves who suddenly were looking into their eyes as equals. Instead of hope, inside the region the South's leadership was now itself running on resentment and galvanizing the white yeomanry by uniting them against the Yankee on the outside and the black family down the road. Loyalty could be expected and even demanded because, at bottom, it was perceived that both of these groups somehow threatened all that had been fought for—the validity of the South.

The near-mandatory hatred of those from the outside, either geographically or ethnically, would result in the stifling of all internal dissent as the postwar leadership unified the body politic to fight the Yankee in the only way the region could—through absolute political unity. There could be no such cohesion if the dirt-poor white farmer came up with a new idea that went against the grain of what his Democratic, quasi-military leaders had ordained. And there certainly would be no unity if the black man were once again bringing back the despised Republicans, even to positions of local power.

And the small bone that they could throw to their increasingly more humble dirt-farmer followers was that, no matter how poor one became, when he went into town at least he could drink out of a "Whites Only" water fountain, use a "Whites Only" urinal, and when traveling could sit in a "Whites Only" railroad car.

This is not to imply that racial animosities ran deep everywhere or that other approaches were not explored. On a personal level there was then, and there still remains today, an evolved compatibility between whites and blacks in the South that is purer and more honest than in any other region of the country, and this closeness grew most profoundly after slavery ended. As Wilbur Cash pointed out, over the generations in the South, "Negro entered into white man as profoundly as white man entered into Negro— subtly influencing every gesture, every word, every emotion and idea, every attitude."[9] And as I mentioned to a gathering of Confederate descendants in a speech at the Confederate War Memorial in 1990, "Americans of African ancestry are the people with whom our history in this country most closely intertwines, whose struggles in an odd but compelling way most resemble our own, and whose rights as full citizens we above all should celebrate and insist upon."

Although whites believed emphatically in racial separation, the true battle lines for most people during this era and also later were not personal so much as they were political and economic. My late father summed up this distinction rather neatly when I was a child: *In the South they didn't care how close the black folks got, so long as they didn't get too rich or too powerful. In the North they never cared how rich or powerful blacks got, so long as they didn't get too close.* As the years following Reconstruction went by, jobs became even scarcer and farms smaller, subdivided among descendants as opportunities for growth and expansion bypassed the region. The thin veneer of white leadership in the South knew full well that as long as poor whites and poor blacks were blaming each other for their misery, the prospects were small that they would join together and address their mutual plight along class, rather than racial, lines.

If evidence of this tendency were needed, one could find it in the way the South's white leadership put down the Populist movement of the late 1800s. The movement, an outgrowth of a national agrarian revolt that had its origins in the Midwest, was based on the essentially Jacksonian principles that "society was to be judged not by its apex but by its base. The quality of life of the masses was the index by which to measure social improvement."[10] Its political basis was the belief, again Jacksonian in its undertones, that existing law in America had become class law, a disguise that allowed certain privileges to flow to a few dominant groups at the expense of the many. Although an acute agricultural crisis had kick-started the movement, it is not difficult to find ancient glimmers of the Scottish Kirk in the rhetoric and style of its leaders. The Scots-Irish migrations through Pennsylvania and the Ohio Valley and into the Great Midwest had left their mark on governing bodies there. Their insistent, bottom-up style of democracy was well represented in the agrarian revolt of the Granger movement in the late 1870s, the Farmers' Alliance of the 1880s, and finally the Populist Party itself. Not only that, but Jackson himself had planted the seeds of "radical democracy" in the North as well as the South, among his chosen political base of "farmers, mechanics and laborers" who rallied under his leadership.

The aim of the Populists was to displace the Democratic Party as the principal national party in competition with the dominant Republicans. Had they succeeded in the South, they well may have done that. And had the leadership of the South been less concerned about preserving the hierarchical pattern of the old slave system and more attuned to the traditional Jacksonian principles of the Scots-Irish culture, the Populists would have made serious and perhaps permanent inroads into that region.

The Populist platform was extreme for the times, although not in its entirety outlandish. Among other things it called for abolishing the national banks (an issue that echoed of Andrew Jackson), electing senators by direct vote (achieved after the party's demise by the Seventeenth Amendment to the Constitution in 1913), a graduated income tax (largely achieved by the Sixteenth Amendment to the Constitution, also in 1913), civil service reform (an issue that Theodore Roosevelt used to his political advantage), an eight-hour workday (modern America should hardly complain about this one), and government ownership of all forms of transportation and communication. Its principal goal was the full democratization of both the economy and the social classes in an effort to aid the advancement of the underprivileged and those who were submerged below the waterline of normal governmental interests.

James Baird Weaver, the Populist candidate for president in 1892, received more than a million votes and carried six western states. An Ohio-born Methodist who reflected the Scots-Irish migration pattern to the Ohio Valley and beyond, Weaver's "Call to Action" during that campaign resonated with language that reflected the traditional Jacksonian hatred of government-sponsored plundering. "If the master builders of our civilization one hundred years ago had been told that at the end of a single century, American society would present such melancholy contrasts of wealth and poverty, of individual happiness and widespread infelicity as are to be found today throughout the Republic, the person making the unwelcome prediction would have been looked upon as a misanthropist and his loyalty to Democratic institutions would have been seriously called in question. But there is a vast difference between the generation which made the heroic struggle for Self-Government in colonial days, and the third generation which is now engaged in a mad rush for wealth."[11]

In the South, many Populist leaders proposed full political justice for blacks—not in retribution against other whites, as had been the case with many Yankees during the Reconstruction era, but as a matter of pure equity, advancing the notion that political and economic democracy were one and the same.[12] While never advocating full social equality or racial integration, the Populist leaders in the South were still well ahead of the nation and their traditional regional leaders on the issue of race. Thomas Watson, a Populist elected to the House of Representatives from Georgia, dared to utter the unspeakable in 1892 when he wrote, "Why should the colored man always be taught that the white man of his neighborhood hates him, while a Northern man, who taxes every rag on his back, loves him? . . . [T]he crushing burdens which now oppress both races of the South will cause each to make an effort to cast them off. They will see a similarity of cause and a similarity of remedy. They will recognize that each should help the other in the work of repealing bad laws and enacting good ones. They will become political allies, and neither can injure the other without weakening both."[13] After the failure of the Populist movement, Watson later recanted on many of these positions, possibly because he had changed his mind, but more likely because he may have had to survive in the world brought on by the backlash against the movement itself.

The retaliation against those who had associated with this movement in the South was real and overwhelming. Rather than embracing a solution that might have provided a formula for rejuvenation, Democratic Party leaders obliterated the Populist movement with a determined assault. These latter-day hybrid aristocrats saw in the Populists not only a threat to the existing order, but also the possibility that the Democratic Party's carefully constructed hegemony could quickly collapse. And in that fear was what Wilbur Cash called "the fateful lesson of Populism. To attempt to carry out a tangible program in their behalf would inevitably be to raise class conflict, and to raise class conflict would inevitably be to split the Democratic Party into irreconcilable factions. And that, again, would be to threaten the Proto-Dorian front and lay the way open to the return of the Negro in politics."[14]

But not only the "Negro"—such a result would also have freed the less-advantaged white from the bonds of his obligatory loyalty to the latter-day Great Captains. And so any white man who dared support the Populist Party was branded as a "nigger lover." Black lynching gained fresh momentum, as did the hard-core separatist Jim Crow laws that carried on well into the twentieth century, just to make sure everyone understood the point. After the Democrat hierarchy was done with them, to be a Populist in the South was hardly better than supporting a Republican. And to be a Republican was just short of committing actionable treason. These implicit but very real demands for absolute loyalty to the Democrats became an unalterable fact of life in the South. They remained so strong that even in 1977 when I began working for Congressman John Paul Hammerschmidt, the first Republican congressman from Arkansas since Reconstruction, one of my favorite great aunts, who when I was young had doted on me, would no longer even let me inside her house.

As Populism was failing in the South, the rest of the country was opening up on other fronts and changing dramatically. Between 1890 and 1910 a new wave of immigration, principally from Ireland, Italy, Germany, Scandinavia, and Eastern Europe, poured into the ports of Boston, New York, Philadelphia, and Baltimore, rarely reaching any part of the South as it moved westward. Millions of new Americans filled the great, old cities along the East Coast and fed workers into the factory towns of Pennsylvania, the Northern cities in Ohio, Indiana, and Illinois, and the automobile assembly lines of Detroit. America began to change, and those Southerners who wished to change with it found it necessary to leave their homes.

The South itself remained frozen in its own time and cultural dimension, ever more isolated, until it was as if it were another country altogether. Also, with this new growth in the factory belt and the continuing expansion of the nation toward the far northwest, the South largely became irrelevant to the nation's growth. The Northern elites had already accomplished an economic takeover of the region. Unable to break its political or cultural spine, they simply lost interest in the rest of it. And the South, still reeling from war and Reconstruction and still, quite frankly, xenophobic, continued to spiral further downward.

The Appalachian Mountain settlements that had provided the springboard of Scots-Irish migrations into the heartland suffered far more isolation than the rest of the South. Even such basic American amenities as electricity did not reach many parts of the region until well after World War II. In an odd twist, this isolation actually created an even sturdier self-sufficiency among the Southern mountaineer than that which belonged to his rough-hewn ancestors. As Wilbur Cash so eloquently wrote, "Mured up in his Appalachian fastness, with no roads to the outside world save giddy red gullies, untouched by the railroad until the twentieth century was already in the offing, this mountaineer had almost literally stood still for more than a hundred years. He no longer wore the coonskin cap of his fathers . . . [but] no other such individualist was left in America—or on earth."[15]

When the roads and railroads did come, the people of Appalachia greeted them with mixed reviews, for it was largely Yankee interest in timber and especially coal that caused them to be built. The ever-hungry industrialists had discovered that West Virginia, eastern Kentucky, and southwest Virginia sat atop one huge vein of coal. And so the rape began. The people from the outside showed up with complicated contracts that the small-scale cattle raisers and tobacco farmers could not fully understand, asking for "rights" to mineral deposits they could not see, and soon they were treated to a sundering of their own earth as the mining companies ripped apart their way of life, so that after a time the only option was to go down into the hole and bring the Man his coal, or starve. The Man got his coal, and the profits it brought when he shipped it out. They got their wages, black lung, and the desecration of their land. Oil made the Middle East rich. Coal made this part of Appalachia a poverty-stricken basket case while the rest of the mountain region remained mired in isolation.

By the turn of the century, swarms of mountaineers had begun departing their long-held hamlets and hollows, pouring east into the mill towns of North and South Carolina or westward into the farmlands of Ohio, Indiana, Illinois, Missouri, Iowa, Kansas, and beyond. My great-grandfather left southwest Virginia for eastern Kentucky, in his later years bringing his family to Missouri, where they worked their way across the state year by year as tenant farmers and finally settled on its western edge. Struck with the wanderlust that so characterizes the Scots-Irish culture, James T. Webb then headed south to Texas, where he was soon killed in a logging accident. My grandfather Robert Lee Webb, born in Kentucky, tried Colorado for a while and then returned to Missouri, where he married a woman descended from three men who had fought brilliantly at King's Mountain and another who had fought at Cowpens. Mary Smith's family, made up also of Condleys, Lains, Millers, and McKnights, had migrated from the mountains of eastern Tennessee and Virginia into the rich farmlands of Scotland County in Missouri's northeastern corner.

This sort of exodus was repeated countless times. People became the South's most important export, whole families again departing, bringing their traditions with them, fueled by "the itch" to roam and by the failed political and economic structure they were forced to leave behind. By 1920, nearly 3 million people born in the South were living outside the region.[16] Those who left had brought with them strong backs, an even stronger sense of individualism, zero money, and very few academic skills. And those who stayed behind displayed the same characteristics, although the prospects for a better life continued to be bleak inside a region that was dominated by a small elite and had come to be alternately forgotten or feared by the rest of the country.

2

Fight. Sing. Drink. Pray.

THE STRONG SCOTS-IRISH tradition of soldiering, its unique musical style, and its emphasis on Calvinist theology all continued,
both in the mountain and backland communities of the region and
wherever else they settled.

The warrior ethic has always been the culture's strong suit. The
Scots-Irish emphasis on soldiering builds military leaders with the
same focus and intensity that Talmudic tradition creates legal
scholars. The tendency of this culture's "best and brightest" to
choose a military life actually increased in the wake of the Civil War
for a variety of reasons. First, the most nobly remembered creature
throughout the South and in many border areas such as Indiana,
Ohio, and southern Pennsylvania was the Civil War soldier memorialized by the ever-present statue in the town square. In the South,
despite the travails of Reconstruction and the poverty that followed, the dignity of those soldiers—and of the ancestors who had
preceded them on other battlefields—was the linchpin of regional
pride. And, as always with this culture, wherever it resides, honorable military service remained one of the surest stepping-stones to
respect and even advancement inside the community.

Second, and more subtly, the appointment system to West Point
and Annapolis allowed every member of Congress to send young

men from his district to these elite military academies, thus guaranteeing a steady flow of young Southerners into quality educational systems of the sort not available in the South. Although the actual practice of congressional appointments was heavily tilted toward the more influential families, it nonetheless allowed Southerners to be educated in national schools, and the Scots-Irish influence to continue at the military's highest levels. Military people may have had their regional prides, but the military as an institution lived separate from and was not responsive to normal political bickering. Yankee Republicans by and large controlled national politics and Southern Democrats reigned supreme in regional affairs, but the military traditions that had long preceded these vicious political debates remained in many ways pristine and even above them.

And finally, this long-held tradition did indeed serve the interests of the nation. Southerners and others from the Scots-Irish cultural base were willing soldiers, in both the officer and enlisted ranks, and their style of soldiering was well matched to the American concept of democracy itself. The informal but powerful notion of Celtic kinship had always bred a different type of leader and follower than most other armies. It was built on a seemingly conflicting set of premises, at the same time autocratic and democratic, that had been tested and found valuable for more than a millennium. On the one hand, every soldier's life was viewed as equally valuable, and despite his power to discipline, an officer owed his soldiers a measure of humility in order to be fully respected. On the other, these soldiers galvanized around strong and daring leaders who "led from the front" and who, despite a measure of command informality, would not hesitate to discipline troops when necessary. The very character of the American military, especially in its ground forces, was built around such concepts, and their Celtic origins are one reason that so many descendants of later Irish immigrations also found their way naturally into military careers.

Further, as World War I commenced and the Marine Corps

prepared for extended ground combat for the first time in its history, many Southerners whose families still winced at the notion of their sons wearing the army blue of Yankeedom opted instead for Marine Corps green. This accentuated an earlier trend and reinforced a strong tradition of Scots-Irish and Southern influence on the culture and leadership style of that elite Corps, which continues to this day. Many of the Marine Corps' most hallowed heroes—two among a legion far too numerous to list in detail would include the legendary Lewis B. "Chesty" Puller and combat genius Gen. Raymond Davis, the most highly decorated Marine of the Korean War—have come from the states represented on the Confederate battle flag. So also have a majority of the Marine Corps' commandants since World War I.[17]

During World War I, soldiers from those thirteen states were awarded 38 Medals of Honor out of a total of 118 given in the war, a rate well exceeding their proportion of the overall population despite the regional and other political sensitivities that often attend the awarding of this hallowed medal. These numbers do not include many soldiers from other states, particularly Pennsylvania, Kansas, Ohio, California, and Colorado, whose surnames clearly indicate Scots-Irish heritage.[18] Many forget also that Douglas MacArthur, whose combat record in World War I brought him out of the shadow of an ethnically Scottish father who had won the Medal of Honor for heroism in the Civil War, was also a son of the South. His mother, Pinky Hardy, who had a profound—some would say unnatural—influence on MacArthur well into his fifties, was a native Virginian whose two Confederate veteran brothers refused to attend her wedding because she was marrying a Yankee.[19] The mother of Missouri-born John J. Pershing, the overall military commander of American battle forces, was of Scots-Irish ancestry, her family having moved to Missouri from Kentucky. And the most celebrated heroic act of the war came at the hands of Alvin York, an unassuming corporal from the Tennessee mountains who, during a battle in October 1918, took command of his platoon after its leaders had become casualties. York, who became *Sergeant York* in the famous film about his exploits, led a seven-man assault directly into a German machine gun nest, creating such havoc that in the end all the guns were captured along with four German officers and 128 soldiers who surrendered to the small American force.[20]

In the mountains and the backcountry, the music got even better. And throughout the region the religion became even more fundamentalist.

In August 1927 sisters Sara and Maybelle Carter left the little village of Hiltons, a few miles east of Big Moccasin Gap, for a historic recording session in Bristol, a town twenty-five miles farther east that straddled the Tennessee–Virginia border. At this session, sponsored by the Victor Talking Machine Company, the Carter sisters were joined by another future legend, Mississippi-born Jimmie Rodgers, who in his audition sang, rather appropriately, a song called "The Soldier's Sweetheart." Rodgers later became known not only as the father of country music, but also as the man who first popularized a style called "the white man's blues." Three decades later another Mississippian, Elvis Presley, would ratchet up that style another notch into "blue-eyed soul," mingling his early music directly with "juke joint" African-American rhythms in such songs as "That's All Right Mama," "Mean Woman Blues," and "Lawdy, Miss Clawdy," and bringing it into mainstream rock and roll.

But in 1927 the Bristol recording sessions were not just about music; they represented a leap into the phenomenon of mass audiences. The Victor Talking Machine Company was cutting records, a new phenomenon that, combined with the technology that made radio an accessible luxury, soon exposed the entire nation to the gut-level influence of a musical form that was truly American. For the first time the haunting acoustics and powerful storytelling of ordinary Scots-Irish people reached beyond their mountain hollows and country stores. And if Jimmie Rodgers, "the blue yodeler," became the father of country music, the talented Carter family thereafter claimed the title of First Family.

This music was simple in its verbal structure but emotionally potent in its acoustics and its message. The old Celtic lyrical and instrumental traditions had melded with a deep religiosity in the mountains and backcountry. Much of the music that had evolved during the century of isolation had sprung from church and evangelical settings as a way for an increasingly illiterate population to share the teachings of a Bible that many of them could not read. Other songs reflected life's hard lessons, or the playful and even sly humor of a people who were on the one hand intensely religious but on the other unapologetically wild. From those origins came modern country music. And the wonder of live radio provided country music its principal forum, the Grand Ole Opry. Soon the entire nation was being treated to the deliberately cornball humor of the rural South and its contradictory musical patterns of intricate instrumentals mixed with simple lyrics.

The traditions continued. The Carter family recorded more than three hundred songs between 1927 and 1942, including the classics "Wabash Cannonball," "Wildwood Flower," and "Keep on the Sunny Side," most of them written and arranged by A. P. Carter, Sara's husband. In the late 1940s, Hank Williams, born in a sharecropper's cabin in Alabama, became one of country music's first "bad boys," singing of hard living, cheating hearts, and good-looking women. True to form, Williams died drunk in the backseat of a Cadillac at the age of twenty-nine, on the way to a concert in rural West Virginia. His son, Hank Williams, Jr., would carry on the family tradition of hard living and unapologetic lyrics.

Maybelle Carter's daughters frequently performed with her, and one of them, June, eventually married Johnny Cash, the fabled Man in Black. Cash, in the tradition of a score of great country performers, had lived the life of which he sang, from the turmoil of booze, drugs, and busted marriages to the insistently deep religious feeling that seemed so contradictory to those who did not understand the culture. The Arkansas-born, Scots-Irish Cash also wrote and sang "Forty Shades of Green," one of the most memorable

paeans to Ireland ever written, symbolic of the emotional bonding
of the two formerly warring ethnic strains that had journeyed from
the Emerald Isle to America. Johnny and June Carter Cash assumed a royalty all their own and dominated the hearts of country
music lovers for decades.

As a Greek philosopher once said, life reduces to art, and art reduces to music. And country music, like the Scots-Irish culture itself, has evolved in the public consciousness to the point that it is in
many ways the bedrock of what it means to be American. Indeed, if
one were to look back at the music industry's political message over
the past forty years, one would find few songs outside the realm of
country that are even mildly empathetic to a soldier's plight. The
Vietnam era was inundated with antiwar songs and others that glo-
rified the leaders of the countercultural movement. Country—with
such songs as Kenny Rogers's "Ruby, Don't Take Your Love to
Town," Merle Haggard's "Fighting Side of Me," Glenn Campbell's
"Galveston" (written by Oklahoman Jimmy Webb), Steve Earle's
brilliant "Copperhead Road" and "Johnny Come Lately," David
Ball's "Riding with Private Malone," and the Dixie Chicks' "Traveling Soldier"—has been almost alone in directly capturing the military experience from the lives of those who were called upon to
fight.

Writing from that perspective was natural for many country
singers and songwriters. Military service is central to their heritage,
and their brothers, fathers, and friends are more likely to have
served during wartime than those from any other culture. Country
singers were the first to react musically to the 9/11 terrorist attacks,
notably Alan Jackson with "Where Were You?" and Toby Keith
with "Courtesy of the Red, White and Blue," which began with a
tribute to his father's army service. And the most moving popular
song of the 2003 Iraq war, "Love Me When I'm Gone," was written
and sung by Three Doors Down, a Mississippi group.

Other powerfully creative American musical forms swirl around country music, and its own styles frequently change and adapt. But when country music changes, it does so slowly, always sensitive to the people and traditions from whence it sprang. And just as the culture itself has quietly infused its power on the national mind-set a person and a family at a time, so has the music reached far beyond its original audience, a listener at a time. Despite the pervasive hype from other musical forms, in today's America there are more radio stations playing country music than any other format. In 2002 there were almost twice as many country music stations (2,139) than the next two formats combined, 1,167 with a news/talk format, and 1,136 playing adult contemporary music. Surveys indicate that country music radio reaches more adults than any other format, and in 2001 five of the ten most-listened-to singers in the United States were country artists: Faith Hill (1), Tim McGraw (3), George Strait (6), Alan Jackson (7), and Garth Brooks (9). Country music stations currently rank number one or number two in 27 of America's top 100 markets, including such seemingly unlikely places as Akron, Ohio; Albany, New York; Fort Myers/Naples, Florida; Riverside/San Bernardino, California; Seattle/Tacoma, Washington; and Indianapolis, Indiana.[21]

This phenomenal success was not predictable eighty years ago. And when it did come, it would contrast, as always, with the serious side of the Scots-Irish culture, the straitlaced fire and brimstone of its religious leadership that over the generations gave birth to America's deeply conservative Bible Belt.

In the post-Reconstruction years, as the South became more isolated and even less educated, many of its religious leaders took Calvinist doctrine into the realm of an extreme, literal fundamentalism. Parishioners were taught, and warned, that every word of the Bible, despite its centuries of varying linguistic interpretations and its frequent internal contradictions, was "the Gospel truth." The theological rigidity of many Protestant fundamentalists sometimes dovetailed with the equally strong intolerance of the Democratic Party's political hegemony, reinforcing the regional taboo against dissent of any kind and galvanizing mistrust against outsiders. This combination of forces, which still exists in muted form in many areas of the South, came to a spectacular and rather embarrassing head in July 1925 at the Rhea County courthouse in the eastern Tennessee mountain town of Dayton. For it was in this remote county halfway between Knoxville and Chattanooga, from which my grandmother Mary Smith's family had migrated to Missouri a generation or two before, that the Scopes "Monkey" trial—also known as the Trial of the Century—was held.

Biblical fundamentalism had been threatened and frequently ridiculed since the 1859 publication of Charles Darwin's *On the Origin of Species*, which argued that mankind had grown from lifeless matter over millions of years, cell by cell, animal by animal, through a natural biological evolution. Such theories were anathema to fundamentalist "creationists" who believed that humans had been directly designed by the hand of God within the past ten thousand years. This confrontation between religious and scientific theories is still unsettled even today, as creationists rationally argue that the living world could not have been fashioned without an "intelligent designer," and that the theory of evolution as presented by the Darwinists still rests on scientific speculation that has yet to be proven.[22]

However, the political debate over the impact of Darwinian theory went well beyond religious views, again pitting the touchstones of Southern culture against what many viewed to be an assault from the outside. As the debate over Darwinism intensified, it became to many "a drama in which science could be pitted against religion, city against rural, and North against South."[23] In short, as Duke University professor Grant Wacker observes, "Evolutionary teaching undermined the authority of the Bible in general. . . . Fundamentalists took note, for example, of the social location where Darwinism arose: among agnostic intellectuals in Britain. . . . Fundamentalists also noticed that evolutionary assumptions flourished among upper-class academic elites, especially in the urban Northeast and Midwest. . . . One thing remained clear for such conservatives: the battle for the schools would serve as a battle for the historically Christian character of American civilization itself. . . . Between 1923 and 1925 four Southern states (Oklahoma, Florida, North Carolina and Texas) tried, with mixed success, to stop the teaching of evolution in the public schools. In the spring of 1925 Tennessee joined the fray by passing the Butler Act . . . [which] made it illegal to 'teach any theory that denies the Story of Divine Creation of man as taught in the Bible, and to teach instead that man has descended from a lower order of animal.'"[24]

And so here it was yet again, the core leaders of the Scots-Irish culture attempting to face down theories tossed at them by English intellectuals and New England elites. But this time they had stumbled into ridicule. After twenty-four-year-old science teacher John Scopes was arrested for violating the Butler Act by rather reluctantly agreeing to teach such a class, the American Civil Liberties Union descended on tiny Dayton, followed by more than a hundred newspapermen from around the world. The trial was on, and despite its remote location, its dimensions were huge: modernity against antiquity, science versus superstition, sophistication against backwoods crudity. Famed defense lawyer Clarence Darrow represented the increasingly uneasy Scopes while the government's case was argued by the aging William Jennings Bryan, a Midwestern Baptist and three-time Democratic nominee for president who died of a heart attack only five days after the trial's completion. The trial would be further memorialized by the 1960 film *Inherit the Wind.* Darrow lost the case, although the Tennessee Supreme Court threw out Scopes's conviction two years later on a legal technicality. But the damage done to Bryan as well as the clownish image of the people of rural Tennessee that resulted from the intense press coverage far transcended the issues of the trial itself.

Most famous among the observers was the irascible and brilliant essayist H. L. Mencken, whose caustic coverage for the *Baltimore Sun* caused an uproar in the South. Mencken began his reporting from Dayton with a typically acidic observation "that the Tennessee anti-evolution law, whatever its wisdom, was at least constitutional—that the yahoos of the State had a clear right to have their progeny taught whatever they chose, and kept secure from whatever knowledge violated their superstitions."[25] But rather than covering the issues of the trial itself, Mencken found himself fascinated instead by the culture that had spawned the law. The Baltimorean who loved to deride the typical American as a "Boobus Americanus" had discovered a whole new crop of people to laugh at. And he also found powerful symbolism in the curious motivations of the aging Bryan's decision to defend this narrow application of the fundamentalist cause at such a late point in his life.

As the trial began, Mencken fired a shot right into the bull's-eye that marked the eternal contradiction of the Scots-Irish culture. "Exactly twelve minutes after I reached the village I was taken in tow by a Christian man and introduced to the favorite tipple of the Cumberland Range: half corn liquor and half Coca-Cola. It seemed a dreadful dose to me, but I found that the Dayton illuminati got it down with gusto, rubbing their tummies and rolling their eyes. . . . They were all hot for [the Old Testament Book of] Genesis, but their faces were far too florid to belong to teetotalers, and when a pretty girl came tripping down the main street, which was often, they reached for the places where their neckties should have been with all the amorous enterprise of movie actors."[26] After filing this dispatch to the *Baltimore Sun*, replete with a tongue-in-cheek description of a spooky, nighttime revival meeting in the nearby mountains, Mencken narrowly escaped being run out of town on a rail.

Mencken's comments on William Jennings Bryan were similarly wicked but at the same time filled with an implicit pity. During the trial, Bryan had even taken the witness stand as an expert on the

Bible, where he was thoroughly humiliated by the more intellectually adept Clarence Darrow, at one point being manipulated into arguing against the notion that man was a mammal. "I am glad I heard it," wrote Mencken, "for otherwise I'd never believe it. There stood the man who had been thrice a candidate for the Presidency of the Republic—there he stood in the glare of the world, uttering stuff that a boy of eight would laugh at. . . . Upon that hook, in truth, Bryan committed suicide, as a legend as well as in the body."[27]

Mencken's final conclusion about Bryan could have served as an observation of the entire political structure that had attempted to decree by law that such a simple and easily debatable theory as Darwinism should be kept from the minds of an entire generation of students while at the same time mandating that the Bible should be taught as science. Although writing about Bryan, Mencken could also have been commenting on the leadership of the South some sixty years after Appomattox. "What moved him, at bottom, was simply hatred of the city men who had laughed at him so long, and brought him at last to so tatterdemalion an estate. He lusted for revenge upon them. He yearned to lead the anthropoid rabble against them, to punish them for their execution upon him by attacking the very vitals of their civilization. He went far beyond the bounds of any merely religious frenzy, however inordinate."[28]

Bryan had his downfall (and his physical demise). The people of Tennessee, and by implication the rest of the South as well, had their ridicule. And much of America grew accustomed to a stylized version of this stubbornly proud but increasingly poverty-stricken people. The barefoot, turnip-devouring creatures of Erskine Caldwell's popular novels such as *Tobacco Road* were only one click away from true reality, but that click moved them in many minds from sympathy to ridicule. The hooded, cross-burning rallies of the Ku Klux Klan, many of whose members were motivated not by illusions of white supremacy so much as by bitterness at being dominated, came to symbolize the mores of an entire region. The gaunt and poverty-stricken emigrants from the South to other regions symbolized to many not the hardships that the people had faced, but an inbred "white trash" cultural inadequacy. Too many Americans could not look past the laughable caricatures to comprehend the brutal and often hopeless state in which the average Southerner, both white and black, existed. And in many parts of America, particularly among the upper crust of academia and the pampered salons of Hollywood, they still do not today.

3

Poor but Proud —
and Stubborn as Hell

AS THE NATION spiraled into the Great Depression following the
stock market crash of October 1929, the South did not regress as
far as other regions for the perverse reason that it had already been
in economic crisis for more than two generations. This did not
mean that the region was freer from trouble than the rest of the
country; in fact, the reverse was true. The years since 1865 had
brought such deep and enduring fault lines that the entire South
had become the North American equivalent of a banana republic,
replete with colonialism from the outside and abuse by a thin patrician class from within. This disparity became ever clearer during
Franklin Roosevelt's presidency, and as the innovative Democrat
reached the midpoint of his second term, he asked the National
Emergency Council to report to him on the economic conditions of
the South. In his letter of transmission, Roosevelt stated his conviction that "the South presents right now the Nation's No. 1 economic problem—the Nation's problem, not merely the South's,"
and wrote bluntly of "the long and ironic history of the despoiling
of this truly American section of the country's population."[29]

On July 25, 1938, the National Emergency Council reported its
findings to the president. The document issued by the council is
one of the most telling—and damning—pieces of evidence ever as-

sembled in illustrating the impact of the long decades of rapacious abuse of the region following the Civil War. Chapter by chapter, issue by issue, the report to the president unmasked the long-term damage caused by the policies of exploitation and retribution that had begun during Reconstruction coupled with the failure of the South's old aristocracy to adapt to modern ways. But the heaviest blame clearly lay with the outside forces that had bought up and effectively colonized the region during the turbulent years after the war.

The report's factual conclusions, while stunning, were no surprise to any thinking Southerner and in some measure validated much of the resentment expressed toward the Yankee and his minions. On the evidence, the South had clearly become an owned place. As the report mentioned, "The public utilities in the South are almost completely controlled by outside interests. All the major railroad systems are owned and controlled elsewhere. Most of the great electric holding company systems . . . are directed, managed and owned by outside interests. Likewise, the transmission and distribution of natural gas, one of the South's great assets, is almost completely in the hands of remote financial institutions. The richest deposits of the iron ore, coal, and limestone . . . are owned or controlled outside the region. . . . Most of the rich deposits of bauxite, from which aluminum is made, are owned or controlled outside the region. Practically all important deposits of zinc ore in the South are owned elsewhere. . . . Over 99 percent of the sulphur produced in the United States comes from Texas and Louisiana. Two extraction companies control the entire output. Both are owned and controlled outside the South."

And there was more. "For mining its mineral wealth and shipping it away . . . the South frequently receives nothing but the low wages of unskilled and semiskilled labor. . . . On the one hand, it is possible for a monopolistic corporation in another region of the country to purchase and leave unused resources in the South which otherwise might be developed in competition with the monopoly.

On the other hand, the large absentee ownership of the South's natural resources and the South's industry makes it possible to influence greatly the manner in which the South is developed and to subordinate that development to other interests outside the South."[30]

Additionally, in policies reminiscent of issues that John C. Calhoun had so vigorously debated a century before, both tariff rates and domestic charges for the use of railroad freight blatantly discriminated against the South, impeding its ability to grow and compete. The rates charged for shipping goods along the nation's railways had for decades been rigged to protect Northern markets from Southern goods. As the report indicated, "The southeastern manufacturer sending goods across the boundary into [the Northeast] is at a relative disadvantage of approximately 39 percent in the charges which he has to pay as compared with the rates for similar shipments entirely within the eastern rate territory. The southwestern manufacturer, with a 75 percent relative disadvantage, is even worse off. . . . The southern producer, attempting to build up a large-scale production on the decreasing cost principle, finds his goods barred from the wider markets in the Nation's most populous area. . . . On the one hand, the freight rates have hampered its industry; on the other hand, our high tariff has subsidized industry in other sections of the country at the expense of the South."[31]

In short, as John C. Calhoun had warned during the debate over tariffs in 1832—a prediction that was lost in the larger debate over slavery—the South had become an economic colony of the North. Further, the years since the Civil War had in many ways legitimized this colonization, tinting it with an odd morality that flowed from the Republican Party's "rescue" of the region from slavery. As historian Arthur M. Schlesinger pointed out, "The technique of 'waving the bloody shirt'—that is, of freeing the slaves again every fourth year—enabled the Republicans long to submerge the fact that they were becoming the party of monopoly and wealth."[32] The South's resources were being plundered and shipped north. Its citizens were reduced to the status of wage laborers. The profits from these enterprises accrued to Northern corporations, where the infrastructure continued to improve both through the direct advantages of individual wealth that went into such things as luxury spending and bank deposits, and indirectly through the larger tax base that allowed better roads, schools, libraries, and social services.

How bad was this drain?

In 1937 the thirteen Southern states had 36 million people, of whom 97.8 percent were native-born—an important statistic, meaning both that the Scots-Irish culture remained predominant among average whites and that none of the South's economic deficiencies were due to assimilating new immigrants from poorer nations. With 28 percent of the country's population, it had, in the words of the report, "only 16 percent of the tangible assets, including factories, machines, and the tools with which people make a living. With more than half the country's farmers, the South has less than a fifth of the farm implements. . . . In 1930 there were nearly twice as many southern farms less than 20 acres in size as in 1880."

Of vital importance, the educational base of the South had been decimated. Illiteracy in the South was almost five times as high as in the North-Central states and more than double the rate in New England and the Middle Atlantic states, despite the recent European immigration into those areas. In addition—and tellingly— "The total endowments of [all] the colleges and universities of the South are less than the combined endowments of Harvard and Yale [alone]. . . . The South must educate one-third of the Nation's children with one-sixth of the Nation's school revenues. . . . In 1936 the Southern States spent an average of $25.11 per child in schools, or about half the average for the country as a whole. . . . At the same time the average school child enrolled in New York State had $141.43 spent on his education."[33]

If there was little money for public education, there was none for much else beyond subsistence, either, and in some cases money had actually disappeared as a medium of exchange. The richest state in the South ranked lower in per capita income than the poorest state outside the region. In 1937 the average annual income in the South was only $314, while the rest of the country averaged $604, nearly twice as much, even in the middle of a depression. An actual majority of the farmers in the South did not own their own land, instead having to operate as tenant farmers or sharecroppers. Tenant farmers averaged $73 for a year's work; sharecroppers varied from $38—a dime a day—to $87, depending on the state. While few black families were on the high end of the economic scale, it would be wrong to assume, as so many social scientists of today immediately do, that they alone dominated the low end. As the report mentioned, "Whites and Negroes have suffered alike. Of the 1,831,000 tenant families in the region, about 66 percent are white [the South's population at this time was 71 percent white]. Approximately half of the sharecroppers are white, living under conditions almost identical with those of Negro sharecroppers."[34]

Tenant farming and sharecropping had evolved from two post–Civil War realities. The first was that many large plantation owners were left with "plenty of land but no capital or labor to work it. Hundreds of thousands of former slaves and impoverished whites were willing to work but had no land. The result was the crop-sharing system, under which the land was worked by men who paid for the privilege with a share of their harvest."[35] The second was the prevalence throughout the South of large tracts of land owned by absentee landlords, some of them from wealthier families that had moved away and others owned by speculators from outside the region. Farmers who lacked the capital to buy their own land "leased" these properties, again usually paying with a percentage of their harvest.

These practices fell even harder on tenant farmers and sharecroppers due to the fragility of the Southern banking system. As the report indicated, "Lacking capital of its own the South has been forced to borrow from outside financiers, who have reaped a rich harvest in the form of interest and dividends. At the same time it

has had to hand over the control of much of its business and industry to investors from wealthier sections. . . . Although the region
contains 28 percent of the country's population, in July 1937, its
banks held less than 11 percent of the Nation's bank deposits. . . .
As a result, the majority of Southern tenant farmers must depend
for credit on their landlords or the 'furnish merchant' who supplies
seed, food, and fertilizer. Their advances have largely replaced currency for a considerable part of the rural population. For security
the landlord or merchant takes a lien on the entire crop, which is
turned over to him immediately after harvest in settlement of the
debt. Usually he keeps the books and fixes the interest rate. Even if
he is fair and does not charge excessive interest, the tenants often
find themselves in debt at the end of the year."[36]

"Even if he is fair" was a very delicate phrase to be put into a report to the president of the United States. And those words were
no doubt carefully chosen, for fairness was not a hallmark of this
system.

In a nutshell, over the decades the national policies of the Republicans had raped the region while the actions of many state and
local Democrats too often were designed to preserve the assets of a
select few at the expense of just about everyone else. Thus, tenant
farmers and sharecroppers, white and black alike—and this means
the majority of the farmers in the South at that time—found themselves to be manipulated and powerless, living under a form of
"double colonialism." First, the entire region had been colonized
from the outside, impoverishing basic infrastructure such as
schools and roads while the banking system and corporate ownership sent revenues from Southern labor to the communities of the
North. And second, in many local areas they and their fellow farmers had become little better than serfs, laboring without hard cash
inside a myriad of petty fiefdoms where the local banker or general
store owner would supply "seed, food, and fertilizer" so that they
could grow a crop, harvest it, and turn it over to the man who had

given them seed and food, in order to live in debt for yet another year.

In White County, Arkansas, my mother grew up inside this system, and it would not be a stretch to say that my grandfather died because of it.

I have seen only two pictures of my grandfather, Birch Hays Hodges, the Kentucky-born son of Civil War soldier Asa William Hodges. The first, taken in his teens during the 1890s, is a tintype showing him with four or five other young students upon his graduation from a teaching "college" in Hartford, Kentucky. He is wearing a suit and tie. His hair is neatly combed above a pair of soft, dark eyes. He is carrying himself, if not with massive self-confidence, certainly with a degree of pride. The second picture was taken in 1936, in front of an unpainted house in Kensett, Arkansas, where, in a few months, after coming in from the fields to take a noontime nap on a corn shuck mattress, he would lie down and die of a stroke. A cloth hat is pulled low over his ears, its brim bent up in front. His worn bib overalls are tucked inside a pair of boots that rise up to his knees. A few chickens peck in the dust at his feet. His gaunt face is baked Indian-brown from the sun. His once-soft eyes have sunk into deep shadows. And he is giving the camera a hard, bitter look that could crack a rock.

My grandfather has always been a mythical figure to me, his tragic, mulelike stubbornness passed on through tales told by my grandmother, mother, and aunts from the time I was old enough to listen to bedtime stories. For although B. H. Hodges died penniless in a shack that lacked electricity, toilets, or running water, if there had ever been an Olympic event called "never give an inch," he would have been world champion. In fact, Georgia-born Tom Petty could have been singing about old B. H. in one of his most popular songs: *"No, I know what's right. I got just one light. In a world that keeps on pushing me around, gonna stand my ground. And I won't back down."*

B. H. Hodges came to Arkansas with a dream. After leaving Kentucky, he had worked for a while in the coal mines near Carbondale, Illinois, then heard that there were diamonds in Arkansas and set out to find them. But Arkansas was hardly South Africa, and in all his years there he never saw a diamond mine. Instead he met my grandmother, Georgia "Frankie" Doyle, fathered eight children, three of whom would die in childhood, argued his way from a chance at teaching school into a migrant's life of picking strawberries and cotton, and finally into a small patch of share-cropped farm. And instead of diamonds, B. H. Hodges found himself a world of trouble.

His problems began when he stood up to a man named A. P. Mills, a local baron who owned both the bank and the general store in Kensett. A. P. had done alright during the hard times, even finding a way to send his son Wilbur to Harvard. Upon his return Wilbur became a local judge, and then a rather famous congressman, both for his expertise in tax law and for his antics with a South American stripper named Fanne Foxe. A. P. Mills was a cheerful man, a true "good old boy" who still would remember my mother by name when she returned to Kensett with her children more than a decade after she had moved away. But he was also very much a creature of his time and place, and my grandfather was not.

As my grandmother, great-aunt, and aunt all told it, my grandfather's sin was to explain to the black folk of Kensett that they were being charged higher interest rates than whites at A. P. Mills's store, thus keeping them in an even worse spiral of debt—and also to suggest to A. P. Mills that this was not a particularly Christian thing to do. My grandfather was pointedly warned that he was causing trouble. By all accounts, my grandfather then told A. P. Mills to go to hell. And A. P. Mills, along with some others who controlled the admittedly sparse purse strings of White County, showed my grandfather that there could be such a thing as hell on earth.

Within a few weeks my grandfather could not get a regular job in White County. He moved back up to the Carbondale coal mines for a while but my grandmother, one of twelve children, got home-sick, so he brought the family back to White County. They began following the crops around the region, picking strawberries when they were in season, picking and chopping other people's cotton, and truck farming. School for my mother and her brother and sisters became intermittent and at times impossible as they picked and chopped alongside the adults.

My grandfather, shunned by the local powers-that-were, never backed down from his beliefs. He had broken a hip badly in a farm accident, and an apparent bone infection eventually caused his skin to permanently split open in that area (I write "apparent" because no doctor treated him), bringing a steady ooze from the joint. My grandmother kept two sets of bandages for the hip, boiling one every day while he wore the other. But this did not keep B. H. from walking six miles round-trip to Searcy several days a week in order to debate others who gathered in the town square to discuss politics. He argued the rights of the black and the poor, and the unfairness of local leaders. And in these spirited debates he was usually, as a wise man once put it, in either a minority or a majority of one.

It was probably the blood infection that killed him. My mother was ten when B. H. Hodges walked inside the house and died. One of her strongest memories of that time was of my grandmother having to steal a few ears of feed corn from a nearby field, silently stripping the kernels off the ears with a knife, and then mixing them with lard in a frying pan to make a dinner. And of brushing her teeth with twigs broken off nearby trees. And of her next-youngest sister dying before her eyes of typhoid fever after the two of them had shared the same drink of stagnant water from a barrel in an old black man's backyard. And of working all night in the woods of absentee farms with two of my great-aunts, secretly cutting and ricking wood on land that belonged to a different class of people in Memphis or maybe New York, hauling it away in a borrowed truck, and delivering it by dawn to fuel the ovens and woodstoves of homes in Searcy and Kensett.

Years of this kind of labor gave my mother arms and shoulders like a weight lifter. When she met my father in Texas at the age of seventeen, his strongest initial reaction was not of her dark-haired, violet-eyed beauty, but that her hands felt as rough as the bark off a tree. And as I myself grew into manhood and progressed through a variety of academic and professional challenges, my mother and grandmother both would seize my hands whenever I first walked into their homes, massaging the palms and feeling their thickness. Whatever else I did in life, it was important to both of them that I never lose my "workingman's hands."

When I became assistant secretary of defense in 1984, the deputy secretary of defense was a protégé of Caspar Weinberger's named William Howard Taft IV. Taft, who had graduated from Yale in 1966 and Harvard Law School in 1969, is the great-grandson of former president and Supreme Court justice William Howard Taft, also of Yale, and the great-great-grandson of one of the founding members of Yale's famous secret society, Skull and Bones. Will Taft and I may as well have grown up on different planets. He had gone to Andover, Yale, and Harvard Law, heading to Nader's Raiders after law school. I had attended seven different public schools in four different states between the sixth and twelfth grades alone as my father moved from one military base to another, then headed off to the Marine Corps and Vietnam after the Naval Academy. But I found Taft likable and proficient despite a certain patrician aloofness. And he did not know it, but he had also inspired me.

During my initial "courtesy call" in Will Taft's office, I noticed that he kept a huge painting of President Taft just behind his desk. And so when I returned to my own office, I called my aunt in Arkansas and asked her to send me the old snapshot of B. H. Hodges standing in his boots and overalls, staring hard back at the world that had tried to stomp him. I had the small photo enlarged as far as technology would allow, which resulted in a four-by-seven-inch black-and-white copy. Then I framed the picture with barn wood. And from that time forward, old B. H. has looked down on whatever desk I happen to be occupying, urging me on but also standing watch over my humility.

Some people have their Skull and Bones. And some people keep their pride, then die of untreated broken bones.

After B. H. Hodges died, my mother's family scattered to the winds, most pouring out of Arkansas into Michigan, Kentucky, Texas, and California, and a few places in between. But it was not simply her father's death that drove them. It was also a war, the innovative policies of a man named Franklin Delano Roosevelt, and the inevitable further migration of a people who were finally deciding to join the exodus into mainstream America. In addition to the 3 million people born in the South who were living in other areas of the country in 1920, another 1.7 million from the states "south of the Potomac and Ohio Rivers and east of the Mississippi" had migrated out of the region during the 1920s, about half of whom were between the ages of fifteen and thirty-five.[37] The 1930s and particularly the 1940s and 1950s would see an even greater escalation of this pace, and also for the first time would see a substantial inmigration initiated primarily by the large number of federal programs and military bases that were either opened up or expanded in the region during the nation's mobilization for World War II.

After World War II the South would begin to resurrect and reshape itself. And those who had left the South and the other areas of the Scots-Irish heartland were also helping to reshape America—not surprisingly, from the bottom up.

4

Hillbilly Highways

THERE ARE A lot of people who do not remember the administration of Franklin Delano Roosevelt with a great deal of fondness. Strong evidence supports the traditional conservative viewpoint that his domestic policies were focused too heavily on centralizing the power of the federal government and creating a quasi-socialist state. It is also undeniable that in foreign affairs Roosevelt persistently maneuvered the nation into World War II, and then threw a monkey wrench into the hard-earned peace by conceding Eastern Europe to Joseph Stalin at the Yalta Conference just before the war ended. Further, this longest-serving president was overtly and unapologetically aristocratic, his attitude toward the poor more the result of a patrician paternalism than an empathetic populism. Roosevelt hardly wanted to eliminate the elites from the American political formula; to the contrary, he was a product of the super-wealthy upper class and thrived on their system of transparent privilege. As one small example, it would boggle the minds of today's media if a mere assistant secretary of the navy, not to mention a president, decided to have a battleship carry him from Washington to his summer vacation home in the very north of Maine, as Roosevelt rather nonchalantly did while holding that lower office.[38] And others argue with some merit that it was mobilization for the war rather than Roosevelt's policies that finally brought the nation out of the grave economic crisis of the 1930s.

But for those Southerners whose families had been trapped inside the generations of unending poverty that long preceded the Great Depression, Roosevelt was a godsend. At last they had found a president who, when it came to their dilemma, was not afraid to lead and who was willing to address key issues rather than simply paper them over with rhetoric. What mattered paternalism when the modern-day descendants of the old Great Captains had remained so powerless against outside economic forces, and yet also continued to completely dominate opportunities within the region? The South had been an economic basket case for generations. The entire nation was now in crisis. And Roosevelt had tossed aside the too-familiar pattern of proposing vague economic policies that would immediately benefit the wealthy and might— perhaps later, if things went right—"trickle down" to those in need or "float everybody's boat" with the rising tide of prosperity. Nor had he decided simply to throw welfare money at those who would not or could not work. Instead, he chose to institute concrete, government-funded programs that actually put people to work.

Many of Roosevelt's vaunted New Deal programs had a profound impact in the South. The Civilian Conservation Corps (CCC) was especially busy in the region, even though its activities spanned forty-seven states. Eventually its ranks swelled to 275,000 young men who were paid the princely sum of thirty dollars a month (as much as some sharecroppers made in a year) to work in American forests and to landscape a growing federal highway system.[39] And the Tennessee Valley Authority (TVA), created in 1933 to manage the Tennessee River, grew over time into perhaps the most important and successful federal project in history. For the people of the Appalachian Mountain region, the TVA meant more than jobs; it brought electricity, and thus the first stages of modernity into the rugged hollows and backcountry. Even today the TVA is America's biggest public power company, bringing in $6.8 billion a year and supplying electricity to more than 8 million people in a seven-state region that comprises much of the principal area of Scots-Irish settlement and influence.[40]

And whether or not the mobilization of the nation's industries and military that began after September 1939 was the true catalyst for turning around a moribund economy, it did bring jobs to the people of the backlands, the kind of cash-paying employment that previously had not been available to those who wanted desperately to work. Further, most Southerners knew that these were the kinds of jobs that easily could have gone elsewhere. They were not wrong to credit Roosevelt's personal sensitivities, as well as the power in the Congress of the Solid South's vaunted seniority in key leadership positions, for this resurgence.

Once mobilization began, factories and military bases sprang up all over the South as well as in states such as Michigan, Illinois, and California, where many Southerners had recently migrated. Importantly, the military bases inside the South brought with them a large influx of people from other regions, for the first time in several generations exposing the curious folkways that had evolved after Civil War Reconstruction to close scrutiny from outsiders. Although some Southern military bases had been used during the 1917 buildup to World War I combat, that mobilization had been brief—a matter of months—and most of the military bases had either been deactivated or reduced to cantonment size after 1918. By contrast, the World War II buildup began in the spring of 1940, when the army's War Plans Division initiated a training program designed to immediately raise an army of 4 million men and that involved a steady influx of soldiers from across the country for the next five years. Actually, construction at some bases, such as Fort Benning, Georgia, had begun as early as 1935, using public works funding from New Deal programs.

Rather than 4 million men, some 16 million Americans would eventually serve during World War II. Along with California, the South held the highest density of these soldiers, a strong percentage of them either coming from the South or spending part of their military years training there. Large-scale training bases became a staple in the recovering economies of virtually every Southern state. Fort Benning, on the Alabama–Georgia border, was home to 100,000 soldiers at any given time. Fort Bragg, North Carolina, had a wartime population of 159,000 soldiers. Fort Polk, Louisiana, was activated as a large training base in 1941. Fort Stewart, Georgia's 280,000 acres were activated in 1940 in an area that had been completely devastated in the final days of the Civil War by the infamous Union general William Tecumseh Sherman and had yet to recover. More than 500,000 soldiers were trained during the war at Fort Jackson, South Carolina, a post named for Andrew Jackson that had been reactivated in 1939 as an infantry training center. Fort Campbell, Kentucky, built in 1942, became home to three armored divisions and an infantry division. Fort A. P. Hill, Virginia, activated in 1940, became a maneuver area for the II Army Corps and three National Guard divisions, and in 1942 was headquarters for the task force that Gen. George S. Patton was preparing to lead into the North Africa campaign. Fort Leonard Wood, Missouri, was activated as a large training base in 1940. Forts Hood and Bliss were activated for similar purposes in Texas, as was Fort Chaffee in Arkansas, all in either 1940 or 1941.[41]

And that was just the army. The Marine Corps opened up its huge base at Camp Lejeune in 1941 originally as the training ground for the 1st Marine Division, which soon thereafter deployed to Guadalcanal. It also vastly expanded its recruit training facilities in Parris Island, South Carolina, where more than 200,000 recruits were trained during World War II. Naval bases dotted the Southern coastline from Norfolk, Virginia, to New Orleans, with Charleston, South Carolina, one of its main hubs. Naval aviation expanded from a small school at Pensacola, Florida, to additional training facilities in the vicinity of Jacksonville, Florida, and Corpus Christi, Texas. Army Air Corps bases—the precursors to today's air force bases—seemed ubiquitous, as pilot training tried to catch up with wartime needs as well as an industrial production rate that eventually reached 8,000 to 10,000 planes a month.

The impact of this phenomenon was cultural as well as economic and had extensive long-term implications. During World War II, millions of non-Southerners of all ethnic backgrounds, most of them citizen-soldiers who had been conscripted (two-thirds of those who served in that war were drafted), were personally exposed to the twin realities of the South. On the one hand, they were often confronted by an honor-bound but frequently backward white culture that was willing to defend its way of life against all outsiders. On the other, the glaring racial humiliations of segregation were visible for all to see. In many eyes, white poverty was attributed to cultural inferiority rather than the generations of Yankee colonialism that had produced it, while the racial inequities they observed would leave a lasting impression, fueling nationwide support for the desegregation and civil rights efforts that began shortly after the end of World War II. And although President Harry Truman may not have had such karma in mind when he announced the policy in 1948, it is interesting to note that the military was the first institution in the country to formally renounce all policies of segregation.

But that would come later.

For those inside the region, mobilization for World War II meant, first and foremost, real cash-paying jobs. My grandmother thought God himself was shining down on her when she found work in an ammunition factory in North Little Rock, making artillery rounds. She and the other backcountry laborers would board a bus at two-thirty in the morning so they could travel the forty miles along narrow roads to the factory in time to begin work, and then the bus would drop them off back in Kensett after dark. My Aunt Ima Jean's husband, Paul, had once left a small family farm to make cars in Detroit, but he got homesick and returned. Then he found work in a sawmill where the principal contracts for decades to come went to making such military items as army cots. In the

1950s, Uncle Paul would lose half of one hand in a sawmill accident, causing him to remain at home for nearly a year as he regrew
the muscles of what remained so that he could again report for
work at the mill. My Aunt Zara left the cotton fields, and Arkansas,
with a boyfriend who had found work as a fireman in Monahans,
Texas, just outside the newly opened Pyote Air Base, where Army
Air Corps bomber pilots—including, eventually, my father—were
being trained. And my Uncle Ercil left a hog farm in Kentucky to
enter the wartime army.

But my grandmother, like so many others, had heard that there
was better work in California. Finally she saved enough money
for two one-way bus tickets to Los Angeles, taking her youngest
daughter, then nine, while sending my mother, then sixteen, to
Texas to live with my aunt. One can only imagine the determination
that propelled this nearly two-thousand-mile journey with a small
child across Arkansas, Oklahoma, Texas, New Mexico, Arizona, and
finally California, to a place where she knew no one and where
there were only rumors about a job. She was a five-foot tall, Popeye-
muscled, forty-nine-year-old widow with literally no money who
had come to Arkansas from Tennessee as a small child and had
never left, other than for a brief stint near the coal mines of southern Illinois. In her later years she would still recall vividly her arrival
at the Los Angeles bus station in the middle of the night, and the
kind man who noted her awestricken confusion and helped her and
her daughter find a place to sleep.

With her physical strength and her size—or more properly, her
lack of it—Frankie Doyle Hodges soon found her way to the
Douglas Aircraft Company, where they hired her to work as a riveter along the tight crawlspaces inside the noses of bomber aircraft.
And so within a few weeks of taking a one-way bus out of Arkansas,
Granny Hodges was living in Santa Monica and working as Rosie
the Riveter. And I doubt there were very many other women on the
assembly line who could match the tiny woman's cotton-chopping
biceps, which were still nearly as large as my own when she was

seventy-one and I was a nineteen-year-old athlete who had been fighting "under the lights" as a boxer for five years.

But as she had in Illinois, Granny got homesick for her extended family in Arkansas. Back in Texas, my Aunt Zara received a letter saying that Granny was again saving her money, this time to go home. Zara, also known as Dot, was the most fiercely ambitious of my mother's siblings. She had been doing her own California dreaming, and as a woman in her early twenties with two children who was getting ready to strike out on her own, that meant keeping Granny in Santa Monica. Dot was also worried because my mother, who was not yet eighteen, had begun dating my father, a twenty-five-year-old pilot with questionable motivations who like all flyboys would soon depart Pyote Airfield for destinations unknown. So she decided to solve two problems at once. She bought my mother a one-way bus ticket to California, reasoning that my mother would reduce Granny's homesickness (and increase the collective price of those one-way bus tickets back to Arkansas) while my father would soon be reassigned from Texas and thus be out of my mother's life.

Aunt Dot was partially successful. Once my mother arrived in California, Granny calmed down. But after my mother left Texas, my father had heated up. Within a few months Dot had made it to California, although my father had by then sent my mother enough money to return to Texas and marry him. And she did, two months after turning eighteen.

My father's family reflected the same fascination with making the jump to the California dreamland, although their starting point was Missouri rather than Arkansas. His two older brothers, Tommy and Charlie, had left school after the eighth grade and were determined that my father and his younger brother, Art, would be the first in the family to finish high school. For the rest of his life he felt an indebtedness to his older brothers that impelled his desire to succeed, remembering their financial help and moral suasion that had kept him in high school. Nor did he stop there. It was one of my life's greatest inspirations to watch my father as he struggled through twenty-six years of night school, all the while carrying a military career filled with overseas deployments and taking care of a family that included four children, until he received a college degree from the University of Omaha during my own senior year of high school.

When the war began, my father was working as an electrician in St. Joseph, Missouri's largest department store, alongside my Uncle Tommy. But the war scattered all of them quickly. My father enlisted the day after Pearl Harbor was attacked and went into the army air corps. His younger brother, Art, went into the army, which after examining his test scores sent him immediately for further schooling, where he became what was then called a "junior engineer." Tommy and Charlie headed for California, followed soon by my grandmother, with Tommy spending the war at the Long Beach Naval Shipyard. And by the end of the war, all of them were living permanently in California except for my father, who returned briefly to Missouri, then re-upped in the air force and spent the next twenty-three years on the road.

These sorts of migrations were hardly unusual; in fact, they were emblematic. In this small microcosm, one begins to understand the flavor of a massive population movement of a scale and scope that approaches the more well-remembered influx to the East Coast from Europe in the late 1890s and early 1900s. Because this migration was internal and because the strongly individualistic people involved had tossed away any overt ethnic identification after generations of assimilation as Americans, historians and political commentators frequently overlook both its scale and its relatively homogeneous nature. And in contrast to the original Scots-Irish migrations into the Appalachian Mountains and beyond, these were not organized family movements, by groups that knew each other, into unpopulated areas in order to begin whole new communities and infuse them with their traditions. These descendants of the original Scots-Irish migrations were now, like most other cultures, immigrants rather than settlers. For most of them, the South or the Border South was their native soil. And even among others who were migrating from the Midwest and Southwest, the Appalachian Mountain communities were the "old sod," the common cultural starting place that had shaped values and habits brought from their ancestors' earlier European migration and then coalesced into a truly American persona.

This emigration played itself out most intensely across the South and Border South as a restless people headed into the industrial areas of the North-Central region and into the distant Mecca of California. The roads into the industrial hubs of Illinois, Ohio, Indiana, and Michigan from the Carolinas, Kentucky, southwest Virginia, West Virginia, and even Arkansas became known as Hillbilly Highways. A motto among the young in the Appalachian hamlets became "Write and read, and Route 23," for the newly built federal highway that cut right through the heart of that region, from northern Georgia to eastern Kentucky, and took them directly to Toledo and Detroit. Hundreds of thousands of other migrants from the South and Midwest poured into California along Route 66, John Steinbeck's *Grapes of Wrath* highway. Referred to pejoratively by more established Californians as Okies and Arkies, they fueled the military-oriented factories of Southern California and made the farmlands from Barstow to Bakersfield a hillbilly enclave. As one example among many, country singing great Merle Haggard, whose parents had just made the trek from Oklahoma, was born in 1937 while his family was living in an abandoned railroad car in Bakersfield.

The scale of this massive out-migration caused the population of many of the Southern and Border States to flat-line during periods of the 1930s and 1940s. Indeed, Arkansas and West Virginia actually lost population between 1940 and 1970 at a time when the overall population of the United States increased by 53 percent, from 132 million to 203 million people. Even today West Virginia still remains well below its 1950 level of 2 million residents.[42]

Importantly, among those of Scots-Irish descent, this migration was different from those that had occurred earlier, for it was bringing a strong percentage of people who had been burned by generations of ill education and poverty. Famed World War II general George Smith Patton, Jr.'s family journey illustrates the success that many earlier Scots-Irish emigrants from the mountain South found on the West Coast. Patton's grandfather George had been killed as a Confederate soldier at the Battle of Winchester in May 1862 (where my own ancestor William John Jewell fought as a member of Stonewall Jackson's brigade) while commanding the 22nd Virginia Regiment in the Shenandoah Valley. His grandfather's brother Walter had also died in that war while commanding a regiment under Maj. Gen. George E. Pickett at Gettysburg. Shortly after the Civil War, Patton's family moved to California, where his father, a graduate of the Virginia Military Institute, ran a ranch. His mother, Ruth Wilson Patton, was the daughter of native Tennesseean Benjamin Davis Wilson, a well-known Indian fighter who had settled in California in 1841 and was known for having started the citrus industry there. Wilson was also the first mayor of Los Angeles, served three terms as a California state senator, and made the first trek up Mount Wilson, which was named in his honor after his death.[43]

There would be no mountains named after the later Okies and Arkies, but their collective contribution was in other ways far greater. Poor they may have been, and uneducated as well, but this infusion of migrants whose American experience had been shaped by the power of the interlocking Scots-Irish communities west of the Appalachian Mountains brought with it a force that would in many ways shape the attitudes of working-class America. In the factories and steel mills of the industrial heartland, and in the shipyards and defense industries along the West Coast, these migrants quickly infected the children of more recent European immigrations with the attitudes that had been nurtured in the Scottish Kirk and then hardened on the American frontier. In a phrase, that attitude might be called, "Take this job and shove it."

Other groups, particularly recently arrived Jewish activists with
a long history in legal theory, brought to the American working
class the concepts of collective bargaining, unionization, and the
use of the strike as a tool to settle worker grievances. Still others,
notably the more recent Irish immigrants with their Jesuit-inspired
rebelliousness, brought a good measure of fierce resistance. But
the Scots-Irish culture—itself so intensely individualistic that few
of its members cared for the unionization process or even collective bargaining—brought a simple, sometimes combative directness when dealing with authority, together with an unbending
demand for personal respect and a complete lack of fear.

Many thinking Americans had worried that the wave of European immigration from 1890 to 1910 would change the nation's
basic character. As Walter Russell Mead pointed out in his well-
regarded essay on Jacksonian American (after mentioning the
Scots-Irish as the originators of what he terms "Jacksonian populism"), "The great cities of the United States were increasingly
filled with Catholics, members of the Orthodox churches and
Jews—all professing in one way or another communitarian social
values very much at odds with the individualism of the traditional
Anglo-Saxon and Anglo-Celtic culture." But something different
happened, at least among America's working classes: the stubbornness of bottom-up won out over the intimidation and manipulation
of top-down. Those from the South and Border South and states
such as Ohio and Pennsylvania that had long Scots-Irish traditions
began to mix among the workers in their factories, neighborhoods,
and local bars, and even began to intermarry with them. Also, one
can never underestimate the impact on those who were exposed to
the power of this culture while serving in America's most quintes-
sentially Scots-Irish institution, the military. By 1975 there were
more than 30 million living veterans in the United States, and the
overwhelming majority had served in the more recent eras of
World War II, Korea, or Vietnam.

As Mead observes, "In what is still a largely unheralded triumph of the melting pot, Northern immigrants gradually assimilated the values of Jacksonian individualism. Each generation of new Americans was less 'social' and more individualistic than the preceding one. . . . The appeal of [the Jacksonian code of honor, self-reliance, equality, individualism, and courage] is one of the reasons that Jacksonian values have spread to so many people outside the original ethnic and social nexus in which Jacksonian America was formed."[44]

Mead goes even further, claiming that Andrew Jackson's "political movement—or, more accurately, the community of political feeling that he wielded into an instrument of power—remains in many ways the most important in American politics . . . Jacksonian populism today has moved beyond its original ethnic and geographical limits. Like country music, another product of Jacksonian culture, Jacksonian politics and folk feeling has become a basic element in American consciousness that can be found from one end of the country to the other."[45]

This observation is correct, at least as it applies to America's vast populist base. Just as the Scots-Irish family networks infused much of the South and the Ohio Valley with their cultural traditions, so also has this powerfully individualistic culture embraced large groups of new Americans, particularly among those of the working classes. Andrew Jackson's core group of "farmers, mechanics and laborers" still thrives in America today and still lives by his code. These are people who measure others not by titles or possessions but by personal honor, dignity, and the willingness to fight for their beliefs. Most are unenvious of wealth, unafraid of the wielders of authority, unconscious of class, and also unwilling to consider themselves ethnically aloof—in most cases, their own ethnicity is less important than their individuality. And more than any other culture, this is the one that new immigrant groups have traditionally gravitated toward in order to call themselves American.

But except for the accessibility given them during Ronald Reagan's presidency—an influence that was often diluted by establishment Republicans—over the past fifty years this movement has rarely seen its issues seriously defended by national leaders. And except for the hard-core Christian Right, which has aligned itself with the Republicans, it represents a large, independent swing vote—whose key concerns are seldom passionately represented by either side in any election—rather than a force that affirmatively shapes the national agenda.

Other than with their support of Reagan—perhaps the most Jacksonian president since Jackson himself—the power of this group's voting patterns has been in their role as electoral spoilers. These are the blue-collar workers and Southerners who swung away from the antiwar Democrats and voted for either George Wallace or Richard Nixon in 1968 (Wallace carried five Southern states), and Nixon in 1972. They were the enthusiastic Reagan Democrats who still will argue passionately about the Gipper's greatness and who in the South finally began supporting Republican candidates. They reluctantly pulled the lever for George Bush in 1988, but many could not do it again for Bush in 1992 or for Bob Dole in 1996, opting instead to sit it out or to vote for Ross Perot. And they are the "red state" individualists who went for George W. Bush in 2000 rather than aligning themselves with the "blue state" voters representing the "new" Democratic Party of political correctness who went for Al Gore. Indeed, the argument can be made that Gore's position on gun control cost him the election, not in Florida but in the Scots-Irish redoubts of Tennessee and West Virginia, both of which through history and logic should have been slam-dunk electoral votes in his favor.

They have become spoilers because in their view America's political elites, both Republican and Democrat, have grown together into an almost indiscernible "hybrid royalty" that offers them little to choose from in terms of how the nation is actually being governed. Grand, useless speeches are made on issues such as flag-burning, homosexual marriage, and abortion, but little is said or done about such vital matters as the near-nationwide breakdown of public education, the mind-boggling rate of incarceration in America's prison systems, or the blatant, government-sponsored reverse discrimination inherent in what are now called diversity programs. And while minor but emotionally charged issues are used to inflame their passions and get their vote, the other wielders of cultural power such as Hollywood, academia, and major media relentlessly chip away at the core principles that have defined the traditions and history of their people. For if the Scots-Irish culture and its Jacksonian derivative have provided the building blocks for America's working classes, no other group has been so denigrated, attacked, and even feared by America's ever more interconnected ruling elites.

For nearly two thousand years, in one form or another, this culture's unbending individualism—and its ingrained hatred of aristocracy—has been in conflict with a variety of authoritarian power structures, and it remains so in today's America. The culture in its embryonic form stood fast against the Roman and Norman nation-builders who created a structured and eventually feudal England. The unique emphasis on individual rights and responsibilities that sprang from Calvinism and the Scottish Kirk caused it to resist the throne and finally brought down a king. The fierceness of its refusal to accommodate the Anglican theocrats in Ulster created the radical politics of nonconformism, and this attitude was carried into the Appalachian Mountains. Its people refused to bend a knee to New York and Boston either before, during, or after the Civil War, standing firm against outside forces that would try to tell them how to live and what to believe. And even today, an individual and an issue at a time, it refuses to accept the politics of group privilege that have been foisted on America by its paternalistic, Ivy League–centered, media-connected, politically correct power centers.

America's ruling classes have carried a visceral dislike of this culture from the earliest days of the colonial experience, when the first Scots-Irish parcels from Ulster—turned away from the Puritan settlements in Massachusetts—headed for the hills of New

Hampshire. Those who plotted their towns so carefully and wished to form a society based on order, reason, and compliance felt little more than disgust for the chaotic, often sensual rebelliousness of a people who refused to be controlled from above. The Quakers who ran early Pennsylvania found them frightening and lawless. The Cavalier aristocrats of Virginia saw them as useful, if only they would remain far away in the mountains and not disrupt the quasi-royal system that had evolved along the coast. The occupiers during Reconstruction found them, frankly, impossible. Modern military commanders, plant foremen, union bosses, and government commissars of political correctness all learn and relearn the same lesson every day—that this is a people who respond to good leadership but will never allow themselves to be dominated or controlled if an edict from above violates their beliefs.

The ethnic makeup of America's ruling class has changed over the generations, just as the ethnic composition of what Mead calls the Jacksonians has been leavened by assimilation. The methods of enforcing dominance from above have also undergone many alterations, from sword and spear and royal prerogative to the ability to manipulate power structures through a network of elite academic institutions, media suasion, and judicial activism. But the basic issues that drive the controversy have remained remarkably consistent. On the one hand, there has always been a form of power that believes it holds the answers to society's problems and wishes to impose those answers from above, its members being the arbiters of what is right and wrong, proper or antisocial. And on the other are the people who are sure of who they are, loyal to strong leaders who affirm their basic beliefs, and who reserve their greatest dislike for those who would abuse governmental systems in order to create special favors for anyone who does not deserve them.

Andrew Jackson's admonishment from long ago still rings true to these people. "Equality of talents, of education or of wealth can not be produced by human institutions. . . . Every man is equally entitled to protection by law; but when the laws undertake to add to these natural and just advantages artificial distinctions, to grant titles, gratuities, and exclusive privileges, to make the rich richer and the potent more powerful, the humble members of our society—the farmers, mechanics and laborers—who have neither the time nor the means of securing favors to themselves, have the right to complain of the injustice of their Government."

The most visible fault line between the people of this culture and those who so adamantly shape modern America's intellectual and political agenda began during the turmoil of the civil rights movement and continues today in a variety of related issues. Just as slavery needed to end, so did the practice of legal segregation. But as with the aftermath of slavery, the real question became, What should happen after the end of segregation, and who should decide, and on what grounds? Arthur Schlesinger pointed out that during the period before the Civil War, the Yankee industrialists shied away from speaking of issues of class while debating slavery in order to avoid the "explosive possibilities" of class warfare if their arguments were then applied to labor problems in the North.[46] For slightly different reasons, so also did the radical activists who were using much of the civil rights movement as a step toward larger political goals.

First, the class issue was a difficult card to play. The socialists and economic Marxists had failed to excite a following in the United States, or for that matter to find a willing proletariat, even during the darkest days of the Depression. Many activists who had pressed for economic Marxism had then joined what some political commentators call the cultural Marxists, with a large segment of the activist Left now claiming that society was flawed along the lines of ineradicable conditions such as race, sex, and sexual preference rather than lack of opportunity and poverty per se. For them to spotlight the dirt-poor legacy of a substantial percentage of white Southerners would be to deny this faction of the antisegregationist movement its principal rallying point, the very hate-object of their cause. For if the supposedly evil, tobacco-chewing South-

ern redneck in his pickup truck with the Confederate flag on the
bumper represented not a fringe but a plurality that had suffered in
economic terms just as deeply as the black, a whole new dynamic
would be necessary. And it also would illuminate by implication
the frequently well-off circumstances of many liberal activists who
were making the case.

If the legal aspects of segregation were cut and dried, the social
and economic elements were anything but. Poverty and hardship
have never traveled completely along racial lines, even in the
South, and particularly in Southern urban areas, where a black professional class had thrived for decades before the civil rights movement even began. Indeed, when former white segregationists
Lester Maddox and Strom Thurmond and Atlanta's first black
mayor, Maynard Jackson, all died within a few days of each other in
June 2003, *The Economist* magazine was careful to point out in an
article that, of the three, "Mr. Jackson had the most privileged
background. His father, a Baptist minister, came from an influential
family in Dallas; his mother from another in Atlanta; both parents
had been university educated." Thurmond, hardly poor, was the
son of a judge. But Maddox, the son of a steelworker, had finished
high school through a correspondence course.[47]

One does not need to defend the conduct of those who opposed
racial integration in order to understand it, and one does not need
to condemn the actions of those who pushed for integration in order to call into question some of their long-term motives. After a
hundred years this issue was balled up in a Gordian knot that was
almost impossible to untie. One could never question the motives,
or even the tactics, of Martin Luther King, Jr., whose equanimity
was Lincolnesque in its breadth of vision. But others, white and
black alike, were bent on using the issue to foment a larger revolution.

As one example, the Students for a Democratic Society, better
known as the SDS, would become the vanguard of the Vietnam antiwar movement, and its members were the instigators of deliber-

ately provocative violence at many antiwar rallies. But it was originally formed in 1962, before there ever was a Vietnam War, with a goal of bringing revolutionary changes to America principally through the issue of race. Indeed, the first agenda item mentioned in its formative Port Huron Statement was "the permeating and victimizing fact of human degradation, symbolized by the Southern struggle against racial bigotry," and many of its members first worked on the racial issue in cities such as Newark and in the South. That its key leadership would later gain notoriety as principal antiwar organizers—including Tom Hayden, who with former wife Jane Fonda ran the Indochina Peace Coalition, and several members of the Chicago Seven, who organized the riots that shut down that city during the 1968 Democratic Party Convention—demonstrates the sweep of their intended goals.

By working so hard to convert an issue of social justice designed to eradicate demeaning laws of exclusion into a full-blown war against the entire value system of a region, these radical activists terribly misread that region's basic culture and turned many of the very people who might have worked for racial justice into their most virulent enemies. To provoke and blame disadvantaged whites for the plight of disadvantaged blacks was either naive or politically manipulative. And to expect that the disadvantaged whites would happily assist in revamping the entire social and economic order without attention being paid to their own situation was absurd. In the largest terms of solving the problems of the region, the racial issue could have been presented as only a first step—one capable of summoning the deepest of emotions, but a step nonetheless along a road that would bring fairness on a far larger scale.

Without such reassurance, the fight over ending legal racial segregation ended up demonizing people who had shared the same social and economic dilemma as the blacks themselves. In reality, once the "Whites Only" water fountains and bathrooms and restaurants went away, there was very little left to distinguish the past several generations of history between a substantial percentage of whites and blacks alike. The demagoguery of many of the South's white political leaders, perhaps borne of the recognition and even fear of that very reality, did not help. But the end result of this approach was more than ironic. For if the scions of the plantation aristocracy had kept poor whites in line for generations by convincing them of their status just above the former slaves, now the liberals and the cultural Marxists were coalescing blacks and unthinking Northerners around the notion that the barriers to black economic advancement had somehow for generations come at the hands of the equally neglected less-advantaged whites.

Or to put it another way, if these were the people who took something away from black America, where did they hide it—inside their corn-shuck mattresses?

As the civil rights movement progressed, and even as it was memorialized, the Southern redneck became the enemy, the veritable poster child of liberal hatred and disgust, even today celebrated in film after film, book after book, speech after speech (along with his literary godson, the skinhead), as the emblem of everything that had kept the black man down. No matter that the country club whites had always held the keys to the Big House, or that many of them had done well at the expense of disadvantaged whites and blacks alike. No matter that the biggest race riots took place outside the South, in that Promised Land where blacks were still being held down by policies, many of them unwritten, which precluded them from assimilating into the American mainstream. Harlem and Bedford Stuyvesant erupted in 1964. Malcolm X was killed in New York a year later. The Watts section of Los Angeles blew up in 1965, in large-scale violence that left 34 dead and more than 1,000 injured. Chicago rioted in 1966, as did Cleveland. Newark and Detroit followed in 1967. Many of these same cities as well as others saw renewed rioting in 1968.

No matter, actually, that except in his fierce resistance, both to forces from the outside and to a misreading of his own history, the redressing of wrongs to African-Americans was not a Southern red-neck phenomenon at all. It was an American phenomenon, for which the Southern redneck has been held up as the whipping boy.

Why was he singled out? Partly because the Southern redneck was such an easy target, with his intrinsic stubbornness, his capacity for violence, and his curious social ways. And partly because something else was going on, something deeper and more fundamental to the social and political makeup of the country: a feeling that the culture so dramatically symbolized by the Southern redneck was the greatest inhibitor of the plans of the activist Left and the cultural Marxists for a new kind of society altogether.

From the perspective of the activist Left, Jacksonian populists are the greatest obstacles to what might be called the collectivist taming of America, symbolized by the edicts of political correctness. And for the last fifty years the Left has been doing everything in its power to sue them, legislate against their interests, mock them in the media, isolate them as idiosyncratic, and publicly humiliate their traditions in order to make them, at best, irrelevant to America's future growth.

In the classic film *Cool Hand Luke*, the warden of the Arkansas work camp was fond of saying over and over to the irascible, unbreakable title character, "Luke, we got to get your mind right. Is your mind right, Luke?" But the warden never got Luke's mind right. He put Luke into solitary confinement inside what was called The Box. He made him work all night, digging a hole and filling it up and then digging it again, until Luke was crying for mercy. He put him in chains, and then in double chains, to keep him from running away. But Luke kept running, and kept resisting, because he would rather die than have the warden make his mind right.

Luke was nothing more than an unpretentious wild man, a good old, unreconstructed, unreeducatable redneck. And whatever these societal manipulators may want to do with their lawsuits and their movies and their constant mockeries, they must understand that they are dealing with a whole lot of Lukes, millions of them, who are only now beginning to comprehend the depth of cynicism and unfairness that has attended so many national policies over the past generation, to their disadvantage.

Change the fabric of their culture? It hasn't happened yet, not in two thousand years. And it won't happen now.

PART SEVEN

Reflections:
The Unbreakable Circle

Again and again I come across the assertion that a society cannot grow and thrive without a culturally superior stratum which generates the impulse toward excellence and greatness. . . . The happenings in this country refute this assertion. . . . [T]here is evidence on every hand that the vigor and health of a society are determined by the quality of the common people rather than that of the cultural elite.

—ERIC HOFFER,
Working and Thinking on the Waterfront (1958)

1

Glad Soldiers,
Accidental Scholars

WORLD WAR II and its aftermath were heady days for those of Scots-Irish descent, elevating this culture with its unique mix of individualism, self-reliance, kinship, and courage from its regional dominance of the Southern backcountry to a subtle but powerful position of national prominence. In international affairs, every element of the Scots-Irish ethos was vital to the strength of the American military while at the same time its values were naturally opposed to the Soviet Union's repressive, expansionist form of communism. Domestically, Scots-Irish folkways had become deeply embedded into the nation's blue-collar communities in every region except the Northeast. And at the individual level, people whose families had for so many generations lived in utter poverty were for the first time reaping the benefits of the American dream on a meaningful scale.

During this same period, the intense philosophical debates that opposed the values of this culture, and the radical political movement that was part and parcel of those deliberations, were being nurtured in geographic, intellectual, and academic venues where the Scots-Irish themselves seldom ventured. Quite often, the grist of the arguments for revolutionary change was the product of social and political experiences in a Europe that the Scots-Irish had long ago left behind. But the intellectual and social forces that were growing in the universities and cultural enclaves of "progressive" America were little more than distant noise to the Scots-Irish, who were fighting an entirely different political and economic monster. Some of them were climbing out of more than seven decades of poverty and colonialism in the South. Others were packing scant belongings and setting out on their rough journeys north or west.

When war ultimately came to America in 1941, their cause was simple, and true to their long history: to defeat their country's enemies on the battlefield. In the war's aftermath, the occupation and rebuilding of Japan and Germany seemed to them a ratification of their own version of democracy. That the Soviet Union immediately pursued an expansionist agenda once the war was over, even as its ugly repression of its own people continued apace, only convinced them further. And the postwar economic boom in America, which brought many of them jobs and cars and decent houses in suburban neighborhoods, was icing on the cake. America was the land of the free, the hope of the world, and they had helped make it so.

No sooner had World War II ended than the Cold War began, and the country was forced to confront an aggressive, competing system of government in a variety of dangerous crisis points around the world. From 1950 to 1953, a war in Korea consumed the country's emotional and intellectual energies as well as the blood and sacrifice of its citizens. A few years later, in 1957, the Soviet Union was the first to enter the space age, the launch of Sputnik bringing with it all the military dangers inherent in intercontinental ballistic missiles capable of delivering nuclear weapons thousands of miles away. And America found itself both bewildered and unprepared.

After Sputnik was launched, my father, then an air force major, brought our family tradition of pioneering into a new generation. Still lacking a college education, he was nonetheless chosen by the air force to become part of one of the most urgent missions in the nation's history: to build a missile system capable of protecting the country against the very real Soviet threat. On short notice our family of six traveled from Alabama to the isolated wilderness of California's central coast, where an old, eighty-five-thousand-acre National Guard training base named Camp Cook was being transformed into Vandenberg Air Force Base.

In the space of one year the military population at Vandenberg expanded from nearly zero to twelve thousand people. At the beginning, the base had no family housing. We lived for a while crammed into a five-dollar-a-night motel room in Pismo Beach, my father driving more than fifty miles each way every day along narrow, two-lane mountain roads to and from the base, leaving before dawn and coming back well after dark. Later we rented a small home in Santa Maria, cutting his commute in half but seeing him just as seldom, and finally we moved into a base housing project that had been scratched into the rough, vine-covered hillsides of Vandenberg. Having spent the fifth grade in England, the sixth in Texas, and the seventh in Alabama, I went to three different schools in the eighth grade alone, the third school a converted World War II hospital complex on the base. The old, yellow, wooden buildings sagged with age and disrepair. Chalkboards and desks had been erected in the low-ceilinged, dimly lit wards. The original hospital had been built above ground, with crawlspaces under it for ventilation. Snakes, jackrabbits, and skunks often found their way below the creaking floors of the classrooms. Rather than purchasing dead frogs pickled in formaldehyde to dissect in science class, my partner and I would simply crawl underneath the building and catch a few toads.

It was chaos in the classrooms, kids from military towns and bases across the nation thrown suddenly into this remote, old hospital complex with its long interconnecting hallways and its odd, haunting memories of wounded soldiers who had once suffered in rows of beds where now we sat in lines of desks. Most of us, including me, were unwilling and unruly students, jarred from normality, frequently disruptive, and always cynical. Fights broke out routinely, on the playgrounds and even in the classrooms. It was not unusual for firecrackers to be thrown across the classroom when a teacher turned toward the freestanding blackboard. The shortstop on my Babe Ruth League baseball team left us in midseason, heading off to jail. Two years later my second baseman on that team was shot while trying to rob a store. We were accused by a few teachers of being "military trash," which, one surmised, must have been somewhere below white trash, because some among us were black and others were brown. But we laughed that off—what kind of teacher would settle for a job in this isolated, intellectually barren region, anyway?

Vandenberg at its beginnings had all the chaos of an isolated frontier town; a raw but accessible wilderness where I spent much of my time hiking and camping, a social structure that saw air force enlisted men dating high school girls, and a lack of contact with the more sophisticated world. More important, it was serious work that our fathers were doing far away along the fringes of the sea, where they had built block houses and launchpads and were testing scientific concepts that no one in history had ever before put into play. Our fathers were not scientists, although civilian scientists and engineers frequently worked alongside them. But they were doers, fixers, mechanical geniuses, risk-takers, and, more than we even understood, they were on an urgent mission involving national survival, with little time to lose.

For two years I rarely saw my father except on holidays and on Sundays, even though we were living in the same house. He was gone before I got up. He was usually still gone when I went to bed. He took no leave and had no vacations. Now and then we would be sitting in our hospital ward of a classroom and the ground would shake and the sky would roar and we would rush outside, hundreds of kids emptying out of the buildings within a blink so that we could stand in the school yards and look westward toward the sea where the latest attempt to launch a missile would fill our eyes. The Thor missiles particularly were the world's greatest firecrackers. More often than not during those first years they went off course and had to be destroyed. Some blew up on the launch pads, some just above them. Sometimes they went sideways instead of following their planned trajectory out into the sea. One of them ended up soaring ever higher, never rolling into its turn toward the sea, and finally exploding just outside the farm town of Santa Maria, where large pieces of metal showered the strawberry fields. We would cheer even when they blew up, for if nothing else we knew that we were watching an attempt to make history somewhere out there in the block houses next to the sea.

Despite Vandenberg's remoteness, we knew viscerally of its importance. In 1959, Soviet premier Nikita Khrushchev made a train journey from Los Angeles to San Francisco during a visit to the United States. The rail route passed through the outer fringes of Vandenberg, near the sea. As the train left the little village of Surf and entered the base's property, Khrushchev famously folded his arms and turned his back on the facility, staring out into the Pacific Ocean until his railroad car was again on civilian soil.

Other strangers knew of us as well.

One summer day as we were playing baseball on a field next to our housing project, we heard that a group of protesters was on its way to Vandenberg, presumably from San Francisco far to the north, in order to march against the Bomb. Stuck as we were in this remote outpost that had no recreational outlets save a base gym, an old movie theater, and a one-room "teen club," the thought of a group of outsiders traveling to the base in order to protest its activities seemed preposterous. Several friends and I made our way to the main gate, where the base commander had augmented the normal air police contingent with a fire truck. Dozens of military kids gathered at the edge of the base perimeter, looking querulously through the chain-link fence.

The protesters were standing in the ice plants and sagebrush on the other side of the dusty, lonely highway, a scraggly, rather confused group of no more than a hundred people holding "Ban the Bomb" signs and gathering their courage to try to enter the base.

Suddenly—almost resignedly—they began walking across the highway. When they neared the gate, the fire hoses opened up, washing them back to the other side. Their mission somehow accomplished, they took a few pictures, mostly of themselves, and then walked slowly away, as wet and beaten as whipped puppies.

We laughed and cheered, more at their oddity than at their cause, which from the confines of our lives seemed too ludicrous even to be taken seriously. How could they not comprehend the seriousness of Russia's missile advantage? And who would even notice that they had come? But less than ten years later, after I returned from a hard year of combat in Vietnam, those protesters and their soul mates would own the streets. Seeing me in my Marine Corps uniform, it was they who would laugh. And it was I who would feel odd.

The missile program at Vandenberg succeeded beyond anyone's expectations, and over time Vandenberg itself eventually became a stable and thriving community. My father flourished as well, finally working in an area with so many unknowns that his natural intelligence trumped the sophisticated education of many around him. He "wrote the book" on the complicated process of bringing together the many pieces of civilian and military hardware and technology into the actual assemblage of workable Atlas missiles on their launching pads. He was promoted early to lieutenant colonel and assigned to the Strategic Air Command's headquarters at Offutt Air Force Base, Nebraska. Predictably for us, this meant three new homes and two new schools in the next two years.

When the Cuban missile crisis erupted in October 1962, the nation was fortunate that the officers and airmen at Vandenberg had done their work, for if the United States had not developed a strong deterrent program of its own, Soviet missiles would have remained in Cuba, only ninety miles away from our shores. If this had happened, certainly the politics not only of the Cold War but also of the Americas themselves would have evolved far more dangerously. As that crisis unfolded, my father spent an entire week without sleep other than catnapping on military aircraft as he shuttled endlessly between Vandenberg and Offutt, coordinating the air force's preparedness to launch missiles at a moment's notice should the president so decide. Finally he passed out at a conference table at SAC headquarters and had to be hospitalized.

For this and other such work my father was again promoted early, this time to colonel with only two years as a lieutenant colonel, which was almost unheard-of, even for better-educated and more urbane academy graduates. Just after I graduated from high school, he was chosen to command the only composite missile squadron in the military, taking a unit responsible for launching Thor, Atlas, and Scout Junior missiles from a success rate of 11 percent to a perfect record of thirteen successful launches in a row. One of his tasks was shooting Atlas missiles into the Johnston Atoll while a version of Nike antiaircraft missiles attempted to intercept them from facilities on the island of Kwajalein—the first, embryonic efforts at an antimissile defense program.

In addition to all this, the old man was steadily sneaking up on his life's great dream—a college degree. He had been the first to study beyond the eighth grade; the first to finish high school; and for twenty-six years, whenever the chance had presented itself, he had been accumulating college credits. A night school class at some isolated military post; a correspondence course; a military school that might qualify for credit by one college or another; even the electrician's course he had taken after high school; all were piled together year after year until he crossed the magic threshold. Once assigned to Offutt Air Force Base, he spent three nights a week at the University of Omaha in addition to carrying his sensitive and demanding workload at SAC headquarters. Fats Domino released a song during that time called "Three Nights a Week You're Gone," and we joked that it was written especially for him.

Finally, in the winter of my senior year of high school, James Henry Webb, Sr., bagged his diploma. It was, shall we say, a Great Santini Moment. My father was never given to subtlety or understatement. As my granny used to put it, and not in a complimentary way, "Your daddy likes it loud."

I watched him from where I sat in the front row of the expandable bleacher seats at the University of Omaha's men's gymnasium, trying to comprehend the depth of his pride. His chin was lifted; he was high on adrenaline. His prematurely gray hair looked almost fluorescent as he walked toward the podium in the midst of a long line of men and women half his age. The presenter put the cherished paper in his hand. And then he broke out of line and walked across the gymnasium floor, drawing immediate attention in front of perhaps a thousand people. He looked like he'd just won the Super Bowl, or maybe the heavyweight championship. And his burning eyes were on me.

I groaned inwardly, looking at the floor and holding on to the top of my head, stunned that he would really be doing this. In seconds he was standing before me, sticking the diploma into my face as if it were a pointer. He began yelling at me, sky-high with the emotion of a dream that I was already beginning to take for granted. I had just been selected for a scholarship to the University of Southern California, and in a year would be off to the Naval Academy. But this simple piece of paper had been my father's unreachable fantasy for nearly three decades.

What was he telling me? What was he screaming in his moment of triumph, as dozens of others watched in amusement and mild puzzlement? *"You can get anything you want in this country, and don't you ever forget it!"* Yes, I thought, swallowing back my cynicism in the face of his raw energy. Even if it takes two hundred years.

There was little that the upperclassmen at the Naval Academy could teach me about military leadership when I reported to that institution in the summer of 1964. Leadership, he had told me time and again, was simple. Forget the textbooks. You can make somebody do something, or you can make him want to do something. Who would you rather work for? I had watched my father for a lifetime, learning both from his example and from the wisdom of his mentorship. And every time I told myself how much I hated the regimen and the numbing routine of Annapolis—which was almost daily for four years—I would also give myself a humility check. For how quickly would he have traded twenty-six years of night school for four years of this?

But hard times were coming, for him, for myself, and for a lot of others who shared our history and our traditions. The Vietnam War put the brakes on the Scots-Irish ascendancy that had begun with the outbreak of World War II. In the coming two decades, the traditional notions of military service as well as the very foundations of what it meant to be an American would take a terrific beating. The Scots-Irish, whose ethos has always been so closely identified with patriotism and respect for military service, would serve in great numbers during this war and in a historic anomaly would, in many cases, be ostracized from many academic and professional arenas as a direct result of their service.

During the summer of 1964 the two most glaring issues on which disagreement had been simmering between the Scots-Irish Jacksonians and the emerging radicals erupted into public view concurrently, with the signing of the Civil Rights Act and the Gulf of Tonkin incident that led to a full-scale war in Vietnam. And it was above all the war in Vietnam that allowed the radicalism that had been spawning for two decades in academia and the professorial journals to burst forth as a political movement that would challenge many of the basic presumptions about American society.

For the Scots-Irish Jacksonians, Vietnam was a real and often brutal war, one in which a high percentage of their sons and brothers fought. As two examples among many, the South had by far the highest casualty rate during the war, a rate 32 percent higher than the Northeast,[1] and the Scots-Irish stronghold of West Virginia had the highest casualty rate of any state. This service, and these casualties, were occurring at a time when the draft laws gave liberal exceptions to those who remained in college, and when the more advantaged members of the age group were actively counseled on how to avoid military service. Only 11 percent of the draft-eligible males in the Vietnam age group actually went to Vietnam, and only 33 percent served in the military at all. To have one's life interrupted for years at an early age, and then to return not only without honor but also shouldering the blame for all the supposed evils of a war that others avoided, is the formula for long-term societal disability. And this is exactly what occurred.

Contrary to popular mythology, the baby boomer generation was far less liberal than the media images of the day seemed to portray. As Michael Lind documents in his book *Vietnam: The Necessary War*, "Few American students in the sixties were radical. At the height of the antiwar movement in 1970, only 11 percent of American college students identified themselves as 'radical or far left.' "[2] These numbers became magnified in the mind-set of most Americans and over time impacted heavily on the respect shown to those who had served. Small though it was, the radical movement that opposed the war was heavily represented in major academia, where it affected the minds of an entire generation of intellectually gifted students and also had a wide and lasting impact on other institutions, such as major media and the arts, through which Americans historically have gained emotional insights and formed their opinions. And the ever-growing unpopularity of the war allowed the radical movement to expand its reach to a large number of well-meaning Americans who simply wanted the war to end, and to develop alliances with an array of political groups whose causes went much farther than the conflict in Vietnam.

Despite the political misfeasance that characterized the course of the war, it is important to remember that the causes that brought the United States into Vietnam were not unsound. Forty years ago Asia was at a vital crossroads, moving uncertainly into a future that was dominated by three different historical trends. The first involved the aftermath of the carnage and destruction of World War II, which had left its scars on every country in the region and also had dramatically changed the role that Japan played in East Asian affairs. The second was the sudden, regionwide end of European colonialism, which created governmental vacuums in every second-tier country except Thailand and, to a lesser extent, the Philippines. And the third was the emergence of communism as a powerful tool of expansionism by military force, its doctrine and strategies emanating principally from the Soviet Union.[3]

The governmental vacuums created by Europe's withdrawal from the region dramatically played into the hands of communist revolutionary movements, especially in the wake of their takeover of China in 1949, for unlike in Europe, these were countries that had never known Western-style democracy. In 1950 the partitioned country of Korea exploded into war as the communist North invaded South Korea, with the Chinese army joining their effort six months later. Communist insurgencies erupted throughout Indochina. In Malaysia the British led a ten-year antiguerrilla compaign against Chinese-backed revolutionaries. A similar insurgency in Indonesia brought about a communist coup attempt, also sponsored by the Chinese, which was put down in 1965.

The situation inside Vietnam was the most complicated. First, for a variety of reasons the French reversed their withdrawal from their long-term colony after World War II, making it easier for insurgents to rally the strongly nationalistic Vietnamese to their side. Second, the charismatic, Soviet-trained Ho Chi Minh had quickly consolidated his anti-French power base just after the war by assassinating the leadership of competing political groups that were anti-French but also anticommunist. Third, once the Korean War armistice was signed in 1953, the Chinese shifted large amounts of sophisticated weaponry to Ho Chi Minh's army. The Viet Minh's sudden acquisition of larger-caliber weapons and field artillery such as the 105-millimeter howitzer abruptly changed the nature of the war and contributed heavily to the French humiliation at Dien Bien Phu. And fourth, further war became inevitable when United States–led backers of the incipient South Vietnamese democracy called off a 1956 election that had been agreed upon after Vietnam was divided in 1954.

In 1958 the communists unleashed a terrorist campaign in the South, followed later by both guerrilla and conventional warfare. Within two years, Northern-trained terrorists were assassinating an average of eleven government officials every day. President John Kennedy referred to this campaign in 1961 when he decided to increase the number of American soldiers operating inside South Vietnam. "We have talked about and read stories of 7,000 to 15,000 guerrillas operating in Viet Nam, killing 2,000 civil officers a year and 2,000 police officers a year, 4,000 total," said Kennedy. "How we fight that kind of problem, which is going to be with us all through this decade, seems to me to be one of the great problems now before the United States."[4]

The United States entered the war reluctantly, halfheartedly, and with a confused and ineffective strategy. But its leadership felt morally and politically compelled to do so, and even such major newspapers as the *Washington Post* initially supported the effort. The U.S. recognized South Vietnam as a separate political entity from North Vietnam, just as it saw West Germany as being separate from communist-controlled East Germany, and just as it continues to distinguish South Korea from communist-controlled North Korea. And South Vietnam was being invaded by the North just as certainly (although with more sophistication) as North Korea had invaded South Korea.

There has been little historical recognition of how brutal the war was for those who fought it on the ground. Dropped onto the enemy's terrain twelve thousand miles away from home, America's citizen-soldiers performed with a tenacity and quality that may never be truly understood. Those who believe the war was fought incompetently on a tactical level should consider that the Vietnamese communists admit to losing 1.4 million soldiers, compared to South Vietnamese losses of 245,000 and American losses of 58,000. And those who believe that it was a "dirty little war" where bombs did all the work might contemplate that it was the most costly war the U.S. Marine Corps has ever fought. Five times as many Marines died in Vietnam as in World War I, three times as many as in Korea, and there were more total casualties (killed and wounded) for the Marines in Vietnam than in all of World War II.

That the war was pursued with honorable intentions does not mean that those who conceived and implemented our strategy deserve any prizes. My own father, who had defined for me the notion of loyalty, became disgusted with Defense Secretary Mc-Namara's so-called "whiz kids" after being assigned to the Pentagon in 1965.

When I was commissioned in the Marine Corps in 1968, he was working on a highly classified program he could not discuss openly, but which I later learned was a satellite linkup from Vietnam to Washington, giving civilian leaders full daily oversight of the war. Watching firsthand the Johnson administration's dissembling to the Congress and disrespect of military leaders, he urged me more than once to go into the navy, find myself a nice ship where I could, as he so often put it, "sit in the wardroom and eat ice cream," and not risk myself as a Marine on an ever-deteriorating battlefield. Once I did receive my orders for combat, my father put in his papers to retire from the air force, telling me he "couldn't bear to watch it" while still wearing a military uniform. Sitting at the kitchen table in his government-issue quarters at Andrews Air Force Base, fighting back the temptation to break the law and share classified information with me, he was ferociously intense, this man who had found his life's calling by flying bombers and cargo planes and perfecting the art of shooting intercontinental ballistic missiles. And he was telling me, as a father and a military professional, that this strategically botched war was not worth my life.

Finally he found the words that communicated his unease without violating his oath of office. "Do you realize Lyndon Johnson is going to know you're wounded before your division commander does? And do you know what that says about the ability of the American military to fight a long-term war?"

He was wrong. Lyndon Johnson never knew I was wounded, because by then Richard Nixon was running the show.

My professional career in writing and government is entirely accidental. At the age of twenty-two my dream was to become a general officer in the Marine Corps. Had I not been wounded, I would never have gone to law school. And had I not gone to law school, I would never have fully comprehended the disdain that many of the advantaged in my generation felt for those who had fought in Vietnam, or the ingrained condescension of the nation's elites toward my culture. And had I never been exposed to this unthinking arrogance, I would not have begun the journey of discovery that, over three decades, finally led to this book. And so, in an odd way, it can be said that I owe all of this to Ho Chi Minh, and to Richard Nixon's post-Tet campaign offensive of 1969.

I was fully prepared for what awaited me in Vietnam. At the Naval Academy, I became one of six finalists for the position of brigade commander despite having less than stellar grades, and was one of 18 in my class of 841 to receive a special commendation for leadership upon graduation. At the grueling Marine Corps Officers' Basic School in Quantico, I had graduated first in my class of 243, scoring 99.3 in leadership and also winning the Military Skills Award for the highest average in the areas of physical fitness, marksmanship, land navigation, and military instruction. Few things in life have come as naturally to me as combat, however difficult those days proved to be. And conversely, few things have surprised me so completely as the other world I entered a few years later when I arrived at the Georgetown University Law Center.

1969 was an odd year to be in Vietnam. Second only to 1968 in terms of American casualties, it was the year made famous by Hamburger Hill as well as the gut-wrenching *Life* magazine cover story showing the pictures of 242 Americans who had been killed in one average week of fighting. Back home it was the year of

Woodstock and of numerous antiwar rallies that culminated in the Moratorium march on Washington. The My Lai massacre hit the papers and was seized upon by the antiwar movement as the emblematic moment of the war. Lyndon Johnson left Washington in utter humiliation. Richard Nixon entered the scene, destined for an even worse fate.[5]

I spent my tour in the An Hoa basin southwest of Da Nang, where the 5th Marine Regiment was in its third year of continuous combat operations. As a rifle platoon and company commander, I served under a succession of three regimental commanders who had cut their teeth in World War II, and four different battalion commanders, three of whom had seen combat in Korea. The company commanders were typically captains on their second combat tour in Vietnam or young first lieutenants like myself, who were given companies after many months of "bush time" as platoon commanders in the basin's tough and unforgiving environs.

The basin was one of the most heavily contested areas in Vietnam, its torn, cratered earth offering every sort of wartime possibility. In the canopied mountains just to the west, not far from the Ho Chi Minh Trail, the North Vietnamese Army operated an infantry division from an area called Base Area 112. In the valleys of the basin, main-force Viet Cong battalions whose ranks were 80 percent North Vietnamese Army regulars moved against the Americans every day. Local Viet Cong units sniped and harassed. Ridgelines and paddy dikes were laced with sophisticated booby traps of every size, from hand grenades to 250-pound bombs. The villages, where many battles took place, sat in the rice paddies and tree lines like individual fortresses, crisscrossed with trenches and spider holes, their homes sporting bunkers capable of surviving direct hits from large-caliber artillery shells. The Viet Cong infrastructure was intricate and permeating. Except for the old and the very young, villagers who did not side with the communists had either been killed or driven out to the government-controlled enclaves near Da Nang.

In the rifle companies we spent endless months patrolling ridgelines and villages and mountains, far away from any notion of tents, barbed wire, hot food, or electricity. Luxuries were limited to what would fit inside one's pack, which after a few "humps" usually boiled down to letter-writing material, towel, soap, toothbrush, poncho liner, and a small transistor radio. We moved through the boiling heat with sixty pounds of weapons and gear, causing a typical Marine to drop 20 percent of his body weight while in the bush. When we stopped, we dug chest-deep fighting holes and slit trenches for toilets. We slept on the ground under makeshift poncho hootches, and when it rained we usually took our hootches down because wet ponchos shined under illumination flares, making great targets. Sleep itself was fitful, never more than an hour or two at a stretch for months at a time as we mixed daytime patrolling with nighttime ambushes, listening posts, foxhole duty, and radio watches. Ringworm, hookworm, malaria, and dysentery were common as was trench foot when the monsoons came. Respite was rotating back to the mud-filled regimental combat base at An Hoa for four or five days, where rocket and mortar attacks were frequent and our troops manned defensive bunkers at night.

We had been told while in training that Marine officers in the rifle companies had an 85 percent probability of being killed or wounded, and the experience of "Dying Delta," as our company was known, bore that out. Of the officers in the bush when I arrived, our company commander was wounded, the weapons platoon commander was wounded, the first platoon commander was killed, the second platoon commander was wounded twice, and I, commanding the third platoon, was wounded twice. The enlisted troops in the rifle platoons fared no better. Two of my original three squad leaders were killed, the third shot in the stomach. My platoon sergeant was severely wounded, as was my platoon guide. By the time I left my platoon I had gone through six radio operators, five of them casualties.

These figures were hardly unique; in fact, they were typical.

Many other units—for instance, those that fought the hill battles around Khe Sanh, or those with the famed Walking Dead of the 9th Marine Regiment, or that were in the battle for Hue City or at Dai Do—had it far worse.

When I remember those days and the very young men who spent them with me, I am continually amazed, for these were mostly recent civilians barely out of high school, called up from the cities and the farms to do their year in Hell and then return. Visions haunt me every day, not of the nightmares of war but of the steady consistency with which my Marines faced their responsibilities, and of how uncomplaining most of them were in the face of constant danger. The salty, battle-hardened twenty-year-olds teaching green nineteen-year-olds the intricate lessons of that hostile battlefield. The unerring skill of the young squad leaders as we moved through unfamiliar villages and weed-choked trails in the black of night. The quick certainty with which they moved when coming under enemy fire. Their sudden tenderness when a fellow Marine was wounded and needed help. Their willingness to risk their lives to save other Marines in peril.

In July 1969, I was hit by two grenades while clearing a series of bunkers along a streambed in a place of frequent combat called the Arizona Valley. The first grenade peppered me lightly on the face and shoulders. The second detonated behind me just after I shot the man who threw it and a second soldier who was pointing an AK-47 at me from inside the same bunker. I was hit in the head, back, arm, and leg, and the grenade's concussion lifted me into the air and threw me down a hill into the stream. I still carry shrapnel at the base of my skull and in one kidney from the blast. But the square, quarter-sized piece that scored the inside of my left knee joint and lodged against the bone of my lower leg would eventually change the direction of my life.

I did not pay much attention to my wounds. I had seen dead Marines, multiple-limb amputees, high-arm amputees, severed spinal cords, bladders ripped open by shrapnel, sucking chest wounds, even one Marine who had been shot between the eyes and out the jaw only to come back to our company after three months in a Japanese hospital. Like so many others during this woefully misunderstood war, I rejoined my unit as soon as possible. I belonged in the bush. Returning to my company before the leg wound had completely healed, it soon became infected. I ignored the infection and the joint itself eventually became septic, complicated by a small, razor-sharp piece of shrapnel that migrated into the joint's open spaces and chewed on the cartilage whenever I walked or ran. I would not learn the full extent of this damage until I completed my tour and returned to the United States.

There followed two years of surgeries and physical therapy as I tried to rehabilitate my leg and remain in the Marine Corps. In 1971, I was put on limited duty and assigned to a desk job on the secretary of the navy's staff. Following a surgery in early 1972, the joint unexpectedly swelled and drained heavily through the stitches, an indication of continuing infection in the bone, and I was finally referred to a medical board. The operating surgeon wrote that, because of the infection, the articular cartilage "was so markedly destroyed that one could easily indent it with a hemostat" and commented that "It is remarkable to note the amount of weight he has succeeded in lifting when one considers the condition of his knee pathologically, indicative of the motivational factors that have sustained him as a Marine officer." He then concluded that "This man is highly motivated and wishes to excel in what areas he can perform in the Marine Corps; however he has diligently exercised for three years with no improvement; indeed, with worsening."

I had recently become one of 16 first lieutenants out of a group of more than 2,700 to be promoted a year early to captain. I loved commanding infantry troops. I had never given any thought as to what I might do if I became a civilian. And now I was one.

2

The Invisible People

THE MARINE CORPS, which took 103,000 killed or wounded out of some 400,000 sent to Vietnam, represented one extreme of that volatile era. The better academic institutions such as the Georgetown Law Center, which I entered in August 1972, represented the other. Moreover, the divide between these two extremes was nearly total. In the Marine Corps, virtually everyone I knew had pulled at least one tour in Vietnam. While at Georgetown Law, among a student body of eighteen hundred people who were largely the same age, I can recall meeting only three other students who were combat veterans. There may have been others. If so, they were not anxious to share their experiences in the law school's bitterly antiwar environment.

It is often said that Vietnam was a draftee's war, fought by the poor and the minorities. More accurately, it was a war fought mainly by volunteers, including two-thirds of those who served and 73 percent of those who died, who came heavily from traditionalist cultures such as the Scots-Irish. Minorities were well represented, but not overly so. African-Americans made up 13.1 percent of the age group, 12.6 percent of the military, and 12.2 percent of the casualties. And most glaringly, the generation's academic elites largely sat out the war. Harvard had lost 691 alumni during World

War II,[6] but in Vietnam, Harvard College lost twelve men from the 12,595 who made up the classes of 1962 through 1972 combined. Princeton's 8,108 male undergraduates during this same period lost six. MIT's 8,998 lost two.[7]

The differences between these two extremes went much further than the war. In the eight years since that 1964 summer, when the Civil Rights Act had first been signed and the Gulf of Tonkin Resolution signaled the beginning of a major escalation in Vietnam, the nation had been sundered by war, urban violence, massive protests, and political assassinations. Along the way the baby boomer generation suffered a schizophrenic divide that has yet to fully mend. And forget all the talk of the "generation gap"; this rupture was largely along cultural and class lines, with racial issues sometimes blurring class distinctions. On one side were self-described political radicals, peaceniks, Black Power activists, flower children, and others who believed the American system was irretrievably broken. On the other were the traditionalists who were fighting the war, working in the coal mines and the factories, studying in less eminent colleges and universities, and worrying that the American system as they knew it was being destroyed by the forces of dissent.

Eight years of turmoil had created an irreversible inertia in both camps. This bifurcation of viewpoints had accelerated since the pivotal nightmare of 1968, which had seen the Tet Offensive in Vietnam, the assassinations of Martin Luther King, Jr., and Robert Kennedy, and the street riots during the Democratic National Convention in Chicago. The national uproar following the shooting deaths of four students during antiwar protests at Kent State in 1970 accelerated it even further. To the antiwar movement and even in popular culture, the Kent State tragedy represented the actions of a government gone gruesome and mad. Crosby, Stills, Nash, and Young warned darkly in a huge hit song of "tin soldiers and Nixon coming," and opined that "we gotta get back to where soldiers aren't gunning us down," as if antiwar protesters were somehow being hunted on a daily basis by the army. Among those who had served in combat, the incident was tragic but hardly emblematic, and the media attention given to it seemed disproportionate if not absurd. The ill-trained National Guardsmen, hounded and physically assaulted by protesting crowds for days, had fired above the heads of those who were pursuing them, their bullets accidentally killing innocent bystanders. And how many U.S. soldiers were killed in Vietnam that week? No one in the media seemed to know or care. The bitterness over this disparity in media treatment ran deep. Long after the war ended, many Vietnam veterans kept bumper stickers on their cars that read "Vietnam / Kent State. 58,000 to 4."

At Georgetown Law, the overwhelming preponderance of students and faculty came heavily from America's better universities and were clearly among the dissenters. Years of intellectual conditioning had taught them that the government was corrupt, that the capitalist system was rapacious, that the military was incompetent and even invidious, and that the WASP culture that had largely built America had done so at the expense of other ethnic and racial groups. To many of them the Vietnam War was largely an extension of a racist, colonialist, capitalist system that had its origins in the evils of slavery and the genocide of Native Americans during the nation's westward expansion. And by implication, in their eyes the ones who had agreed to serve in Vietnam were either criminal or stupid.

By August 1972 one could understand the nation's war weariness, although a Harris Poll taken that very month indicated strong support for continued bombing of North Vietnam (55 percent to 32 percent) and for mining North Vietnamese harbors (64 percent to 22 percent), and, by a margin of 74 percent to 11 percent, it showed an overwhelming agreement that "it is important that South Vietnam not fall into the control of the communists."[8] What one could not easily comprehend was the unthinking viciousness of so many among those who had not gone when they spoke of the government and of those who had stepped forward to serve. These were not America's downtrodden sitting in the classrooms of Georgetown Law. Radicalism was an elitist, largely intellectual phenomenon, and America's best and brightest were at the height of their disaffection with their own society.

The mood at the law center was outrageously out of step with the rest of America and yet filled with an unbending, adamant certainty. In a straw poll just before the 1972 election, Richard Nixon received eight votes out of more than a thousand students who voted and was endorsed by no one on the faculty, yet despite the turmoil of Watergate he would receive two-thirds of the votes in the actual election. Nixon was routinely compared to Hitler. Words like "fascist" and "pig" echoed through debates about the war. A few students wore the Viet Cong flag on their jackets in the same manner that others wore college or pro team logos. Professors began discussions with little jokes about "contradictions in terms, such as military intelligence," or humorous analogies such as "military justice is to justice as military music is to music." In criminal law class, the concept of consent in rape was introduced with an example of an American soldier in Vietnam walking into a village, carrying his weapon, and choosing a random female victim who acquiesced in sexual intercourse. "You know how our guys are in Vietnam," the professor winked. "She sees the gun. Did she consent?"

Sometimes it became more personal. Our final exam in criminal law, worth 100 percent of one's grade, began with a supposedly humorous fact pattern about a platoon sergeant named "Jack Webb" who lost two of his fellow soldiers dead while leading a combat patrol in Vietnam. "Sergeant Webb" then decided to smuggle jade that he had bought on the black market in Bangkok by stuffing the gems inside his soldiers' wounds before escorting their remains home for their funerals. And the question: To what extent did the Fourth Amendment allow customs officials to search inside the holes of the dead bodies in order to find the jade? To state the obvious, after all the broken bodies and the nights spent in the rain and the blood-filled operations and the dead friends whose lives to me were sacrosanct, this personalized approach to the constitutional issue of search and seizure did not exactly strike me as funny. I could not bring myself to reread the question, and it was a difficult challenge to finish the rest of the exam.

Nor was this simply an insensitive, unthinking act. I had recently won the law school's first-year legal writing competition with an article about a young black Marine who had been wrongly convicted of a war crime in Vietnam. Six years later I would clear Sam Green's name, although by then I was doing it for his mother, as Green had taken his own life halfway through the process. My professor, only three years older than I and clearly on the other side of the cultural divide, knew of my Marine Corps background and how strongly I felt about those who had fought in Vietnam. The same professor who had defined consent in rape with a wink toward "how our guys are in Vietnam" was now dropping a big one on my lap.

Not wishing to cheapen the memory of the friends and fellow Marines I had lost in combat by protesting my grade, I instead wrote a letter to the dean of the law school pointing out that the professor knew of my background, used not only an odious Vietnam analogy but also my name, and thus at a minimum lacked the judgment to teach at such a prestigious school. If such a fact pattern had been written after World War II, the professor would have been drawn and quartered, probably by the students themselves. At Georgetown Law he was given tenure.

Debates about the shape and direction of American society were similarly skewed. The very legitimacy of so-called WASP America was under relentless attack, both for the supposedly authoritarian society that the WASPs had created and for the unfair advantages that its members allegedly held. Affirmative action programs were in their infancy, and ethnocentric retreat was replacing old notions of America's melting pot, defining the very nature of government benefits to an age group. In this convenient, pseudo-Marxist scenario, anyone who was not a White Anglo-

Saxon Protestant had grounds for complaint about his or her people's collective "struggle." And anyone who was a WASP was by de-
fault a privileged, less-than-deserving whipping post. As one Ivy
League graduate said in my presence, "You don't need the W because they're all white, and you don't need the P because they're all
Protestant. That leaves you with nothing but an ASS."

Over time it became clear that, at bottom, this vitriol was not
really about the war or even about simple political disagreement. It
was instead a larger battle between the cultural forces that were
supposedly behind the creation of a mercantile, racist American society and thus had brought us into war, and a collective group of opposing forces that wished to diminish their power while a new
America was being created from the ashes of their past glories.
History, as the poet T. S. Eliot once wrote, has many cunning pas-
sages, and certainly is not as clear-cut as the activists were trying to
make it. But the WASPs, forever on the defensive, were losing big-
time. And in this academic stratosphere where the attitudes of future policy-makers were being formed, the Scots-Irish culture, like
the Vietnam veteran, was largely invisible.

To be of Scots-Irish heritage as this debate raged on was to lose
twice, for in these arguments the culture's historical journey was
both unknown and irrelevant. First, since the dominant forces in
American society were by assumption the WASP hierarchy, to be
white, Protestant, and of British heritage immediately lumped one
in with the New England Brahmin elites. In this perverted logic,
those who had been the clearest victims of Yankee colonialism
were now grouped together with the beneficiaries. All WASPs were
considered to be the same in this environment, as if they had
landed together on the same ship at Plymouth Rock and the smart
ones had gone to Boston while the dumbest had somehow made
their way to West Virginia.

And second, it was impossible to argue the distinctions among
the cultures that had originally settled the South and Border South.
To be of Southern descent brought with it an immediate presump-

tion of invidious discrimination and cruelty dating back to the slave system and the unequal, segregated society that followed it. Through a false reading of history that focused only on the disadvantages that had accrued to blacks, the white cultures whose ancestors had gained the least benefit from the elitist social structure of the Old South were being grouped together with the veneer that had formed the aristocracy. The occasional Southerners who had studied alongside these students and professors at the better universities typically reinforced this premise, either through their own privileged origins, or by ducking the debate, or by becoming self-hating stereotypes who deflected criticism by denouncing the culture that had spawned them.

These debates and the presumptions that fed them were based on an enormous, palpable falsity fed by the reality that few who were advancing such ideas had ever experienced the intricacies of the cultures in America's heartland with any degree of intimacy. These bright but inexperienced intellectuals had never seen with their own eyes the culture that they were ignoring, and instead were forming hard opinions based on unrealities that were as mythical as the shadows on the wall of Plato's Cave. But it was almost impossible to argue against their presumptions. To speak of one's family journey was dismissed as anecdotal if not unrepresentative of a culture's true journey. And for all the minute details that went into socioeconomic data based on race, there was no available data that would show the vast distinctions among white Americans. And yet it was intuitively obvious to the casual observer, as our professors liked to say in other matters, that the statistical straw man of "white America" being used to determine minority inclusiveness was nothing more than an imaginary facade. Indeed, white America is so variegated that it is an ethnic fairy tale.

In 1974, toward the end of my second year at Georgetown Law, the University of Chicago's National Opinion Research Center (NORC) published a landmark study, dividing American whites into seventeen ethnic and religious backgrounds and scoring them

by educational attainment and family income.[9] Contrary to prevailing mythology, the vaunted White Anglo-Saxon Protestants
were even then not at the top. The highest WASP group—the
Episcopalians—ranked sixth in family income, behind American
Jews, then Irish, Italian, German, and Polish Catholics. Other
white Protestants, principally the descendants of those who had
settled the Midwest and the South, constituted the bottom eight
groups, and ten of the bottom twelve. Educational attainment and
income levels did not vary geographically, as for instance among
white Baptists (who scored the lowest overall) living in Arkansas or
California, a further indication that these differences were culturally rather than geographically based.

Family income in the NORC study varied by almost $5,000 dol-
lars, from the Jewish high of $13,340 to the Baptist low of $8,693.
By comparison, in the 1970 census the variance in family income
between whites taken as a whole and blacks was only $3,600. In ad-
dition, white Baptists averaged only 10.7 years of education, which
was almost four years less than American Jews and at the same
level of black Americans in 1970. This meant that, even prior to the
major affirmative action programs, there was a greater variation
within "white America" than there was between white America and
black America. And in terms of education and income, the whites
at the bottom were in approximately the same situation as blacks.

The past thirty years of affirmative action and the more expan-
sive concept of diversity quotas have not altered this reality; instead, they have exacerbated it. In the technological age, with the
shrinking of the industrial base, the decrease in quality of public
education, and the tendency of those who "have" to protect their
own and utilize greater assets to prepare them for the future, the
divergence in both expectation and reward among our citizens has
grown rather than disappeared. In this context, the untold story of
the programs designed to bring racial diversity into the American
mainstream is that diversity among white cultures has been ignored, with the result that less-advantaged whites have often paid

far beyond their percentage of the white population when quotas have been put into place for the benefit of minorities.

Recent data from the NORC's General Social Survey on white American adults born after World War II indicates that the vast distinctions in educational attainment among whites has not abated. Social Survey data for the years 1980–2000 shows that white Baptists, who are heavily descended from the Scots-Irish culture, as well as "Irish Protestants," who are almost exclusively from that culture, rank well below other white ethnic groups, and also well below the combined national average when all racial and ethnic groups are taken together. This data shows that only 18.4 percent of white Baptists born after World War II and 21.8 percent of Irish Protestants have obtained a college degree, compared to a national average 30.1 percent that includes all races, a Jewish average of 73.3 percent, and an average among those of Chinese and Indian descent of 61.9 percent.

Again, there is no regional variance to this lack of education; the percentage of college graduates among those who grew up in the South is little different from those whose families had migrated out of the South to other places. These figures indicate that, similar to the much-discussed experiences of black Americans, whites who migrated from the South with little capital, and after the generations of educational deprivation that followed the Civil War, often brought their cultural disadvantages with them. Whatever comment one might wish to make about this fact as a cultural feature, these members of our society can hardly be called advantaged in a way that justifies legal discrimination against them as interchangeable members of a supposedly monolithic white majority.

Does this lack of educational access matter? Ron K. Unz, a prominent California businessman and political activist, examined the ethnic makeup of Harvard College in the *Wall Street Journal* not long ago. As he wrote, "Asians comprise between 2% and 3% of the U.S. population, but nearly 20% of Harvard undergraduates. Then, too, between a quarter and a third of Harvard students identify themselves as Jewish." Unz continues, "Thus it appears that Jews and Asians approximate half of Harvard's student body, leaving the other half for the remaining 95% of America [and this is without taking into account the 15% minority quota]. . . . Furthermore, even among non-Jewish whites there is almost certainly a severe skew in representation, with Northeastern WASPs being far better represented than other demographic or religious groups such as Baptists or Southerners. . . . This entire ethnic dilemma is present to a greater or lesser degree at most of our other elite educational institutions. . . . And partly because these universities act as a natural springboard to elite careers in law, medicine, finance and technology, many of these commanding heights of American society seem to exhibit a similar skew in demographic composition."[10]

And so the answer is that it appears to matter a great deal. It is an odd reality that in cultural terms, the dividing line of race and ethnicity in America is steadily becoming blurred, a friendship and a marriage at a time, while in political terms race and ethnicity continue to define government entitlements and, inevitably, power. And in the age of globalization, when so many of America's hands-on manufacturing jobs have been exported to cheaper labor pools in Third World countries, it matters even more, for our society is increasingly diverging along the lines suggested by Mr. Unz.

That those of Scots-Irish descent have failed to use such evidence in order to argue against diversity programs that do not distinguish among the widely varying white ethnic groups is as much a comment on their individuality as it is on their political naïveté. To argue about such disparities would require that they act collectively. And to act collectively would require that they alter their historic understanding of what it means to be an American. And thus the final question in this age of diversity and political correctness is whether they can learn to play the modern game of group politics. For if they do, they hold the future direction of America in their collective hands.

This culture has more power than it understands. It has shaped the emotional fabric of the nation, defined America's unique form of populist democracy, created a distinctively American musical style, and through the power of its insistence on personal honor and adamant individualism has become the definition of "American" that others gravitate toward when they wish to drop their hyphens and join the cultural mainstream. It has produced great military and political leaders, memorable athletes, talented performers, and successful entrepreneurs. It also has the most powerful issue in American politics on its side: simple fairness. Indeed, the Scots-Irish notion of fairness has dominated the most insistent rhetoric about the American democratic system since the days of Andrew Jackson—that the life and access to the future of every human being has equal value, regardless of wealth or social status. And the Scots-Irish people brought this concept to reality through the frequently bloody, brutally confrontational process of refusing, over and over again, to be dominated from above for reasons that benefited only the ruling classes.

In the summer of 2003, a folklife festival on the Mall in Washington, DC, had as one of its features the arts, crafts, and music of the Appalachian Mountain region. During that festival, Phyllis Deal of Clintwood, Virginia, a maker of Appalachian foodstuffs, was more definitive than she probably even intended when asked by a *Washington Post* reporter if her products were being marketed through local food cooperatives. "No," she answered. "There's a traditional resistance to cooperatives in our area. We're not very cooperative."[11]

Dear Mrs. Deal: I admire your independent spirit. But it's time to get more cooperative.

3

Rites of Passage:
The Legacy of Camel Six

You can't stomp us out and you can't make us run
Cause we're them old boys raised on shotguns.
We say grace, we say "ma'am,"
And if you ain't into that we don't give a damn.

—HANK WILLIAMS, JR.,
"A Country Boy Can Survive"

DUE LARGELY TO the odd-couple marriage of rebellious political populism and strict religious Calvinism in the Scottish Kirk during the Protestant Reformation, the traditional Scots-Irish culture is a study in wild contrasts. These are an intensely religious people—indeed, they comprise the very heart of the Christian evangelical movement—and yet they are also unapologetically and even devilishly hedonistic. They are probably the most antiauthoritarian culture in America, conditioned from birth to resist any pressure from above, and yet they are known as the most intensely patriotic segment of the country as well. They are naturally rebellious, often impossible to control, and yet their strong military tradition produces generation after generation of perhaps the finest soldiers the world has ever seen. They are filled with wanderlust and are ethnically assimilative, but their love of their own heritage can move them to tears when the bagpipes play, and no matter how far they roam, their passion for family travels with them.

Underlying these seeming contradictions is an unwritten but historically consistent code of personal honor and individual accountability. For untold centuries this code has required males of the culture to prove through physical challenge that they possess the courage, judgment, loyalty, and survival skills necessary to take their place among the "Celtic kinship." Modern sociologists may wish to demean this process and call it sexist or outmoded, but it nonetheless persists, through a series of formal and informal rites of passage. The specifics may vary, but as the generations move forward, the end result is strikingly familiar. Through a system of rewards and punishments, honor and shame, and ultimately acceptance or rejection, the Scots-Irish culture shapes its own version of manhood in accordance with the traditions that have sustained it. One is tempted to call this process the Redneck Bar Mitzvah.

Since the culture is assimilative and also emphasizes collateral kinship, the rites of passage do not always take place inside the family or even the extended family. Group activities such as hunting and athletics often play an important role, as does the proving ground of military service. I like to claim that my two closest lifelong friends are both Scots-Irish, even though one is of Filipino descent and the other is Russian. But the rituals and demands of military service imbued both with the same identifiable traits of courage, personal honor, and loyalty that one would find in the mountain communities of Virginia or Tennessee. While never losing their own ethnic identity, they have also met the test of mine.

These standards were passed down to me hard and early by my father, and I have done the same thing with my son. In both cases it was automatic, even more the role of a father than checking homework or making sure we went to church. In this culture, if one is to be recognized as a leader, he must know how to fight and be willing to do so, even in the face of certain defeat. He must be willing to compete in games of skill, whether they are something as traditional as organized athletics, as specialized as motorcycle or stock car racing, or as esoteric as billiards or video games. He must know how to use a weapon to defend himself, his family, and his friends. He should know how to hunt and fish and camp, and thus survive. And throughout his young life he should observe and learn from the strong men in his midst, so that he can take their lessons with him into adulthood and pass them on to the next generation. Perhaps, as some claim, the advance of civilization and the sophistication of our society have made many of these lessons irrelevant. But to me, the attitudes they ingrained have been the most consistent sustaining forces in my life.

I began hunting with my father as a very small boy, following him puppylike through dense woods and acting as his retriever when he shot rabbit and squirrel. He gave me my first rifle at the age of eight, as I did with my son. From age five he took me fishing, cutting a branch off a tree and tying fishing line onto it so that I could pull in sunfish while he went for bass. At about the same age he taught me how to both follow and lay a trail in the woods, and how to make an "Indian fire," large enough to cook over but small enough not to be noticed at a distance. When I was ten he gave me my first bait-casting rod. To him, bait-casting was an art form. At his direction, I spent untold hours in the backyard casting a dummy lure into an old bicycle tire, putting a handkerchief between my elbow and my side to keep me from "throwing" the rod at my target, so that I would learn to snap a rod using only my wrist.

When I was six my father bought me my first pair of boxing gloves and taught me how to use them. In the military housing projects when I was growing up and in the public schools of Alabama and the Midwest where I lived, it was common for young boys to form a human ring and take turns inside it, facing off against one another in an endless set of sparring matches. At a very early age my father laid out the eternal ground rules for street-fighting: Never start a fight, but never run away, even if you know you are going to lose. If you run, you'll still be running tomorrow. And if you fight, win or lose, a bully won't come back. And whomever you fight, you must make them pay. You must always mark them, so that the next day they have to face the world with a black eye or a cut lip or a bruised cheek, and remember where they got it.

My most memorable childhood moments were the ones spent at the outer edges of what other cultures might call the tribal circle, listening to my father and his longtime friends swap tales. This ritual is at the heart of the Scots-Irish culture, still replayed in hunting lodges and fishing camps throughout America as the old and young gather ostensibly to hunt or fish but in reality to celebrate their bonds and pass on their way of life. In the cabins and around the campfires the lions sit at center stage, trading false insults and challenging each other, jesting with the emeritus elders who need no longer fight, telling tales of younger days or of those who have gone before. And on the outer edges, ever quiet, the young boys listen, awed and thankful to be in the presence of the drinking and the swearing, absorbing stories that tell them what it means to be a man, and longing for the day that they can finally sit as full members of the tribe.

I drank my first whiskey straight from the bottle on a cold Missouri night while on a raccoon hunt with my Uncle Dub and two other young cousins. We drove in a column of trucks down dirt roads into the far fields and the half dozen hunters let their dogs go, then gathered at the trucks as the coon dogs yapped along the nearby tree lines, waiting for the telltale baying that would signal they had treed the coon. As always they were fired with the unexplainable excitement of the hunt, telling grown men's stories as if we were not there. Then in the cold, crisp night the hounds began to bay, and the hunters picked up their weapons and headed toward the dogs. As I grabbed mine, the whiskey unexpectedly came to me. "It's cold, boy," an older farmer grinned, nodding at the half-empty bottle. I pulled the burning liquid into my belly and knew that I had moved one step closer to the center of the ring.

I spent untold hours fishing with my father and my Uncle Bud, who was not blood-related but as my father's best lifelong friend may as well have been. When I was young, Bud would simply ignore me, making a point never to rig my bait or help me unhook a caught fish. But as I became a full fishing partner, he took to me as if I were his own son. I learned more about my father and his brothers by listening to the two men talk than from lone conversations with my father himself. Bud Colwell and the Webb boys; those stories shaped me. How as a boy in Oklahoma, Bud had killed a rabbit by throwing a rock and hitting it in the head when it was on the run. And Bud running a labor gang in a Missouri gravel pit before the war, where one day he was suddenly attacked by a man he had not hired from the labor pool, and hitting the man so hard in the forehead that when the man woke up and blew his nose his eyeball popped out. And Bud, the toughest young man in Elwood, Kansas, a tiny river town that once had been Elwood, Missouri, until the spring floods receded and they saw they were now on the river's westward side, holding court in front of the general store the day the Webb boys moved to town. Bud pointing to a puddle in the dirt road, claiming that no man within fifty miles could put him in it. And my Uncle Tommy, inches shorter and rarely given to boasting, walking forward without a word and nonchalantly throwing him into the puddle.

Even in his fifties, fear and an animal respect would stalk Bud's eyes when he spoke of Tommy Lee Webb. How Tommy could throw a knockout punch that never moved more than about twelve inches. And how often that punch would be the only one thrown in a fight as Tommy, never given to arguing, would simply knock a man down within seconds after the first insult. How Tommy could fight three grown men at the same time and beat them all. How Tommy, thoroughly drunk, had driven through the main streets of nearby St. Joseph at fifty miles an hour with a cold focus that was unnerving to watch. How even a knife put straight into his chest in a fight over a woman had not slowed Tommy down once the wound had healed. How Tommy had learned to be a highly successful TV repairman not by going to some class but by buying a TV and taking it apart until he knew from his own intellect what every single tube did. And how Tommy had done the same thing with air conditioners, making a second successful business. Tommy was The Man.

Bud was The Man, too. He had spent almost all of World War II overseas, first in North Africa and then in Italy, serving so little time in this country that he did not even qualify for the American Campaign Medal. When he returned from the war, he began working for Otis Elevator, and a few years later both his retinas had hemorrhaged, destroying his central vision and leaving him legally blind. Taking a settlement from Otis and a small pension from the Veterans Administration, Bud moved to Florida, bought a dilapidated old house, and spent a year redoing it, learning how to use his hands without full vision. With the help of my father and two workers, he then built a silica sand plant from the bottom up, and when he was burned out by a competitor he found a new location and built another one, this time processing Fuller's Earth. Bud then traveled extensively, his wife, Anna, driving and serving as his assistant, selling his product all over America. Few of his buyers even knew he was blind.

One by one, the great lions of my young life died, and finally there was only my father. My generation had made it to the center of the ring, the favored places around the campfire, the main table in the cabin at the fishing camp. For a couple weeks every summer my father and brother and I, along with our sons and other friends, would gather in one Minnesota fishing camp or another, spending mornings and evenings going for bass and northern pike, drinking far too much, cooking for each other, and rekindling our understanding of who we were and from whence we had come. It was now our sons and nephews who gathered at the outer edges, quietly listening to the tales of those who had gone before them, sneaking a cigar or a beer and wondering at the time when their day would come. And my father became the elder emeritus, to be both constantly ribbed and, ultimately, revered.

We ribbed him mercilessly because that was the inevitable, final act for the old lions. My father had not been an easy man to grow up with. He did not spare the lash. He was given to making taunts and impossible challenges. When I was very young he would ask me if I was tough, and then hold out his fist and have me hit it again and again, telling me I could stop if I admitted I wasn't tough. My small fist would crumple against his and I would be unable to stop my tears, but I would never admit I wasn't tough. And now as he advanced to the far side of seventy, I would sometimes greet him in the morning with a clenched fist and a remembering taunt. "Come on, old man. Hit my fist." And we both knew without saying it that the mantle had passed, that his lesson had been learned, and that his methods, while frequently harsh, were never viewed as cruel.

We revered him because, while so many people on this earth had talked the talk, we knew that he had walked the walk. And hey, he was my pa. One summer we decided to name him Camel Six, Camel from a disgustingly funny joke my brother had told, and Six because it was the military designation for a unit commander. He deserved both; Camel because he could be disgustingly funny, drinking too much and talking too loud, never without an opinion; Six because he was indeed the Commander.

My father was The Main, Main Man.

In 1984, I was nominated and confirmed as Assistant Secretary of Defense for Reserve Affairs, responsible for the oversight of all the military's National Guard and Reserve programs as well as the evaluator of their ability to mobilize if the nation went to war. As the date for the swearing-in ceremony approached, the White House called and suggested that I ask Defense Secretary Caspar Weinberger to administer the oath of office, reasoning that the gesture might cement my relations with my new boss. Over time I came to admire Cap Weinberger more than any person I ever worked for outside of the Marine Corps. But I had another idea.

I called the General Counsel's office and asked if a military officer could legally administer the oath of office to a high-level civilian appointee. They said yes. Well, I asked, how about a retired military officer? They checked, and the next day said that this was indeed legal. And so I called old Camel Six and told him he needed to come up to Washington.

Hundreds of people were packed inside the Secretary of Defense's conference room on the day of the ceremony, including a few dozen friends, family members, and Marines who had served with me in Vietnam, plus the service secretaries and most of the Joint Chiefs of Staff. Caspar Weinberger made a short speech that officially introduced me to the Pentagon's hierarchy and outlined my professional experience. I made a few remarks about the challenges of the position and my sense of obligation to those who wore the military uniform. Then my mother stepped forward, holding a Bible, and my father administered the oath of office.

It was a simple moment, over in a minute or so. But as the audience of friends and high-level government officials applauded, my father choked up. I had seen him cry only once in my life, the day I had said good-bye to him as I left for Vietnam, when "Danny Boy" unexpectedly played on the radio. Now, I thought half-humorously, he's crying over a job. He grabbed my arm and whispered into my ear.

"I raised a little boy. But a giant just walked across this room."

If he were regarding me from the perspective of a former colonel, one who had worked his way up without great education, spending long years deployed and other years struggling from base to base and living in rented homes, I could sense his logic. At age thirty-eight, I now held the civilian equivalent rank of a four-star general. Indeed, three years later, almost to the day, I would be confirmed as Secretary of the Navy, and an official at the Naval Academy Alumni Association would call to tell me I was the first

Naval Academy graduate in history to serve in the military and then become Navy Secretary.

But as a man? My father, proud as he was, could not fool me. I had already spent enough time in Washington to know that one did not become a giant just because someone had selected him for a government job, no matter how many aides he had or how many limos drove him around town.

I knew who the giants were. They had made this country, mountain after mountain and dream by dream. They had fought the thin soil and the dense woods and the swamps, and the enemies who came to kill them and destroy their way of life. They had endured whole generations of poverty. They knew the certain dread of having nowhere to turn when the cold wind howled against the door, or when an unidentifiable fever raged up inside their children. Some of them had spent entire lifetimes facing that imposter called hopelessness without ever passing on to their children even a hint of the self-defeating monster of despair.

They had made me, one unbending attitude at a time. And I would never betray either Camel Six or their legacy.

4

Kensett, Arkansas

BIRCH HAYS HODGES and Georgia Frankie Doyle are buried in a small cemetery where the hamlet of Kensett gives way to a patch of still-untamed east Arkansas farmland. The knoll where they lie side by side overlooks an unending repetition of lush cow pastures and smoky tree lines. It brings me no comfort, but at the right time of summer I can stand at my grandparents' graves and feel my mind drift easily to visions of the thick, torn fields of Vietnam's Quang Nam Province, where I once patrolled as a Marine. Indeed, eastern Arkansas is heavy into rice these days, and driving along the back roads out of Memphis past wide fields and thin stands of trees always calls up in me an eerie resonance that will not go away. Longtime Vietnam correspondent Michael Herr, author of the often-electric memoir *Dispatches*, once opined that sometimes out on operations with the Marines it seemed as though it really was a war between their peasants and ours, and that the Marines conversed as if they were all from the same small town in Arkansas. They weren't, but they may as well have been. And that small town could well have been Kensett.

My mother's parents lie side by side below flat stone markers, next to the graves of two of their children who died before the age of ten. Forty years separated their respective burials. For my grandfather, who began in Kentucky and then left the coal mines of Carbondale, Illinois, dreaming that he might find diamonds in Arkansas, this was just where his body gave out. For my grand-mother, whose family crossed the Mississippi River into Arkansas from western Tennessee in a covered wagon when she was a small child, this grave in Kensett represents her final returning. Decades of dislocation had called her out to California, then back to Arkansas, on to Illinois and Missouri, and finally out to California again to live near her youngest daughter before her death at the age of eighty-three. But all that was nothing more than meander-ing. In the end she belonged beside Birch Hays Hodges on this lit-tle knoll at the outer edge of Kensett.

Granny was a strong force in my life. Behind that quick smile and slow, slow drawl was what I've come to call an acquiescent toughness that so characterizes the Scots-Irish women whose roots go back into the mountain South. Acquiescent because she knew that it did no good to question fate, and fate had brought her hard living. Toughness because no matter how hard things got, she was harder still. Thinking of how she and others so steadily faced the hardships that life brought them somehow brings to my mind a New Testament passage, from Paul's letter to the Romans. *We re-joice in our sufferings, knowing that suffering produces endurance, and endurance produces character, and character produces hope, and hope does not disappoint us, because God's love has been poured into our hearts.*

Well, not exactly rejoice, but certainly endure. Granny could make do with almost nothing. She could grow almost anything out of the ground. She could break a Lucky Strike cigarette in two when she stepped off a bus, knowing just how many drags she could take between the bus and home. The buses. I have to laugh. She was seventy-five years old when I finished the Naval Academy, and my father had paid to fly her from California to see me gradu-ate. It was her first airplane ride. She told my dad that she liked it okay, but when it came time for her to go back she took the bus—

three thousand miles. She liked bourbon better. The second night my dad poured her a shot, she declined, telling him that she couldn't drink it anymore because it made her feel too good.

It is not enough to say that I loved my grandmother. She lived with us from the time I was two until I was eight. My father, at that time an air force pilot, was gone for three of those years, to Alaska and then to England and then Germany, where he flew in the Berlin Airlift, and after that to remote bases where there was no family housing. At night during those long years, I would sleep with a picture of him standing at attention on a flight line next to one of his aircraft. For a little boy there could have been no nobler hero to look up to, no greater man in the entire world to honor and to miss, and I still keep that picture in my office today. When he was deployed, my grandmother helped fill the void, but she did much more. From the time I was old enough to listen, every night before I went to sleep she made our family history come alive. Many of the tales she told to me and my siblings had been passed down through the generations, mother and father to daughter and son. As a very young boy I came to know Revolutionary War soldiers, dead Confederates, quietly determined great-grandfathers who cut down trees and laid cordwood roads across swamps to bring horse-drawn wagons from Tennessee into the dark heart of Arkansas, and a mysteriously stubborn grandfather whose harshest phrase was "Dad blame it, Pete," a man crippled by a busted hip who would rather have died poor on his feet than live rich on his knees. And he had done just that.

Nor was old Birch Hodges alone in that respect. My father used to claim, with the disregard of one who had not been born there, that Arkansas had been settled by dreamers and thieves, and that over time the thieves had edged the dreamers out. In the decades following World War II, Arkansas became known for the vastly profitable Wal-Mart chain, the Tyson Foods conglomerate, and the Stephens brokerage, reputed to be the largest securities firm outside of Wall Street. Trickle-down theories haven't exactly taken hold, however, as the state has retained its reputation as something of a banana republic. Arkansas gives us scads of singers and actors, more than its share of athletes, good soldiers, and every now and then a notable but usually roguish politician. But its educational system has always been near rock bottom. Its crime rate, particularly in Pulaski County, home of Little Rock, has always hovered near the top. And in places like Kensett, nothing goes on, good or bad, that's much different from what was happening when my grandfather was still alive.

My great-aunt Lena lies in a pauper's grave at the outside edge of the cemetery. I remind myself that someday I must buy her a marker. She was a hard-living, highly intelligent woman who married late to an older widower, died childless, and suffered the ignominy of having her possessions gone through by strangers when she passed away at the age of ninety-two before family members could make the trip to Kensett and claim them. Standing at her unmarked grave, I remember sitting in the starkness of her living room in 1975 after I finished law school, under her quiet, almost accusing stare, and her finally breaking the silence by saying, simply, "So you've been to law school. Did they teach you how to *lie* yet?"

Another memory, or rather a passed-down recollection, haunts me as I contemplate the simple sack below the earth that holds the departed Lena's bones. For if I close my eyes and think my way into the misty fields and the distant past, I know that somewhere out there I might see an old truck rumbling into the dead of night, occupied by two hard women along with a little girl whose lame daddy had just walked into the house and died, heading out into the tree lines of some swampy absentee farm to cut and rick dead wood and haul it back to town and hamlet, and so to survive. It was Lena who managed to arrange for the truck that she and her sister and my mother used while the rest of Kensett and nearby Searcy slept, in order to deliver wood for cook stoves and fireplaces to front porches by dawn. Family rumor puts a name on it, but respect for the dead causes me to leave it to the imagination as to what Lena had to trade in order to procure the use of the truck. Lena got things done. Suffice it to say that those were hard and bitter times, and if it were not for Lena they would have been harder and more miserable still.

Not that Lena came away unscarred. She herself told me of the morning of her conversion, when she walked into the back door of a packed Baptist church, stood in the aisle with the entire congregation watching her, and threw her hands into the air and admitted, "I declare, I'm a sinner before God!" And her growing more fervent with old age, refusing to let me inside her house after I began working for a Republican congressman in 1977, standing instead in her front yard dressed only in a bathrobe in the cool April morning air, pointing a finger at me as she shouted, "How can you do this? Did you notice Jesus and Jimmy Carter both have the same initials? Every time I look at our president on TV, I see the blood of Jesus Christ, dripping off the cross onto his back!"

I loved my great-aunt Lena, although it wasn't always easy to do that. And I've got to get a marker for her grave.

I thirsted to hear these kin-people talk. I could sit entranced through magic hours in the stark kitchens and quiet, dusky living rooms of those who were willing to reach back like those ancient tribal elders and help me understand that my life is in some sense a continuum that began before I was born, and will carry me with it long after I am gone. Their revelations came in dribbles, sometimes coaxed and at others dropped casually into a conversation like a sly but knowing confession. The tough, enduring men and women who went through this cauldron did not speak openly or even willingly with each other about the bad times when I was growing up. It seems an unspoken axiom that people who have really had it hard are the last ones to sit around and reminisce about how hard they really had it. In fact, I know there are some who will not be happy that I've touched on those days here, however lightly. And I have lightly trod, for they did indeed live hard.

There's much more, the untold stories that have faded into scattered graves on cold and silent lips, the ones that belong to those who are still alive, and the others that I'm not allowed to tell. But just as Big Moccasin Gap defined one end of the trek across a raw continent, so does Kensett bring some of its tangled highways into focus. Two hundred years separate the family journeys at these two remote outposts. In that time a nation like no other evolved and grew. And yet in Big Moccasin Gap and in Kensett, time pretty well stands still.

And what are we left with? On the one hand we live in an America that is always changing. On the other we are looking at a people so individualistic and yet also so embracive that their ethnic history has melded with nearly every segment of our society while the strength of their culture has in so many ways given that same society its unique historical glue.

But to be sure, the Scots-Irish are a people filled with many offshoots and derivatives, with common threads that join them while strong differences obviate any thought of "ethnic purity" or even complete philosophical unity. We are related to those who stayed behind in Scotland and the border areas in the north of present-day England. We count as cousins those who remained in Ulster, not only Protestant but many Catholics as well. We ourselves are those who remained in the rough north of New England and especially along the mountain ridges that stretch from Pennsylvania to Georgia and Alabama; those who settled the backcountry and farmlands of the South, the Ohio Valley, and the Midwest; those who went north to the factories, west to the Rocky Mountains, and farther still to the farmlands and new freedom of the Pacific Coast. Some continued to marry among themselves, and some did not. Some are wildly prosperous, and some are not. Some remember at least pieces of this journey, and some do not. Some care, and some do not. Some think it matters, and some do not.

Who are we? We are the molten core at the very center of the unbridled, raw, rebellious spirit of America. We helped build this nation, from the bottom up. We face the world on our feet and not on our knees. We were born fighting. And if the cause is right, we will never retreat.

Notes

PART ONE: RULERS AND REDNECKS

1. U.S. Census figures. In Korea, West Virginia lost 801 combat dead from a population of 2 million. Connecticut, with a slightly larger population, lost 314. New York, with a population of 14.8 million, lost 2,243. In Vietnam, West Virginia lost 732 combat dead from a population of 1.74 million. Connecticut lost 611 from a population of 3.03 million. New York lost 4,120 from a population of 18.2 million.
2. Alexis de Tocqueville, *Democracy in America* (New York: Bantam Classic, 2000), p. 35.
3. Ibid., p. 34.
4. See James G. Leyburn, *The Scotch-Irish: A Social History* (Chapel Hill: University of North Carolina Press, 1962), pp. 179–83; and David Hackett Fischer, *Albion's Seed* (New York: Oxford University Press, 1989), pp. 608–9.
5. R. F. Foster, *Modern Ireland, 1600–1972* (London: Penguin, 1989), pp. 354–58.
6. Ibid., p. 357.
7. Walter Russell Mead, "The Jacksonian Tradition," *National Interest* (Winter 1999–2000), pp. 5–29.
8. Ibid., p. 15.
9. Ibid., pp. 12–13.
10. Ibid., p. 9.
11. Ibid., p. 11.

PART TWO: THE MAKING OF A PEOPLE — AND A NATION

1. The most concise and historically reliable explication of this period can be found in Nora Chadwick, *The Celts* (New York: Pelican, 1981), pp. 24–63.
2. Ibid., pp. 38–39.
3. Ibid., p. 39.
4. Ibid., p. 53.
5. Winston Churchill, *A History of the English-Speaking Peoples,* vol. 1, *The Birth of Britain* (New York: Dorset Press, 1990), p. 33.
6. Chadwick, *The Celts*, p. 66.
7. Ibid., p. 43.
8. See, e.g., John Boyd Brent in www.Scotland.com, at Hadrian's Wall.
9. Churchill, *Birth of Britain*, p. 40.
10. Cassius Dio, *Roman History*, bk. 77, chap. 12.
11. Ibid., chaps. 13 and 14.
12. Churchill, *Birth of Britain*, p. 41.
13. Ibid., pp. 36–37.
14. Ibid., p. 38.
15. Ibid., p. 169.
16. Ibid., p. 174.
17. T. C. Smout, *A History of the Scottish People, 1560–1830* (London: Fontana/Collins, 1981), p. 20.
18. For general reference see Chadwick, *The Celts*, pp. 75–76, 89–94; Smout, *A History of the Scottish People*, pp. 18–21; and J. D. Mackie, *A History of Scotland* (New York: Dorset Press, 1985), pp. 16–27.
19. Chadwick, *The Celts*, p. 76.
20. Smout, *A History of the Scottish People*, p. 19.
21. Ibid., p. 20.
22. Ibid., p. 22.
23. Ibid.
24. Ibid., p. 20.
25. Mackie, *A History of Scotland*, p. 41.
26. Smout, *A History of the Scottish People*, p. 22.
27. Ibid., p. 23.
28. Ibid., p. 24.
29. Joseph R. Strayer, *Western Europe in the Middle Ages* (New York: Appleton-Century-Crofts, 1955), p. 199.
30. Mackie, *A History of Scotland*, p. 63.
31. Churchill, *The Birth of Britain*, p. 304.
32. Ibid., p. 305.

33. Ibid.
34. Ibid., p. 308.
35. Mackie, *A History of Scotland*, p. 74.
36. Churchill, *The Birth of Britain*, p. 313.
37. Ibid., pp. 314–15.
38. Mackie, *A History of Scotland*, p. 76.

PART THREE: THE ULSTER SCOTS

1. R. F. Foster, *Modern Ireland, 1600–1972* (London: Penguin Books, 1989), pp. 12–13.
2. James G. Leyburn, *The Scotch-Irish: A Social History* (University of North Carolina Press, 1962), p. 85.
3. Joseph R. Strayer, *Western Europe in the Middle Ages* (New York: Appleton-Century-Crofts, 1955), p. 223.
4. Foster, *Modern Ireland*, p. 3.
5. Ibid., p. 35.
6. Leyburn, *The Scotch-Irish*, p. 88.
7. Ibid.
8. Foster, *Modern Ireland*, p. 44.
9. Ibid.
10. Leyburn, *The Scotch-Irish*, p. 88.
11. See Foster, *Modern Ireland*, p. 26.
12. Ibid., p. 60.
13. Ibid., p. 14.
14. Walter Harris, *Hibernica, or Ancient Tracts Relating to Ireland* (Dublin, 1770), quoted in Leyburn, *The Scotch-Irish*, pp. 90–91.
15. Henry Grey Graham, *The Social Life of Scotland in the Eighteenth Century*, 4th ed. (London, 1937), p. 185, quoted in Leyburn, *The Scotch-Irish*, p. 26.
16. David Hackett Fischer, *Albion's Seed* (New York: Oxford University Press, 1989), p. 624.
17. T. C. Smout, *A History of the Scottish People, 1560–1830* (London: Fontana/Collins, 1981), p. 32.
18. Ibid.
19. Leyburn, *The Scotch-Irish*, p. 7.
20. Fischer, *Albion's Seed*, p. 624.
21. See, e.g., Fischer, *Albion's Seed*, pp. 626–29; Leyburn, *The Scotch-Irish*, pp. 9–10; and Smout, *A History of the Scottish People*, p. 97.

22. Smout, A History of the Scottish People, p. 97.
23. Quoted in Fischer, Albion's Seed, p. 629.
24. Smout, A History of the Scottish People, p. 33.
25. Ibid., pp. 38–39.
26. Leyburn, The Scotch-Irish, p. 11.
27. Smout, A History of the Scottish People, p. 36.
28. Fischer, Albion's Seed, pp. 628, 660–62.
29. Mackie, A History of Scotland, p. 140.
30. Leyburn, The Scotch-Irish, p. 48.
31. Smout, A History of the Scottish People, pp. 50–51.
32. Mackie, A History of Scotland, pp. 141–43.
33. Smout, A History of the Scottish People, pp. 52–53.
34. Ibid., p. 53.
35. Biographical sketch of John Calvin, H. Henry Meeter Center for Calvin Studies, Calvin College, Grand Rapids, MI.
36. Charles H. Sylvester, ed., Progress of Nations (Hanson-Bellows Co., 1912), vol. 3, p. 457.
37. Smout, A History of the Scottish People, p. 56.
38. See Winston Churchill, A History of the English-Speaking Peoples, vol. 2, The New World (New York: Dorset Press, 1990), pp. 104–19.
39. See Mackie, A History of Scotland, pp. 145–58; Smout, A History of the Scottish People, pp. 56–77; and Leyburn, The Scotch-Irish, pp. 54–67.
40. Mackie, A History of Scotland, pp. 156–57.
41. Ibid., p. 158.
42. Smout, A History of Scotland, p. 142.
43. Churchill, The New World, p. 150.
44. Ibid., p. 275.
45. Foster, Modern Ireland, p. 84; Leyburn, The Scotch-Irish, p. 124.
46. Foster, Modern Ireland, p. 86.
47. Ibid., p. 87.
48. Ibid., p. 89.
49. Ibid., p. 93.
50. Leyburn, The Scotch-Irish, p. 126.
51. See Fischer, Albion's Seed, pp. 618–30.
52. Leyburn, The Scotch-Irish, p. 127.
53. Ibid., p. 125.
54. Churchill, The New World, pp. 338–39.
55. See Leyburn, The Scotch-Irish, pp. 164–68.

56. Ibid., pp. 146–47.
57. Foster, *Modern Ireland*, pp. 157–59.
58. Ibid., p. 147.
59. Churchill, *A History of the English-Speaking Peoples*, vol. 3, *The Age of Revolution* (New York: Dorset Press, 1990), p. 9.
60. Foster, *Modern Ireland*, p. 140.
61. Leyburn, *The Scotch-Irish*, pp. 129–30.
62. See Brian Walker, "Remembering the Siege of Derry," in William Kelly, ed., *The Sieges of Derry* (Dublin: Four Courts Press, 2001); Ian McBride, *The Siege of Derry in Ulster Protestant Mythology* (Dublin, 1977); Philip Dwyer, *Siege* (1893); and Thomas Witherow, *Derry and Enniskillen in the Year 1689* (1885).
63. Foster, *Modern Ireland*, p. 156.
64. See ibid., p. 148.
65. Ibid., p. 272.
66. Ibid., p. 162.
67. Leyburn, *The Scotch-Irish*, p. 166.
68. Ibid., p. 175; Fischer, *Albion's Seed*, p. 787.
69. Smout, *A History of the Scottish People*, pp. 92, 224.
70. "A Hotbed of Genius," *The Economist*, January 22, 1983, p. 83.

PART FOUR: THE SPIRIT OF A REVOLUTION

1. Ned Landsman, *Scotland and Its First American Colony, 1683–1765* (Princeton University Press, 1985), p. 46, quoted in David Hackett Fischer, *Albion's Seed* (New York: Oxford University Press, 1989), p. 665.
2. Landsman, quoted in Fischer, *Albion's Seed*, p. 666.
3. Fischer, *Albion's Seed*, p. 667.
4. James G. Leyburn, *The Scotch-Irish: A Social History* (Chapel Hill: University of North Carolina Press, 1962), p. 185.
5. Ibid., p. 183.
6. Gaius Jackson Slosser, ed., *They Seek a Country: The American Presbyterians* (New York: Macmillan, 1955), p. 8.
7. Fischer, *Albion's Seed*, pp. 666–67.
8. Leyburn, *The Scotch-Irish*, p. 237.
9. Ibid., pp. 238–41. See also Ian McBride, *The Siege of Derry in Ulster Protestant Mythology* (Dublin, 1977).
10. Leyburn, *The Scotch-Irish*, p. 244.
11. Taken from Frederick B. Tolles, *James Logan and the Culture of Provincial Pennsylvania* (1957).

12. Cited in John H. Finley, *The Coming of the Scot* (New York, 1940), pp. 58–59, quoted in Leyburn, *The Scotch-Irish*, pp. 191–92.

13. George Chambers, *A Tribute to the Principles, Virtues, Habits and Public Usefulness of the Irish and Scotch Early Settlers of Pennsylvania* (Chambersburg, 1856), p. 10, quoted in Leyburn, *The Scotch-Irish*, p. 192.

14. Daniel Rupp, *History and Topography of Northumberland, Huntington, Mifflin, Union, Columbia, Juniata, and Clinton Counties, Pa.* (Lancaster, 1847), p. 17, quoted in Leyburn, *The Scotch-Irish*, p. 193.

15. Leyburn, *The Scotch-Irish*, p. 199.

16. Ibid.

17. John Dalzell, "The Scotch-Irish in Western Pennsylvania," *Proceedings of the Second Scotch-Irish Congress*, p. 175, quoted in Whitelaw Reid, *The Scot in America and the Ulster Scot* (London: Macmillan and Co., Ltd., 1912), p. 31.

18. Leyburn, *The Scotch-Irish*, p. 196.

19. Fischer, *Albion's Seed*, pp. 748–49.

20. Ibid., p. 787.

21. 1911 Encyclopedia, statistics at www.1911encyclopedia.org

22. Ibid.

23. Leyburn, *The Scotch-Irish*, p. 201.

24. See generally Ibid., pp. 201–5; see also www.1911encyclopedia.org at Virginia.

25. Leyburn, *The Scotch-Irish*, pp. 201–5.

26. Winston Churchill, *A History of the English-Speaking Peoples*, vol. 3, *The Age of Revolution* (New York: Dorset Press, 1990), p. 133.

27. Leyburn, *The Scotch-Irish*, p. 213.

28. John Solomon Otto, *The Southern Frontiers, 1607–1860* (New York: Greenwood Press, 1989), p. 65.

29. Patrick Griffin, "The People with No Name: Ulster's Migrants and Identity Formation in Eighteenth-Century Pennsylvania," *William and Mary Quarterly* 58, no. 3 (July 2001).

30. Penn MSS, Official Correspondence, 1683–1727, II, 145, quoted in Leyburn, *The Scotch-Irish*, p. 330.

31. R. D. W. Connor, *Race Elements in the White Population of North Carolina* (Raleigh, 1920), p. 83, quoted in Leyburn, *The Scotch-Irish*, p. 215.

32. Reid, *The Scot in America*, p. 28.

33. Leyburn, *The Scotch-Irish*, pp. 330–31.

34. R. F. Foster, *Modern Ireland, 1600–1972* (London: Penguin Books, 1989), p. 216.

35. See www.1911encyclopedia.org at Virginia.

36. Bernard Bailyn, *Voyagers to the West* (New York: Alfred A. Knopf, 1986), p. 26.

37. Ibid., pp. 30–31.

38. Ibid., p. 37.

39. Ibid., p. 40.

40. James Anthony Froude, *The English in Ireland* (London, 1872), vol. 1, p. 392, quoted in Reid, *The Scot in America*, p. 35.

41. T. C. Smout, *A History of the Scottish People, 1560–1830* (London: Fontana/Collins, 1981), p. 43.

42. Foster, *Modern Ireland*, p. 216.

43. Charles Woodmason, *The Carolina Backcountry on the Eve of the Revolution* (Chapel Hill: University of North Carolina Press, 1953), p. 14.

44. Ibid., p. 60.

45. Fischer, *Albion's Seed*, p. 644.

46. Ibid., p. 646.

47. Reid, *The Scot in America*, p. 6.

48. Leyburn, *The Scotch-Irish*, p. 305.

49. Robert Leckie, *The Wars of America* (New York: Harper & Row, 1968), vol. 1, pp. 205–6.

50. See Leyburn, *The Scotch-Irish*, p. 308.

51. Wilma Dykeman, *With Fire and Sword: The Battle of King's Mountain* (Washington, DC, Department of the Interior Publication, 1978), p. 17.

52. Ibid.

53. Ibid., p. 18.

54. Leckie, *The Wars of America*, vol. 1, pp. 198–99.

55. Ibid.

56. Dykeman, *With Fire and Sword*, p. 21.

57. Leckie, *The Wars of America*, vol. 1, p. 199.

58. Dykeman, *With Fire and Sword*, pp. 21–22.

59. Ibid., p. 34.

60. Ibid., pp. 35–36.

61. Ibid., p. 37.

62. Ibid., p. 40.

63. Ibid., p. 49.

64. Ibid., p. 67.

65. Leckie, *The Wars of America*, vol. 1, p. 205.

66. Ibid., p. 209.

PART FIVE: RISE AND FALL: THE HEART OF THE SOUTH

1. James G. Leyburn, *The Scotch-Irish: A Social History* (Chapel Hill: University of North Carolina Press, 1962), p. 317.
2. "Growth and Expansion of the United States in the Era of James Madison," part 3, p. 2. James Madison University document, available at www.jmu.edu/madison/1810pop.htm
3. Wilbur Cash, *The Mind of the South* (New York: Vintage Books, 1969), p. 27.
4. David Hackett Fischer, *Albion's Seed* (New York: Oxford University Press, 1989), pp. 635–39.
5. Ibid., p. 753.
6. Ibid., p. 758.
7. Numerous sources, as quoted in Robert V. Remini, *Andrew Jackson* (New York: Perennial Library, 1966), p. 19.
8. Fischer, *Albion's Seed*, p. 642.
9. Remini, *Andrew Jackson*, p. 20.
10. Ibid., p. 25.
11. Ibid., p. 28.
12. Fischer, *Albion's Seed*, p. 775.
13. See generally Remini, *Andrew Jackson*, pp. 57–61.
14. Robert Leckie, *The Wars of America* (New York: Harper & Row, 1968), vol. 1, p. 273.
15. Ibid., p. 275.
16. Remini, *Andrew Jackson*, p. 61.
17. Ibid., pp. 57–58.
18. Leckie, *The Wars of America*, vol. 1, pp. 287–90.
19. Ibid., pp. 307–13; Remini, *Andrew Jackson*, pp. 68–72.
20. Remini, *Andrew Jackson*, p. 76.
21. Ibid., p. 82.
22. Arthur M. Schlesinger, Jr., *The Age of Jackson* (Boston: Little, Brown & Company, 1953), p. 37.
23. Ibid., p. 93.
24. Joseph Nathan Kane, *Facts about the Presidents* (New York: H. W. Wilson, 1981), p. 57.
25. Vernon Louis Parrington, *Main Currents in American Thought* (New York: Harcourt Brace & World, 1958), vol. 2, pp. 146–47.
26. *London Times*, November 20, 1828.
27. Remini, *Andrew Jackson*, p. 103.
28. Ibid., p. 150.

29. Parrington, *Main Currents in American Thought*, vol. 2, p. 149.
30. Schlesinger, *The Age of Jackson*, pp. 92, 96.
31. Ibid., pp. 74–76.
32. Ibid., pp. 84, 86, 89.
33. Remini, *Andrew Jackson*, p. 154.
34. Parrington, *Main Currents in American Thought*, vol. 2, p. 149.
35. Schlesinger, *The Age of Jackson*, p. 90; Remini, *Andrew Jackson*, pp. 151–52.
36. Schlesinger, *The Age of Jackson*, p. 30.
37. Ibid., p. 97.
38. Parrington, *Main Currents in American Thought*, vol. 2, p. 69.
39. Ibid., p. 70.
40. John C. Calhoun, "A Disquisition on Government," quoted in Parrington, *Main Currents in American Thought*, vol. 2, p. 79.
41. Ibid., p. 82.
42. Numerous sources as quoted in Remini, *Andrew Jackson*, p. 133.
43. Ibid., pp. 134–35.
44. Parrington, *Main Currents in American Thought*, vol. 2, pp. 151–52.
45. Henry Steele Commager, ed., *The Blue and the Gray* (New York: Fairfax Press, 1982), p. xxxiv.
46. Ibid., pp. xxxiii, xxxiv, xxxviii.
47. The Tenth Amendment reads: *"The powers not delegated to the United States by the Constitution, nor prohibited by it to the States, are reserved to the States respectively, or to the people."*
48. Schlesinger, *The Age of Jackson*, pp. 505–6.
49. Neal T. Jones, ed., *A Book of Days for the Literary Year* (New York: Thames and Hudson, 1984), March 20, November 26.
50. John Hope Franklin and Alfred A. Moss, Jr., *From Slavery to Freedom*, 7th ed. (New York: McGraw-Hill, 1994), p. 123.
51. Ibid.
52. Cash, *The Mind of the South*, p. 14.
53. Ibid., p. 55.
54. Parrington, *Main Currents in American Thought*, vol. 2, p. 63.
55. Ibid., p. 64.
56. Ibid.
57. As quoted in the James Madison University document, "Growth and Expansion of the United States in the Era of James Madison," part 3, p. 9. See http://www.jmu.edu/madison/1810pop.htm
58. Cash, *The Mind of the South*, pp. 23–24.
59. Ibid., p. 45.

60. Fischer, *Albion's Seed*, pp. 854–55.

61. Ibid., pp. 856–59.

62. South Carolina Declaration of Causes of Secession, quoted in Commager, *The Blue and the Gray*, pp. 6–7.

63. Shelby Foote, *The Civil War: A Narrative* (New York: Random House, 1958), vol. 1, p. 48.

64. Fischer, *Albion's Seed*, p. 860.

65. Douglas Southall Freeman, quoted in Commager, *The Blue and the Gray*, pp. xxix–xxx.

66. James Webb, *Fields of Fire* (New York: Bantam, 2001), pp. 35–36.

67. Foote, *The Civil War*, vol. 3, p. 1040.

68. Commager, *The Blue and the Gray*, p. xxxvi.

69. Cash, *The Mind of the South*, p. 32.

70. Ibid., p. 45.

71. See John A. Scott, ed., *Living Documents in American History* (New York: Washington Square Press, 1964), pp. 644–45. The Emancipation Proclamation specifically excluded much of southern Louisiana including the entire city of New Orleans, most of eastern Virginia including the cities of Norfolk and Portsmouth, and all of West Virginia, plus the Union slaveholding states of Missouri, Delaware, Maryland, and Kentucky in their entirety.

72. Professor Parrington won the Pulitzer Prize for *Main Currents in American Thought* in 1928, receiving two thousand dollars, double the usual prize award, for his book.

73. Parrington, *Main Currents in American Thought*, vol. 2, p. 84.

74. Ibid., p. 85.

75. Ibid., p. 88.

76. Ibid., p. 92.

77. Ibid., p. 91.

78. The slave states were Alabama, Arkansas, Delaware, Florida, Georgia, Kentucky, Louisiana, Maryland, Mississippi, Missouri, North Carolina, South Carolina, Tennessee, Texas, and Virginia.

79. As quoted in Paul M. Angle, *The Civil War Years* (New York: Doubleday, 1967), p. 41.

80. Ibid.

81. Foote, *The Civil War*, vol. 1, p. 86.

82. Ibid., p. 88.

83. Statistics are derived from an article by Omer Addington in the *Scott County, Virginia Star*, March 28, 1990.

84. See, e.g., Professor William Winston Fontaine, "The Descent of

General Robert Edward Lee from Robert the Bruce, of Scotland," papers of the Southern Historical Society, March 29, 1881.

85. Grady McWhiney and Perry D. Jamieson, *Attack and Die* (Tuscaloosa: University of Alabama Press, 1982), p. 180.

PART SIX: RECONSTRUCTION. DIASPORA. REEDUCATION?

1. James Webb, *Fields of Fire* (New York: Bantam, 2001), p. 29.
2. Wilbur Cash, *The Mind of the South* (New York: Vintage Books, 1969), p. 116.
3. Ibid., pp. 106, 114.
4. David Hackett Fischer, *Albion's Seed* (New York: Oxford University Press, 1989), pp. 861–62.
5. Frederick Douglass, "Reconstruction," *Atlantic Monthly*, December 1866.
6. John Hope Franklin, *From Slavery To Freedom* (New York: Alfred A. Knopf, 1974), p. 280.
7. As quoted in www.nv.cc.va.us/home/nvsageh/Hist122/Part1/Douglass Recon.html
8. Cash, *The Mind of the South*, pp. 121, 134–35.
9. Ibid., p. 51.
10. Norman Pollack, ed., *The Populist Mind* (Indianapolis: Bobbs-Merrill, 1967), p. xx.
11. George Brown Tindall, ed., *A Populist Reader: Selections from the Works of American Populist Leaders* (New York: Harper & Row, 1966), p. 60.
12. Pollack, *The Populist Mind*, pp. xxiv, xxviii.
13. Thomas E. Watson, "The Negro Question in the South," *The Arena*, VI (October 1892), pp. 540–50, quoted in Tindall, *A Populist Reader*, pp. 118–28.
14. Cash, *The Mind of the South*, p. 251.
15. Ibid., p. 219.
16. Ibid., p. 283.
17. John A. Lejeune (LA), Wendell C. Neville (VA), Alexander A. Vandegrift (VA), Clifton B. Cates (TN), Lemuel C. Shepherd, Jr. (VA), Randolph M. Pate (SC), Leonard F. Chapman Jr. (FL), Louis H. Wilson, Jr. (MS), Robert H. Barrow (LA), Carl E. Mundy, Jr. (AL), James L. Jones, Jr. (MO), and Michael W. Hagee (TX).
18. *The Congressional Medal of Honor* (Forest Ranch, CA: Sharp & Dunnigan Publications, 1984), pp. 504–42. These numbers discount

double awards (army and navy) for the same action, and also one incident that occurred outside of combat.

19. William Manchester, *American Caesar* (New York: Little, Brown & Company, 1978), p. 24.

20. *Congressional Medal of Honor*, p. 542.

21. Country Music Association statistics, October 2002.

22. For a concise analysis of the issues as well as a bibliography that covers both sides of the religious debate, see Christopher Armstrong and Grant Wacker, "The Scopes Trial," published by the National Humanities Center, October 2000. Available online at http://www.nhc.rtp.nc.us:8080/tserve/tkeyinfo/tscopes.htm

23. George M. Marsden, *Religion and American Culture*, p. 185, quoted in Armstrong and Wacker, "The Scopes Trial."

24. Armstrong and Wacker, "The Scopes Trial."

25. H. L. Mencken, "In Memoriam: WJB," quoted in Alistair Cooke, ed., *The Vintage Mencken* (New York: Vintage Books, 1955), p. 166.

26. H. L. Mencken, "The Hills of Zion," quoted in Cooke, *The Vintage Mencken*, p. 154.

27. Mencken, "In Memoriam: WJB," quoted in Cooke, *The Vintage Mencken,* pp. 165, 167.

28. Ibid., p. 165.

29. "Report to the President on the Economic Conditions of the South," July 25, 1938 (Library of Congress Document), pp. 1–2.

30. Ibid., pp. 53–55.

31. Ibid., pp. 58–60.

32. Arthur M. Schlesinger, Jr., *The Age of Jackson* (Boston: Little, Brown & Company, 1953), p. 507.

33. "Report to the President on the Economic Conditions of the South," pp. 5, 7, 8, 19, 26–27.

34. Ibid., pp. 22, 46.

35. Ibid., p. 46.

36. Ibid., pp. 49–51.

37. Ibid., p. 26.

38. This battleship visit is memorialized at Roosevelt's former summer home in Campobello, off the coast of Maine along the Canadian border.

39. Manchester, *American Caesar*, pp. 156–57.

40. "A Valley in the Shadow of Debt," *The Economist*, July 19, 2003, p. 23.

41. Dates and figures on the World War II mobilization impact on mili-

tary bases are taken from the command histories of each military base mentioned.

42. U.S. Census Bureau figures. Arkansas' population in 1941 was 1.97 million. By 1956 it was 1.7 million. In 1970 it was 1.92 million. West Virginia's population in 1940 was 1.9 million. By 1950 it had risen to 2.0 million. By 1970 it was 1.7 million. Today it is 1.8 million.
43. See www.pattonhq.com
44. Walter Russell Mead, "The Jacksonian Tradition," *National Interest* (Winter 1999–2000), pp. 11–12.
45. Ibid., pp. 8–9.
46. Schlesinger, *The Age of Jackson*, p. 506.
47. "My How You've Changed," *The Economist*, July 5, 2003, p. 28.

PART SEVEN: REFLECTIONS: THE UNBREAKABLE CIRCLE

1. David M. Halbfinger and Steven A. Holmes, "Military Mirrors Working-Class America," *New York Times*, March 30, 2003, at www.nytimes.com
2. Michael Lind, *Vietnam: The Necessary War* (New York: Free Press, 1999), p. 109.
3. Portions of this narrative first appeared in an article written by the author in *American Legion* magazine, September 2003.
4. Presidential news conference, April 21, 1961, at www.jfklibrary.org/jfk_press_conference_610421.html
5. Portions of this narrative first appeared in an article written by the author in *American Enterprise* magazine, August 2000.
6. *Harvard* magazine, September–October 1995, p. 47.
7. The numbers are for members of those undergraduate classes who died while serving in the military, according to telephone inquiries with the registrar's office of each university, 1986.
8. Harris survey, August 1972, Survey Collection Harris / 2234, available online from the Odom Institute at http://cgi.irss.unc.edu/tempdocs/20:52:35:1.htm
9. As published in Andrew M. Greeley, *Ethnicity, Denomination and Inequality* (Beverly Hills: Sage Publications), Series Number 90-029, 1976.
10. Ron K. Unz, "Some Minorities Are More Minor Than Others," *Wall Street Journal* editorial page, November 16, 1998.
11. Ken Ringle, "The Celt Belt," *Washington Post*, July 3, 2003, p. C1.

Index

About the Author

JAMES WEBB is the author of six best-selling novels, including *Fields of Fire* and *The Emperor's General*. He is also a filmmaker *(Rules of Engagement)*, an Emmy Award–winning journalist, and has taught literature at the university level. One of the most highly decorated Marines of the Vietnam War, he served as Assistant Secretary of Defense and Secretary of the Navy during the Reagan administration.